THE
SOUTHERN
NATION

THE SOUTHERN NATION

The *New* Rise *of the* Old South

R. Gordon Thornton

PELICAN PUBLISHING COMPANY
Gretna 2000

*The word "Pelican" and the depiction of a pelican are
registered trademarks of Pelican Publishing Company, Inc., and are
registered in the U.S. Patent and Trademark Office.*

Library of Congress Cataloging-in-Publication Data

Thornton, R. Gordon.
  The southern nation : the new rise of the Old South / by R.
Gordon Thornton.
      p. c.m.
  ISBN 1-56554-697-0 (alk. paper)
    1. Southern States—Politics and government—1951- 2.
Nationalism—Southern States—History—20th century. 3.
Southern States—Social conditions—1945- 4. United States—
History—Civil War, 1861-1865—Influence. I. Title.

  F216.2 .T48 2000
  975'.043—dc21

                                                99-051592

Printed in the United States of America

Published by Pelican Publishing Company, Inc.
1000 Burmaster Street, Gretna, Louisiana 70053

To my daughter, Chelsea,
and her generation.
They are the ones
who must live with our results.

Contents

Acknowledgments 9

Introduction 11

Chapter I.   A Brave New World 21
Chapter II.   The Walls Come Tumbling Down 29
Chapter III.   Life Behind the Cotton Curtain 39
Chapter IV.   The Birth of a Nation 73
Chapter V.   The Southern Phoenix 101
Chapter VI.   The Irresistible Gray Force of Freedom 111
Chapter VII.   The Personal Quest for Freedom 123
Chapter VIII.   The Community Quest 141
Chapter IX.   Stand and Be Counted 155
Chapter X.   The Cause and the Cure 177
Chapter XI.   The Greatest Conquest 195
Chapter XII.   Conclusion: Deo Vindice Resurgam 217

Appendix A: Declaration of Constitutional Principles 223
Appendix B: The New Albany Declaration 227
Appendix C: Suggested Reading for Southrons 233
Appendix D: Some Southern Resources 237

Notes 241

Index 252

Acknowledgments

I must thank a number of people for making this book possible. The kind ladies at the Crossett and Hamburg, Arkansas libraries were a great help. I am sure they are still wondering what I needed with all the information they conjured up from such obscure sources. The Cooley family of Crossett really kept this project moving along. I have a talent for turning the most marvelous and foolproof high-tech equipment into an expensive paperweight. The Cooleys' talents were on call at all hours to restore the damage wrought by my computer illiteracy. I also owe the many publishers and organizations who allowed me to quote their material a huge debt of gratitude.

Then, there are those who pioneered the trail of modern Southern nationalism. Michael Grissom and the Kennedy brothers led the way. I merely followed with my perspective of the Southern cause. All Southrons also owe a huge debt to Dr. Milburn Calhoun and the staff of Pelican Publishing Company. They allowed the South a voice when few others would risk listening. It is not easy to risk your capital or your neck in today's world of politically correct attitudes and corporate censorship. Allowing the expression of unconventional ideas is the mark of true courage in the modern marketplace.

Most of all I would like to thank my family for their support while I worked on this project. They worked hard to make my efforts a success. It is no small chore for a wife to ignore endless reams of used paper lying about that her husband says he can't afford to throw away. It is an even harder task for a five-year-old to leave all that mess alone. For all their hard work, my wife, Barbie, and our daughter, Chelsea, have my undying love and appreciation. Chelsea and her generation were the inspiration for this book. May the Empire never succeed in deceiving her generation the way it did mine.

Introduction

The Southern Nation sprang to life on February 6, 1861. Representatives of six seceded Southern states christened their new child with a constitution that day. Actually, our Southern Nation was conceived long before. After a gestation of about a hundred years, it burst from the womb with a cry that deafened the world. Our other Southern states rejoiced at the new arrival and joined the celebration.

Our Northern relatives reacted with typical in-law jealousy toward our new infant in the family of nations. The new pharaoh in Washington was especially jealous. After all, he was elected king. Seeing the new star floating in the breeze above Montgomery alarmed him. He winced at the thought of a new toddler rambling through the house, scarring up the furniture and kicking over his favorite toys. In true pharaoh fashion, he ordered his army to slaughter the South's firstborn. Two of his most trusted Yankee generals executed their orders with fanatical determination. Then, they proudly announced the job done. Congress read the last rites. Northern writers took up the chant as they wrote a new batch of history books. They pronounced the Southern Nation dead.

Still, our Southern Nation lived. Our infant sheltered in a tightly woven basket as his wounds healed. He drifts safely down a long muddy Nile somewhere between St. Louis and New Orleans. Soon, the basket will burst open and he will spring to his feet full-grown. It won't be long. He has already cracked the lid. Then, the world will see that the history books were all wrong. We will add the Southern Nation to the long list of things that Yankees are wrong about.

Some of these history writers amuse me. I freely admit that most are supposedly far more learned and knowing than I am, but some switch in the brain's circuitry seems to short out about the time a Ph.D. is conferred. This cognitive short-circuit forces them to waste good time and reams of paper. Mrs. Ferrell, my high-school English teacher, used to describe it as "dead wood." That is line after line, page after page, volume after volume of the same thing. All of which amounts to only so many dead trees, never any new ideas or observations. Any modern school or public library has a broad selection of so-called Civil War history. It is a broad selection in terms of mass, but its substance is usually written from a narrow historical point of view.

There are many books about history, but there are very few about how to make history. Almost all published histories of what we down here refer to as the War for Southern Independence do nothing more than recite the official imperial Yankee dogma. They always say the same old thing. Dusty pages retell the tale of how the benevolent Squarehead liberated our ancestors from their barefoot, backward ways to give them the ultimate gift of devastation and poverty as they sang "Glory, glory, hallelujah" all the way.

For me, reading these tiresome drones that worship the Yankee establishment is a unique personal exercise in tolerance. The other night, against my better judgment, I read one of these propaganda pieces of tired mythology and Websterian grammar. Before I finally consigned it to the compost pile, I ran across something that really challenged me. It was a reference to how amazing it was that the South held out for four long years against the glorious Yankee imperialist bluecoats. The moment overcame me. I couldn't help myself. I took out my pencil and paper. Then, I purged.

Outside of having Granny Clampett in the ranks, I can think of one particularly good reason why the South held out against the odds for so long. That reason was the Southern cause. What was our cause? Liberty. That's all. There was no Freudian psychobabble or magic resourcefulness, just liberty. What held the South together was that same vision of freedom that held men in the ranks at Bunker Hill. It was a vision of freedom that was common to all Southerners, from the lowest rear-rank-two private, to the Confederate president, and the women who kept things running at home. Their vision fed upon the same fire that kept men warm at Valley Forge, just the same as it did in the trenches outside St. Petersburg. That same vision drove men up Cemetery Ridge and the Columbia Pike. For four long years of bitter warfare, Southerners could see and feel their goal almost within reach. Their freedom from Northern meddling, freedom from oppression, freedom to live as they chose, think as they chose, all were at stake. They observed in despair as their dream escaped them.

Liberty was the spark that King George fanned into a flame in 1776. In 1861, Lincoln tried to extinguish that same flame in the South. Abe got singed. Our little smoldering pile burst into a wildfire as his invasion force assembled. The flame is always at home in the South. Ours is the land of liberty. The architects of American freedom, with its right to life, liberty, and property, were Southern men. The Gaelic-Southern heart immediately recognizes the fire and its warmth as an old friend. Its spark quickly caught in the tinderbox souls of the sons of Erin and Robert the Bruce. With such fuel, the flame needs no fanning. It quickly grows in intensity and consumes all it contacts. Along with the Southern fire comes a new mind.

Our Southern fire may smolder, but it never dies. It always rekindles from the smallest remaining spark. Our fire is a self-fulfilling prophecy. Living long after its original prophet, it is unquenchable even in death. Have you ever noticed? The grass grows warmer and greener over the mass graves at Shiloh. The fire that dwells within the resting souls of fallen Southrons keeps its growth full and lush.

Why did the Yankees invade and destroy our beloved home? They feared us. A tyrant fears our fire more than pestilence and plague. The South blazed long before an arsonist named Sherman marched to the sea. Our Yankee neighbors feared the fire that grew here freely and naturally. A contagion it is, spreading from mind to heart to soul, infecting all within influence. The Yankees knew it would spread hotter and further if unchecked. They feared what might happen if their minions and employees were infected. God forbid, their servants might begin to think for themselves.

The Yankees and their empire still fear us today. That is the reason they continue to persecute us. The American Empire dissects and revises our Constitution and its Bill of Rights until nothing is left. They flood the airwaves with distortion that explains how they want us to think. The empire constantly bombards us with its promotion of multiculturalism and "alternative" lifestyles. The university elite and their big business partners demand that we shuck our natural speech with its twangs and drawls. They want to better homogenize us to the rest of their financial domain. The imperials fear Southerners and their little flame. They are not afraid of what we are. They fear what we can be.

Of course, that fear is what all the recent talk of Southern nationalism and Southern independence is all about. The Yankees and their other imperial subjects do not have to love us, just so long as they fear us. (They've never loved us anyway.) That is what captive nations the world over, from Latvia to Quebec, have realized as the age of empire perishes in its sleep. The idea is catching on again here, too. Southerners are again turning to thoughts once locked deep within our genetic memory. Thoughts like liberty, self-reliance, and even independence are part of our make-up dating back to our earliest common ancestors. Thoughts of Southern nationhood are natural and healthy for us. These thoughts develop an attitude of hope. That is what this book is all about—hope for the Southern future.

The South is the last bastion of western civilization. We are the holdouts of Anglo-Celtic and Christian culture. This book and others like it are kindling for the flame of the Southern cause. *The Southern Nation* aims to teach and persuade you to conduct your own personal secession from the empire. I encourage you to reject the mindless, generic plastic world that Northern corporations are pushing on a lost generation of Southern consumers. In addition, you will learn how to take your family, friends, and community from under the emperor's thumb as well. More importantly, this book tells you why you need to make the change to Southern nationalism. Together, we can rebuild our Southern Nation, one family at a time, one community at a time. It will occur to you that Southern nationhood is our only viable option if we wish to retain the blessings that we inherited from our ancestors.

In a way, this book is the third episode in an unplanned trilogy of Southern nationalism published by Pelican. Each installment was seen as radical when it was first published. Each message mellowed into approval by the time the next was published. This is the third stage of the traditionalist Southern viewpoint in its published evolution since the 1980s. Michael Andrew Grissom started the new Southern rights revolution with *Southern by the Grace of God*. In its pages, he taught us that it was normal to be proud of our Southern heritage. He gave us a glimpse of the priceless treasures we inherit from preserving our nationality, but he tempered this bounty with a survey of what we have already lost. He gave Southerners a preview of the cell walls we will inhabit if we discard the precious legacy of Southern civilization.

In *The South Was Right!*, brothers James R. and Walter D. Kennedy revealed that our ancestors' Southern cause was the right cause. They led us in seeing the truth. Though our ancestors have passed, we inherited their unfinished works. Their cause, now more than ever, is worth fighting to fulfill. The South not only was right, it still is right. As always, a free Southern homeland is the utmost desire of the Southern cause.

As for my part of the trilogy, *The Southern Nation* tells you why and how to fight for our Southern legacy. This is a Southern how-to book. It teaches you to resist the forces that threaten to exterminate the last shreds of both Southern and western civilization. I do not question the cause and our need for action. That is a given. We know our homeland is worth fighting to defend. My goal is to teach you to fight smart, how to win while maximizing our Southern uniqueness.

Many people are confused about what Southern nationalism actually is. Over the last few years, Southern nationalism as been described as everything from an evil racist plot to just another manifestation of multiculturalism. Both of these descriptions are equally absurd. The growing number of blacks and Hispanics that are joining in support of the Southern cause rules out racist intentions. As for multicultural fantasies, the empire offers ample evidence that Southerners never have been and never will be welcome in any scheme that celebrates so-called diversity. As with any other imperial program, we remain only as captives. It is plain that we are not wanted. Aside from our usefulness as cannon fodder, Southern participation is never welcome in the new Third World of the New World.

Southern nationalism draws its existence and its strength from a Southern conservative tradition with roots extending all the way back to the plain of Runnymede. This tradition is different from mainstream American conservatism. It shares more of the Gaelic and old continental European heritage as it opposes the continuing conversion into a Leviathan of our original republic of sovereign states. Southern nationalism opposes any form of imperial meddling outside of the original constitutional obligations, such as providing for the common defense. This means it is definitely opposed to the welfare state. Southern nationalism is the natural Southern reaction to government that oversteps its bounds and runs wild.

As despair seeps into the ranks of traditional American conservatives, many are breaking their former political ties. They search for an alternative. Many are finding their answer in Southern nationalism. Even many Northern conservatives now recognize that the American imperial system is broken beyond repair. Again, they look to the

Southern bedrock of the original constitutional American republic as the answer. People everywhere look to the South for the fix. So far, they have looked to the wrong Southern citizens for the answers.

Southern nationalism is a drive to preserve the social, religious, political, and cultural traditions of the Southern people. True Southerners denounce the secular humanist tendencies that have guided the empire since Appomattox. These Northern intellectual fantasies value nature above man and man above God. Meanwhile they place commercial greed and materialism above all. Southerners are tired of the lies of both major political parties. We are equally tired of fighting the empire's brush-fire wars and dying in some foreign backwoods while trying to play the world's policemen.

Southrons agree that it is time to look out for our own people for a change. We lost control of our borders 130 years ago and have been living on borrowed time ever since. As the empire's open-border policy is rapidly changing America into just another Third World entity, we find that Southern nationalists and their paleo-federalist cousins are not just limited to the South. All across the empire the cry is rising for reduced immigration and increased self-sufficiency, combined with a strong agricultural base. However, the Southern nationalist's main concern is for the South first. It is our nation. Let the others fend for themselves for a while. Besides, no preservation of our traditions or return to our old ways is possible while we remain captives of the empire. As the League of the South's president, Dr. Michael Hill, stated:

> All we want is to be left alone, left alone to raise our families, worship our God, and enjoy the fruits of our own labors. . . . We have declared that the Southern republic exists, if for now only in our minds and hearts. But one day, our flags will be unfurled over a new nation of our own making.[1]

It is only fitting that the Southern dream of 1861 was reborn in the 1990s. In that decade, the U.S. government confirmed it lacks any authority to prevent Southern nationhood. This is unquestionable. From 1990 to 1994, the American Empire extended full diplomatic recognition to twenty new secessionist republics that were formerly part of the USSR, Yugoslavia, and Czechoslovakia. Even without this precedent, most serious students of American history and constitutional law agree that secession is just as much a right belonging to any American state. Still, the imperial government cares little for the rights of a state or citizen. The empire lends its blessing to other lands. Here, its policy is that secession is a right no American state will ever be permitted to exercise. Thomas Jefferson and the other founding fathers knew that secession was the yardstick that judged whether or not a people were truly free. With the Soviet Union gone, who is the evil empire now?

Open your mind. Open your heart to the familiar warmth of your Southern Nation. The fire is a dear close friend who longs to dwell again in his hereditary home. As a Southron, you are incomplete without the fire within. Whether your outside shell is white, black, yellow, or red, your inside is dark and vacant until lighted and warmed by your fire. That is the way God intended a Southron to be. His gift of fire makes us Southern. It makes us men, makes us whole. The fire is our tool, our friend. Let it come home by kindling one small spark. Then, you begin a journey that is as sweeping an adventure as anything that ever quickened the pulse of Odysseus or Beowulf. Like the deeds of ancient mythical heroes, the work of our generation is the legend and legacy of the next. Come with us. Be the seed of legends. It is our birthright, given by the hand of God.

Unlike past generations in other captive nations, we do not have to kill, burn, or bleed to assert our birthright. It is ours already. We just have to exercise our claim and take ownership. Our fathers have already paid the price in blood for Southern nationhood. All the interest they require on our legacy is faith and sweat. The Southern Nation will become reality if we only believe. If we demand our legacy and it is not delivered, our faith will gain it for us. The South is our Promised Land. It is our choice. We can play the part of Esau or Israel.

True freedom lives in the heart, the mind, and the soul. Government can never take it away. Only we can forfeit it. Sure, the American Empire wins some battles, but the imperials will not be here for the finish. They can't win. The Southern fire outlasts us all. Feed the flame. Use your hearts, your minds, and your souls to win back freedom for our Southern Nation. Then, when I pass over, notice if the grass grows greener over me; if not for the flame, then maybe for the sweetness of the Southern soil that gave me life.

Occupied Hamburg, Arkansas
July 20, 1999

THE SOUTHERN NATION

CHAPTER I

A Brave New World

Liberty is always won where there exists the unconquerable will
to be free.   Jefferson Davis[1]

Sometimes Arkansas's weather stinks. It was already the coldest
night of the winter of 1992. Now, freezing rain fell and added to
the misery. My pickup, a relic of the early seventies, started sliding
around curves, and I wondered if I would even reach the
Smackover Library. I hate to be late, but I hate hiking around in
the cold even more. Finally, I made it. Sleet bounced off my wind-
shield as I half-slid, half-wrestled my truck into a parking space.

Bracing myself against the wind, I hurried up the steps to the
meeting room. Then, I slipped and sprawled on the porch. The icy
wind that followed me through the door did not ease my self-con-
sciousness. The chill disrupted the gathering, and about forty heads
turned to see who had let in the cold. As I slumped into a seat, the
camp commander introduced the evening's speaker.

A friend had invited me to several of these meetings over the last
few months. For some reason, I finally found time to show on the
most miserable night of the year. It just so happened that this
night's speaker also chose to brave the weather and fight his way up
from Simsboro, Louisiana. I had never heard of Don Kennedy or
his brother, Ron. I also had never heard of their first book, *The
South Was Right*, but Don soon impressed me. His appearance and
manner seemed more like that of a Sunday-school teacher than it
did a revolutionary. The ideas he spoke of, however, were revolutionary. They shocked me. I had never heard their equal spoken in
public. That night, I knew only one other person in the room, but
quickly found I was among friends. My awakening began.

A logger seated next to me introduced himself. I shook his ragged middle-aged hand and said, "I like your speaker. I never had any idea that I am not the only person who feels this way. Mr. Kennedy thinks the way I do."

Wiping his glasses, my new friend grinned. "That's the key. Mr. Kennedy thinks."

That night I cast off my shackles. I had heard lip service to liberty and reason from politicians and their kind. This was different. That night, I broke free. I became not just a free man, but a free Southerner. I found that I was no longer a closet Confederate. In one miserable night, I met with a reality that all people crave. I became a part of something larger than myself. I left that meeting with a new outlook and a treasured memento, an autographed copy of the Kennedy brothers' book.

Books are warm and trusted friends to me. Ideas flow freely from their familiar pages. I may be old fashioned, but I do not find familiarity or warmth in the radioactive glow of a computer screen. Information age or not, computers remain just another tool. My books are tangible, embraceable friends. The book I purchased that night is the same. It was not just a keepsake. I devoured its substance and content. I studied and reflected on every thought. Skeptical by nature, I checked the sources and the validity of each point. I was not disappointed. The Kennedy brothers' argument is irrefutable. Their research is flawless. If anything, their message is understated. There is not a misstatement or half-truth in their work.

It took some hunting, but I found many other friends in this unknown branch of Southern literature. As I pored over their contents, my study left me with only one conclusion. The South *was* right! It also left me with a dilemma. What could I do about it? How many more people felt the way I did? The cause, my cause, is not the Lost Cause—it is the Right Cause.

As we emerged from the meeting room, the storm was gone. I breathed the damp night air freely, with a clear head, under a clear sky. The stars showed brighter in the Arkansas sky than anywhere else in the world that night. I am sure that I was not the only one of Don's audience who cast his eyes and thoughts toward the heavens that evening.

The rebirth of the Old South frightens New South liberals. It terrifies their yellow scalawag sidekicks. A similar lament awaits their Yankee establishment mentors. Poor in spirit, but not in pocketbook, they cannot hurt us anymore. Before the force of truth all their power and influence is nothing. It is "gone with the wind."

Even with all the powerful forces of Yankeedom behind them, the scalawags and liberals cannot stand against the new breed of Southerner. This new Southerner is simply mad as hell, and he just won't take it anymore. This is not a sudden genetic shift sweeping our nation, just an idea. It is not even a new idea. What they fear is the common spirit of historic defiance that permeates every molecule south of the Ohio River. This remarkable zeal is nothing supernatural, just a simple, hereditary dream. The Southern dream passes like a torch from generation to generation. It is the ruling class's fault. They are the ones who fanned our torch into a bonfire. Then, they ordered their agents to quench the fire by pouring gasoline on it. The resulting conflagration is rapidly catching in a new generation. It consumes us wholly. A new breed, we are still amazingly similar to the old breed. We even share the same surnames. Our battle cry is "No More Oppression! No More Compromise! No More Lies!"

Our native sons increasingly realize that though we lost the war, we can still win the peace. The goal of this new generation of Southrons is to finally win the peace. We reject the brush of lies and bigotry that tars us. Unlike generations passed, we also reject the hand that wields the brush. We know what we are up against. We must win the peace, if we ever wish to live in peace. Freedom to exercise our right to be left alone is forever the goal of the Southern cause.

Now, more than any other time in history, we have the needed resources and advantages. We have everything we need to restore our people to freedom and prosperity. Our problems are not the responsibility of Washington bureaucrats. If the South's character and way of life vanishes, the fault is ours alone.

Yes, I admit it. I am a cheerleader for all things Southern. Unlike many of my peers, I feel no need to apologize for my convictions. I despise the prospect of apologizing for what I am. I also defy the prospect of having the blood of Southern civilization coat my hands. Perhaps my deep Southern agrarian roots are the source of that faith. It is a faith that has served me well all through the so-called "Culture Wars." The front lines of the Culture Wars furnished me many wounds. What surprised me was that blood did not flow from my wounds, or those of my peers. Pride flowed from them, Southern pride, and a feeling of Southern nationhood. That feeling outlives any fate that may befall us. It swells up out of oppression and hopelessness. Our pride grows with every outrage, every flag that burns, every monument that falls. That same feeling will be here long after we are gone. Michael Grissom put it into words:

> Repression of the people, suppression of ideas—both breed contempt no matter the name of the oppressor. Two years ago, I would not have broached the subject of Southern nationalism in any conversation. . . . Yet now, not only do I hear discussions about secession (especially in the wake of our Quebec neighbors who want to secede from father Canada), I am reading of it in magazines and newspapers. . . . Count the Southerner down, but count him not out.[2]

Grissom is right. A few years ago, no one ever dared think of Southern nationalism, let alone speak or write about it. Then again, a few years ago a turreted concrete wall divided Berlin. Recently, my young daughter played on a portion of the Berlin Wall while it was on display at Stone Mountain, Georgia.[3] A few years ago, Lithuania and the other Baltic states were firmly sunk in the Soviet quagmire. No one ever predicted the fall of communism without flowing rivers of blood to accompany it. Still, one of those poor oppressed people dared to think. Then one brave (or foolhardy) soul dared to speak. Others dared to listen. Then, those who dared to speak, wrote. Because of their faith, many people thought, then they believed. The rest is now fodder for history books.

It is the same where we live. First, we must dare think. Second, we must dare speak. Then, we must write so others may think. The next step is watching our people forge a new reality as they believe. Once we believe, the Southern Nation will be reality. Unfortunately, standing in the path of our belief are all the years of indoctrination that told us that the Southern dream was not practical. The false prophets of doom did their work well. However, their wall, like Berlin's, crumbles at the sound of truth's trumpet.

What our alternative reality requires of Southerners does not particularly take guts. Neither does it take great bravery or courage. If someone does not agree with what I say or write, they usually just tell me. Sometimes it is polite and well articulated. Other times it is not. Usually the only wound my detractor tries to inflict on me is emotional. Sure, it sometimes hurts, but it takes greater effort to remain silent than it does to speak the truth, even when the truth is not popular or politically correct.

The person who does show guts, bravery, and courage is the student who stood in the streets of Belgrade. He dares to stand up for his rights. He faces off against the trained guardians of a regime and risks a lot more than getting his feelings hurt. The young Serb still stands there defiantly, just as he learned it from our great-grandparents. Occasionally, he waves a Confederate battle flag. He not only has guts; he shows it. We have a lesson to learn from his stand. There, his rulers fear him. Here, we fear ours.

Fear always has its price. Some people choose to sell out to fear. They deny everything that makes them all they could ever be. What they lose is so much more valuable than the wretched thirty pieces of silver they gain. Theirs was a future of promise. Theirs was a future where they could have accomplished much more than they ever will as scalawags. By selling out, they lose that inner strength that would have made them more than mere men. They reject their homeland, their way of life, their people, as well as their strength. No one forced the scalawag to choose his path. He did it freely. Yet, all he gets is the scraps that our conquerors reject. The scalawag frets and growls under the table over a bone with precious little meat. Even a conqueror has no respect for a collaborator.

All over Eastern Europe, those who chose to sell out to the Soviets now live in dim, moldy flats. Theirs is the righteous retirement of a traitor who managed to save his hide. Now only cockroaches are at their call. They are their only friends, sharing a similar niche in the food chain. Once, these men were the feared muscle of Europe. Now, their frequent nightmares feature only a potter's field. This is the cost of betrayal, their choice. Elsewhere in the world people know how to deal with collaborators. The Bill Clintons, Al Gores, and Zell Millers of our world should be grateful that the people they betray are not Dutch or Norwegian.

Selling out is a choice few Southerners make. Our heritage and culture are too precious to squander. It is a comfort and source of strength. Mr. Bill Williams of Little Rock once told me a story that reminded me how powerful a comfort being Southern is. At the time, he was Arkansas's director for the League of the South, and I was laid up in a Little Rock hospital bed. Mr. Bill is also a veteran of the forgotten Korean War. During the war, he was an artilleryman, spending endless days shelling hills that had numbers for names. At the close of one typically long day during the battle for Seoul, Mr. Bill rested.

> I was sitting on the tail of the artillery piece with a friend and we heard a train whistle. This was impossible for we were at least a hundred miles from any railroad and so I said nothing to the man sitting next to me for fear that I might be called crazy. I heard it again and looked at the other man who was looking at me like, "What in blazes?"
> I asked him, "You hear what I heard?"
> He said, "Well, I think I heard a train whistle."
> Then, we heard it again. Some of the others in the unit were getting to their feet when the lead truck of an armored convoy rounded the curve just to our east. It was a large air compressor truck such as used by construction companies. Mounted on the back of the air tank was a steam whistle, which the driver was blowing every little bit. Behind that truck came some smaller trucks, support trucks for the tanks in the unit. After the trucks came the lead jeep and then the first tank, which was painted Confederate gray. It was an Arkansas National Guard Armored Regiment and in the lead tank, the commander was standing in his position in the turret with his upper body showing. He was dressed, at least on his upper body, in a Confederate officer's tunic and campaign hat with the right brim turned up. On his lead tank, he was flying the Arkansas state flag from one radio mast and the Confederate battle flag from the other. Most of the fellows in my unit were from the South. I expect we had at least one representative from every one of the thirteen Southern states and we all sent up a loud cheer for the flag.[4]

I asked Mr. Bill what his reaction was. He said, "I was moved. I had prayed for home and God delivered."

Mr. Bill's story is familiar to many Southern fighting men. Our beloved and tattered emblem flew from the trenches of France during World War I. It returned on the sixth of June 1944. Our flag island-hopped the Pacific with the Marines of CONFORSOLS (The Confederate Forces of the Solomons).[5] Again, it accompanied our men back to the jungles during the Vietnam War. Our beloved and despised banner flew over the deserts of the Persian Gulf. Cradled in the loving arms of a real Mississippi colonel, our flag even hitched a ride in the helicopters of the French Foreign Legion. This excursion ended three hundred miles behind Iraqi lines, on the banks of the Tigris River. There our banner bathed with the French Tricolors in the Foreign Legion's traditional celebration of victory.

Our flag, so despised by our conquerors and so beloved by us, flies wherever men long to be free. It no longer belongs just to us. We freely share it with any man who dares to dream of freedom. Berliners hoisted our flag atop their hated wall as Germany reunited. Lithuanians, Latvians, and Estonians waved our flag when waving even their own meant death. The student protesters of Belgrade braved gas and bayonets to wave our banner. Outside the South people desire our flag as much as blue jeans. It mingles with the *Fleurs-de-lis* all over Quebec. Our version of Saint Andrew's Cross also finds a ready market in Scotland. Our beloved and tattered emblem, tarred with the same brush that paints us, is the universal symbol for defiance of tyranny. Even Zulus wave it in South Africa. Only in America is it considered a negative. Everywhere else our Confederate battle flag is a universal symbol of liberty.

It can be that symbol again here. Our conquerors and their weak-kneed collaborators do not fear what our flag is. They fear what it can make us. Thanks to those daring few who showed us the way, those who dared think, speak, and write, our conquerors' lies are uncovered. The truth unmasked shall set us free. We do not have to apologize anymore. We refuse to bow and scrape anymore. We are the Southern Nation and we know that no political system can buck the truth. All we have to do is stand up for truth.

CHAPTER II

The Walls Came Tumbling Down

Is life so dear or peace so sweet as to be purchased at the price of chains and slavery? Forbid it, Almighty God! I know not what course others may take, but as for me, give me liberty, or give me death! Patrick Henry[1]

It is remarkable. History proves it. The prime example competes against us today. The most profitable venture any country can undertake is to wage war against the United States and lose. It is such an ironic notion that it was the theme of the movie *The Mouse That Roared,* starring the late Peter Sellers. If the antagonist succumbs to U.S. power, does it really lose? The U.S. typically rebuilds its opponents stronger and better than before.

Americans will always remember December 7, 1941 as a "day that will live in infamy." America repaid the Japanese for their unwarranted aggression by making them into an economic superpower. Now, we have Japanese products in every American home. Our workers fear Japanese competition with good cause. The Japanese champion free trade, as long as it excludes American products from entering Japan.

The Allies also rebuilt West Germany as a model industrial powerhouse. The German chemical industry is a vital artery to the western world. Reunification supplied both East and West Germans with a renewed national spirit and pride. Since reunification, much more has developed. Numbers of young Germans are dabbling in Nazi ideology. Will the world forget so easily?

Though our government did not allow our troops to win the Vietnam War, it serves as another good illustration of the policy. Our troops would scarcely clear a Viet Cong stronghold before

American contractors would appear to rebuild the village. The new cinder-block villages furnished much better accommodations for the Viet Cong. The sturdier construction also made them harder to retake—a lot harder than the collection of huts they had once been. The cycle of retake and rebuild continued for eleven years. Many consider the former first lady's construction hands to be the last American troops to leave Vietnam.

As the Persian Gulf War was in its final hours, Allied troops sped across the desert toward Baghdad. Most Americans worried about the casualties and waited for the end. A costly siege of Baghdad loomed as the likely conclusion. As we sat glued to our televisions and wondered, the news commentators voiced different concerns. They and their paid experts speculated about how much money it would cost the allies to rebuild Iraq. They assumed that American taxes would pour in and save Saddam Hussein from himself. At the time, they voiced no concern for the people of pillaged and bleeding Kuwait. Recently, the same rhetoric resurfaced about rebuilding Yugoslavia, as NATO bombed that country back to a Stone-Age level of existence because it refused to allow Kosovar secession.

Contrast this with our fate. As the War Between the States sped to a close, Northern politicians speculated on ways to divide the spoil. As Southern armies crumbled, Northern armies intensified their program of destruction. Father Abraham's victorious legions raped, pillaged, and plundered the South beyond recognition. While foreign antagonists can expect new construction, Southerners, as *fellow Americans,* got Reconstruction. We got the first of Washington's great social programs, "The Raw Deal."

Does it cause bitterness even today? You had better believe it does. When his mill management asked whether he was still angry over the outcome of a ten-year-old labor dispute, one Southron replied, "Hell! I'm still mad about the Civil War!"[2]

In no other portion of the vast American Empire are the citizens held with more contempt than in the South. The empire has occupied and controlled us for more than 130 years. Its ruling elite restricts Southerners to the status of second-class citizens. Because we lost a war more than 100 years ago, the Southern citizen lost his political voice. His choices made for him, even his right of suffrage turns against him. The ruling class makes sure of this through its political hierarchy and the liberal media. In many counties and parishes, the voter views a Soviet-styled ballot with no real options. Voiceless and powerless, we remain as servants of the Washington regime.

The Southern populace desires and deserves better. We can have better. The problem is that we remain unorganized. Modern political campaigns are prohibitively expensive. This bars many of our most promising young minds from the arena. Modern media turns our elections into mob rule through electronic popularity contests. With spin doctors, professional campaign managers, and image consultants, electioneering is a complex science. The masters of this craft restrict system outsiders from learning the ropes.

Barring very few outstanding examples, true Southern conservatives are forbidden political office. In fact, a true traditional Southern politician is now a contradiction in terms. First, they must overcome the 30 to 40 percent of voters who form the liberal, welfare voting block. Then the candidate must carry 80 to 90 percent of the remaining vote to win. Those well-meaning few who ever make it find themselves hobbled by the party system. To remain in office, they must play ball and worship their chosen party's bosses. With their influence thus limited, there is little chance for accomplishment.[3]

History salts our present predicament with tragedy. Ours is a legacy of repeated insult and injury. Our history is an infamous chain of events starting long before 1787 and continuing to this day. The once tightly tethered central government wastes no chance to enlarge its power to the point of tyranny. Our Washington regime constantly flaunts its true purpose. Our rulers' hidden objective is to reduce the common Southern citizen to servitude.

We can change this. Our forefathers did it. We can too. They did it by pledging their lives, property, and sacred honor in 1776. They suffered long and hard so that others might live free from the dictates of kings. Our Confederate forefathers tried again in 1861. They gave all for four long years because they could see what the future held in store. They tried valiantly, but failed. Washington then subjected them to the cruelest peace ever inflicted upon any race of free men. Around us, we can see the fulfillment of their fears.

In our case, we like to think we have taken steps to change history ourselves. Media pundits heralded our revolution of November 1994 as either an electoral tantrum or the beginning of a new era. Again, the elite betrayed us. We only swapped one master for a different one. If anything, we should learn something from our experience. Our present method of butting heads with the establishment is futile.

Many around us are discouraged. They turn to dormancy and whining. As Thomas Jefferson wrote, "all experience hath shown that mankind are more disposed to suffer while evils are sufferable, than to right themselves by abolishing the forms to which they are accustomed."[4]

There is hope. We can do better. Captivity does not have to be our permanent condition. All over the world, people are following the example that Americans first set. People are shaking loose. The children of captive parents are now seeing their descendants born free. More people are looking at the world in the same light that Thomas Jefferson and Patrick Henry saw it. They view the world through the eyes of free men. It is happening all around us. Again, it is our turn to look to our own ancestral example.

Scotland is an ancestral homeland for many Southerners. It is the land of the independent spirit of the Highlander, William Wallace, and Robert the Bruce. It is also the stepchild of British union. With the rise of the Scots National Party, many Scots again intend to rule their own affairs.

Periodically, British authorities uncover plots aiming to recover the Sacred Stone of Scone. The stone is ever a sore spot with Scots. It was once the established coronation seat of Gaelic royalty. Ancient tradition claims that Jacob used the stone as a pillow the night he dreamed of a ladder to heaven. It was brought to Ireland and later Scotland from the Middle East. Saint Patrick is also reputed to have blessed the stone. The thirteenth-century English king, Edward I, stole away the stone as an insult to Scots and a confirmation of the English crown's authority. For seven hundred years, the stone rested in Westminster Abbey as the coronation seat of British monarchs. Many Scots determined that Prince Charles would not defile their sacred seat as his predecessors. A group of youthful Scots succeeded in retrieving the stone temporarily in 1950. It was later recovered in Scotland. Even after its return in what Scots nationalists saw as a British political ploy in November 1996, the stone remains a sore symbol of English domination and treachery.[5]

More recently, the Scots National Party forced Parliament to turn over a greater portion of the North Sea oil royalties. These moneys will find better use with the native Scots than in the coffers of the crown. However, this concession has done little to buy the independent Highlanders' spirit. Despite all the conciliatory efforts of the crown, Scots voted to institute their own parliament on September 12, 1997. With popular Scot advocates such as actor Sean Connery, the crown sees that Scottish independence is uncomfortably close to reality.[6]

Another resistance to the crown's authority festers closer to home. Quebec, the French Canadian province garnered by conquest during the French and Indian Wars, is clamoring for independence. French Canadians have long resented rule by the British Commonwealth. Fifteen years ago Quebec separatists forced the Ottawa regime into many cultural concessions and acknowledgment of Quebec's right to secede. The concessions soon proved to be a carrot dangling from a stick. Ottawa used a typical tactic of suppression by promoting Anglo and Third World emigration to water down the predominately French speaking population. The Quebecois are now less disillusioned than before. Their October 1995 referendum on secession proves it.

The Ottawa regime does not want to lose its captive colony. In preparation for the referendum, the Canadian government orchestrated public displays of affection by Anglo-Canadians. While the European Economic Community threatened sanctions, Pres. Bill Clinton threatened to invoke the North American Free Trade Agreement to coerce Quebec away from independence. Despite the outside pressure and coercion, secession received amazing support, barely failing by less than .5 percent. This was an actual number reported to be less than the number of mangled and unreadable ballots. Even with all the new emigrants and all the scare tactics, 49.6 percent of Quebecois still favored independence.[7]

For some of the greatest illustrations of people achieving their freedom, we must look to the former Soviet Empire. The efforts of labor leader Lech Walesa to bring reform and free elections to Poland were a resounding triumph. We should not underestimate Poland's influence on the breakup of the Soviet Empire. Especially prominent was the example the Poles presented the captive Baltic republics of Lithuania, Latvia, and Estonia.

The Baltic states were indeed the leaders of the Soviet breakup. Seized during World War II and occupied ever since, they are a classic example of undying nationalism. The Soviet overlords in Moscow outlawed every trace of the Baltic republics' history. For fifty years, possession of cultural emblems, the flags, or even the currency of the original governments meant imprisonment or death at the hands of the Communist Party's Politburo and the KGB. Proving that might does not make right, the Baltic states pressed for their independence and won. They did this despite the presence of Soviet troops and large enforced Russian immigrant populations.

In addition, we must never forget the example of tiny Slovakia. The prophets of doom assured that she could never exist independent of the Czech Republic. The Slovaks proved them wrong. Slovakia showed it could be a success. The new nation is developing into an economically sound republic. This new spirit of freedom is making our old maps obsolete.

Perhaps the greatest twentieth-century example of a people achieving nationhood is India. Through persistence, an entire subcontinent won freedom from British domination. Mohandas Gandhi united his people and led them using the innovative principles of moral persuasion and passive resistance. His insistence on nonviolent action declawed the British lion and won the respect of the world. Gandhi's methods proved to be revolutionary. Though a Hindu holy man, he learned his techniques from mankind's greatest teacher, Jesus of Nazareth. True, today India faces many of the same historical problems, but not among them is rule by outsiders siphoning her natural wealth to glut the British crown.

These movements all have several factors in common. They all involved a unified people of largely common heritage. Usually, the ruling class discouraged and suppressed the cultural heritage of the captive people. The people resorted to using their creativity and the limited resources they had at hand. In the cases of the Warsaw Pact countries and India, these resources were indeed very limited. They had to make do with almost nothing. Over the long term, these nations and their movements have shown or show promise of being extremely successful. The amazing factor is that these movements used little or no violence to achieve the peoples' aims. Contrast this with the Russian "People's Revolution," the Chinese "Cultural Revolution," or the other Marxist revolutions of Africa and the Americas.

Plainly, this should teach us several lessons. Political change is best and most permanently evoked without resorting to violence. When the ruling class uses violence or intrigue to suppress such movements, it usually ensures the movements' eventual success. People of common heritage plainly desire to govern their own affairs. History shows that people are more content and are in most cases better off when they control their own government. The overall lesson is a reinforcement of the Jeffersonian principle that people of a common heritage have a natural and God-given right to self-determination. Even the "Great Delineator," Abraham Lincoln, acknowledged this right. Too bad that Lincoln did not practice what he preached. If he did, it would have spared more than six hundred thousand American lives. As an Illinois representative on the floor of Congress, he claimed:

> Any people, anywhere, being inclined and having the power have the right to rise up and shake off the existing government, and form a new one that suits them better. This is a most valuable, a most sacred right which we hope and believe is to liberate the world. Nor is this right confined to the cases in which the whole people of an existing government may choose to exercise it. Any portion of such people that can, may revolutionize and make their own of so much of the territory as they inhabit.[8]

The examples of other nations with resources inferior to our own should encourage the Southerner and teach him an important lesson. We can be happy. We can be self-sufficient. We can be free! We are a blessed people. As one Southron tells us:

> You've got more solid pack, world class, honorable heritage than any other bunch of people, from any other region, in the world. Even the sun shines brighter on you than anyone else in the world. Even God put more of His books in your Southland than in any other area of the world, per capita.[9]

There is a solution to our problems. It involves a return to the constitutional principles of state sovereignty and states' rights. We can find the solution in tightly limited and controlled central government. Citizens must recognize the right and the obligation of their state to impose its protection between the citizen and an abusive central government. In addition, we must support that state's right and duty of secession if the state is lacking any other alternative.

Do you want to shock the average Southerner? Present him with the ideas of nullification and secession as legitimate means of protection from the intrusions of a powerful and abusive central government. He will answer, "Been there. Done that. It doesn't work. The war settled the question."

He is wrong. Violence and conquest are never the answer to any question. These same people teach their children to shun violence. This helps them grow into peaceful, law-abiding adults. They will also advise their children, "If at first they don't succeed, they should try, try again."

They should sample their own advice. To them, I say, "If at first you don't secede . . ."

Like others before us, we must realize that government does not grant us our rights. God gives man his unalienable rights. A government cannot take away these rights. The only way you lose them is if you give them away. You can forfeit them purposefully or by submission to oppressive authority. Rights are like any other gift from God. They are not to be squandered for a myth of security. If you do, you will pay the price. However, most people fail to realize this. It will cost them, and their children. It costs them now. They remain passive only because they do not realize how much it costs them. The Kennedy brothers brought out this tragic fact in their book, *The South Was Right!*

> T. E. Lawrence, the famous Lawrence of Arabia, . . . noted the effort to free the Arab people from Turkish rule was accomplished not when the last battle had been won but when the majority of the Arab people no longer accepted Turkish rule as legitimate. At that point they were free. It only remained for them to stay loyal to their belief in freedom long enough for the struggle to work out the details of when and how the Turks would leave. The same point is true today for us. . . . You are not free because you do not believe you can be free.[10]

That is a potent observation. It is an observation that we, as Southerners, must take to heart. We have work to do. We must prepare ourselves for freedom. As we prepare ourselves, we must prepare our families, and especially prepare our children. They are the ones who must live with our result. Beginning with ourselves, we must ready our nation, the Southern Nation.

We will not win freedom at the time we gain our independence. We will win freedom when we realize several basic truths. Once Southerners believe them, truly believe them, then we will be free. The rest is a matter of course.

> 1. Southerners are a conquered people, oppressed politically, economically, socially, and morally.
> 2. The South is by definition a nation of its own, with its own unique language, culture, history, philosophy, and icons.
> 3. Southern nationhood is practical as well as possible. The South will be better off as a free and independent nation.

4. As a nation, it is our duty and obligation to practice our God-given right of self-determination. Once Southerners determine to free themselves, no force on earth can stop them.

Read the preceding section again. Reflect on it. Then read it some more. Type it out and tape it to your refrigerator door, or tape it to your steering wheel. Place a copy anywhere it will be seen. This will ensure that these important truths become your common thoughts. Pound these truths into yourself and your neighbor. These truths are the key to the control of our own destiny.

Many will be quick to tell us how heavily the empire stacks the deck against us. As the Slovaks did, we must refuse to listen to these professional pessimists. As Southrons, we count our friends, not our enemies. Reality shows that we have a large circle of friends on which to build. Even after the April 1995 Oklahoma City bombing, news agencies conducted polls that showed that as many as 39 percent of Americans feel that the federal government has become too large and powerful. They feel that their own government poses an immediate threat to the rights and freedoms of ordinary citizens.[11] Thirty-nine percent is an amazing figure, especially considering all the *führery* and liberal propaganda that saturated the media after two Northerners came South to kill innocent Southern men, women, and children. That poll reflected the view of the empire as a whole. How do we feel as a Southern Nation?

More polls show that more than 70 percent of Southerners approve of the Confederate battle flag being incorporated into the design of their states' flags.[12] The ruling elite universally malign this show of respect for our past. They would prefer to appease a whining few, while millions suffer.

Another poll conducted by possibly the most reconstructed of the South's Northern-owned newspapers did not quite get the result they had in mind. The *Atlanta Journal-Constitution* poll asked an age-old question of Southrons. The result was conclusive. Southern independence is not the dead issue that the journalists thought. Twenty percent of Southerners, or one out of five, feel that the Southern states would be better off as a separate nation.[13] Consider it. We suffered more than 130 years of occupation, re-education, indoctrination, and constant assault from Washington's ministry of propaganda. The result is amazing.

As of 1995, more than twelve million unreconstructed Southerners supported independence. Judge that figure by the share of colonists desiring independence in 1776. At that time, only about 10 percent of the colonists supported the idea of separation from England. Still, they waged a long war to win their independence. How many Northerners would be just as happy to rid themselves of the burden of association with us?

THE FOUR PRINCIPLES OF SOUTHERN FREEDOM

1. Southerners are a conquered people, oppressed politically, economically, socially, and morally.
2. The South is by definition a nation of its own, with its own unique language, culture, history, philosophy, and icons.
3. Southern nationhood is practical as well as possible. The South will be better off as a free and independent nation.
4. As a nation, it is our duty and obligation to practice our God-given right of self-determination. Once Southerners determine to free themselves, no force on earth can stop them.

CHAPTER III

Life Behind
the Cotton Curtain

We hold these truths to be self-evident: That all men are created equal; that they are endowed by their Creator with certain unalienable rights; that among these are life, liberty, and the pursuit of happiness; that, to secure these rights, governments are instituted among men, deriving their just powers from the consent of the governed.   The Declaration of Independence

Consent. It is a very big word. It is the prime requirement for a just government. To be legitimate, a government must have its citizens' consent. Does the present American government have our consent? If not, it is our duty to change it or withdraw from it.

Once, government had our consent. It was the original American republic. That government ceased to exist in the 1860s. The radical Northern element spoiled it and laid it to waste. The enactment of the Fourteenth Amendment destroyed its last vestiges. Our modern American government bears no more resemblance to the old American republic than imperial Rome bore to the old Roman republic. What we have now is an imperial American government, the "American Empire. The consent of the governed is the difference between a free people and a captive nation held against its will. Remember the first principle of Southern nationhood: "Southerners are a conquered people, oppressed politically, economically, socially, and morally."

The tragedy is that so few people see the Southern condition in its true light. Historically, we are a nation held captive against our will. Time does not miraculously transform the crime of kidnapping into a legal act of adoption. Our fate deprives us of a promised destiny of greatness. Our future remains unfulfilled. As long as we remain the prisoners of union, we will never live up to our God-given potential.

Just as in the prior chapter's examples of captive nations, our masters deprive us of our potential. They oppress us politically. Their empire milks our economy of its natural wealth. They have socially maligned and reconstructed us. They even subvert us morally. All of this, done by the hands of our conquerors, is supposedly for our own good. These tactics are only a ploy to further control us and further enrich themselves. Just like other captive nations, Southerners can rise as a phoenix from our own ashes.

Few of us pay attention to the price of our captivity. Our union nickels and dimes us into oblivion. Meanwhile, we must bow and scrape to our supposed betters in Washington. Once we take time to examine the cost, we see we are terribly short-changed. Our union is a lop-sided arrangement. It is a foolhardy bargain that no intelligent banker or lawyer could recommend to his clients. The sooner the Southern people realize the cost of associating with the American Empire; the sooner we can do something to reduce the bill.

A NATION WITHOUT A COUNTRY

The American South as a captive nation? Yes, just like Poland and the other former Soviet satellites were. The South with a right to exist separately of the other United States? Yes, with just as much right as the original thirteen colonies had to exist separately of England. The faint of heart will object to this idea. Their indoctrination shows. They think the war settled all of this.

Would these same people trust their lawsuits to trial by combat also? Our conquest is no more valid than any other is. Because the Nazis and Soviets conquered Poland, did that make Poland rightfully theirs? What of Japan's conquest of the Philippines? What of Iraq's conquest of Kuwait? Must the Baltic republics return to the Soviet fold? Are we still rightfully British subjects? The queen should not hold her breath while waiting for an apology from Congress. On the other hand, Southerners should not hold their breath, either. Military conquest gives the victor no legal precedent or legitimacy. Trial by combat is an idea forever confined to the Dark Ages, with one exception—the trial by combat of the South locks submission forever into the Southern mind.

It is no secret that the North plundered the South after its invasion and conquest. Did conquest give the North that right? Did our conquest give the North the right to despoil the American republic and subvert it to its own interests? Again, the indoctrinated Southerner will reply that all that ended more than one hundred years ago.

Wrong. It happens now, while we sit idle. As you sit here reading this, somewhere a federal judge is deciding what new part of your privacy to invade. As you sit and watch television, someone else is deciding what version of history your children learn. There is plenty of reason to assume that it will be a politically correct Northern revision of history. Their version of the past is one carefully engineered to make our children feel soul-numbing guilt. While you work at your job, some undeserving individual, whether Washington bureaucrat or constant welfare abuser, is squandering the hard-earned fruit of your labor. While we play this weekend, the last shreds of our culture and heritage are being taken away to show themselves no more. Alert Southrons know that the Empire wants to keep us in our place. Our culture and heritage might remind us of when we were a free people. If we remember, we might try to restore our long lost rights. This would take away our masters' privilege and pleasure.

What rights did we lose? We lost many more than we realize. We lost not only the rights protected under the old constitutional republic but even more rights protected under the Confederate States Constitution. The founding fathers added the first ten amendments, the Bill of Rights, to the U.S. Constitution as an afterthought. The states' constitutions already guaranteed the citizens' rights. However, the states insisted on protecting our unalienable rights within the union, also. Many of the framers of the U.S. Constitution thought that the rights of citizens were obvious. They did not need inclusion in the document. The states disagreed. The Bill of Rights was the price of union.

In the Confederate Constitution, the rights of citizens are not an afterthought. Included in the main body of the document, they are safe. Your rights were also more secure under the Confederate Constitution, because its framers made it more difficult to amend. What has become of these rights? The myth of history shields from view or justifies the loss of many of our most unalienable rights. Here are a few examples.

The freedom of religion guaranteed in the First Amendment embodies the spirit of why many colonists originally came to these shores. The Washington aristocracy now uses the First Amendment as the basis for exclusion of religion from all public or government activity. They give the reason behind this as a protection of minority religious groups. The concern they express is that even a non-denominational prayer might offend or influence an individual, therefore violating his First Amendment rights. They call this the separation of church and state (also known as freedom *from* religion). This separation appears nowhere in the constitution or in the writings of its framers. Before you object because of the popularized myth, remember that Thomas Jefferson was not one of the constitution's framers.

The freedom of speech as stated in the First Amendment is alive and well for some. For the rest of us, the elite and their drive for politically correct expression curtails our right. Therefore, you may still say whatever you like as long as it is not controversial and viewed as offensive or intolerant by anyone. To this you must add the qualifier that what you say cannot be true, historically accurate, or in opposition to the elite's general view of Utopia. If one or more of the Empire's special protected subjects object to what you say, they declare your freedom of speech void. This is, of course unless you are a homosexual, a protected minority, a pornographer (or other special "artist"), or are a member of the Empire's ruling class. Even libel and smut are free speech for them.

Our right to keep and bear arms, as embodied in the Second Amendment, withers and still faces repeal. There should be no controversy. The argument should have ended for all times when President George Washington signed the Militia Act of 1792 into law. The Militia Act enrolled all able-bodied, adult male citizens in the general militia. The same law required all military-aged male citizens to own their own firearm. That should make things clear, but here is the official opinion of our government, written by a Justice Department official on behalf of the Clinton administration.

> The current state of federal law does not recognize that the Second Amendment protects the right of private citizens to possess firearms of any type. Instead, the Second Amendment is deemed to be a collective right belonging to the state and not to an individual. Accordingly, the Second Amendment is interpreted by this administration as prohibiting the federal government from preventing a state government from forming or having a state recognized militia force. With this understanding

in mind, the source of citizens' authority to possess a handgun has never been particularly identified in American law.[1]

There is little doubt, especially among anti-gun activists, why the Second Amendment was thought to be imperative. They know (and conceal) the truth, as Noah Webster understood it.

> Before a standing army can rule, the people must be disarmed; as they are in almost every kingdom in Europe. The supreme power in America cannot enforce unjust laws by the sword, because the whole body of the people are armed, and constitute a force superior to any band of regular troops that can be, on any pretense, raised in the United States.[2]

Nothing could be stated more plainly. The Second Amendment could not be plainer. There is no exclusion of military arms or the mention of legitimate sporting use. Parliament used the "sporting-use" clause of the unwritten British constitution to disarm all but the elite of Britain. Since only the lords and gentry of Britain own land, only they have a place to hunt. To cut down on supposed poaching, the British government disarmed the rest of the populace. Now only the elite and the military of the British Empire have arms.[3] There can be no doubt about the meaning of the Second Amendment. The Second Amendment guarantees the people of the several states the means to resist tyranny.

Your Fourth Amendment protection against search and seizure is also under attack. As a means of fighting illegal drugs, some seek to limit your protection from prying officials. Such measures could remove the issue and execution of search warrants from even the superficial scrutiny of our courts. If the government enacts this legislation, who will protect the citizen?

The Fifth Amendment protected us from the seizure of private property by government. At least, it did, until agencies such as the Internal Revenue Service, Farmer's Home Administration, and the Environmental Protection Agency came along. During the rampage of farm foreclosures of the 1970s and 1980s, the FHA made it a point to seize any personal property that could be remotely considered a farm asset, along with mortgaged property. This was a clear violation of the principles embodied in the Fifth Amendment.

You will find there is little that resembles due process of law when the Internal Revenue Service arbitrarily seizes property or assets. It may be for accounting errors or non-compliance with any of the many volumes of Internal Revenue codes. Why? The IRS code is not law. Your congressman never debated or voted on the code. It is agency-enforced regulation. Every April, stories fill the press about law-abiding citizens whose lives and businesses the IRS destroys with a mere accusation followed by seizure. Most of those seizures never passed a judge's scrutiny. Even with all the new laws that require the IRS to provide proof of its allegations, do not expect them to suddenly become a taxpayer-friendly agency. So much for rights.

The list goes on and on. The freedom of association, property rights, and states' rights, all died hideous deaths. This includes the most basic right of all, the right of self-determination. What is self-determination? It is the right to band together with other citizens and chose your own destinies and form of government. That is what the citizens of the Confederate States did. We can see that this was their right according to the Declaration of Independence. Remember to exercise your rights or you will lose them.

> But when a long train of abuses and usurpations, pursuing invariably the same object, evinces a design to reduce them under absolute despotism, it is their right, it is their duty, to throw off such government and to provide new guards for their future security.[4]

Our Creator endowed all people with the right of self-determination. What of the South? Why do federal judges hobble our legislatures? Obviously, we do not lack representation at the state level. At the state level, we can apply effective pressure for change. Ask former governor Jim Guy Tucker of Arkansas if he wants to tamper with school consolidation any more. After being battered with eggs by a hostile crowd in Cabot, Arkansas, he is convinced. The same can happen in any state, but how do you get within egg-range of congress? A faceless federal judiciary? A president? They are out of range to anyone using conventional means. The Empire fears us, so it places itself beyond our reach. Nothing short of a return to our original form of republic will restore them to being within range. No matter what you are told at campaign time, they are not voluntarily going to place themselves back within egg-range.

The South is a victim, and the Empire wants to keep it that way. The Empire killed more than six hundred thousand to keep it that way. All other states have the right to qualify voters. The Voting

Rights Act of 1964 (renewed during the Reagan administration) assures that only the South does not.[5] In turn, the welfare system makes sure that the imperial oligarchy has a steady stream of bought votes to keep it in power. Vote buying, of course, is illegal and unethical, unless you are one of the privileged classes sitting in Babylon on the Potomac.

Ever since the North illegally invaded the South in 1861, no traditional Southern conservative is allowed a seat on the Supreme Court. If the South had real representation on the Supreme Court, could the nightmarish events of the 1950s and 1960s have taken place? Could the Empire single out the South for social engineering?

We are the victims of political discrimination, to say the least. To state it correctly, we are serfs. More than once we have challenged the order. A force of federal marshals and the 101st Airborne Division suppressed Arkansas's challenge in 1957. This was just months after Soviet tanks suppressed Hungary's challenge to Moscow's dominion. President Eisenhower condemned the Soviets for using military force against civilians. Shortly thereafter, he used troops against civilians in Little Rock. Hypocrisy has always been the Yankees' strong point.

Little Rock just started the trend. The next use of federal muscle against Southern civilians was in 1962. That beloved emperor, John F. Kennedy, decided to send thousands of heavily armed troops to lay siege to Oxford, Mississippi. The Feds started a small war to ensure that one young black man could force his way into Ole Miss. As shots rang out night and day, it soon became apparent who was doing all the shooting. For days soldiers tear-gassed dormitories, arresting and holding students in basements without food or sanitation. When it was over, scores were wounded. One innocent student and a French reporter lay dead.[6] Thanks to Hollywood, everyone remembers "Mississippi burning," but it seems no one remembers who lit the fire. The scene at Ole Miss resembled some of Sherman's earlier work. Because it was down South, Washington was automatically right.

> Families were arrested along the highways leading into Oxford, herded into animal sheds, held for as long as twenty-four hours without food, water, or blankets, and clubbed by Federal marshals whose mercurial moods were often foul. A twelve-year-old boy was severely beaten for falling asleep against a marshal's orders.[7]

There was no national outrage for Mississippi's killed and wounded. Especially none like the outcry that later characterized the Northern shooting commonly known as the Kent State Massacre. The whole affair served to remind a new Southern generation just who was boss. It also showed just whose rights counted the most with the empire.

Leaders rise among us, determined to restore our rights. George Wallace was shot for his effort. How many more were censured? Suppressed? Discouraged? Murdered? What about Huey Long?

To understand where we must go, we must understand where we have been. A quick study of the U.S. Constitution and amendments one through twelve reveals where we started. Before our unsuccessful defense of constitutional liberty and self-determination, the president had very limited power. The executive branch was a shadow of what it quickly became under and after Lincoln.

The federal government began no more powerful than the states, themselves. The only instance where an average, law-abiding, state citizen noticed the federal government was through the census, military service, or at the post office. Our forefathers designed it that way. They had a very real fear of big government. The founding fathers feared large standing armies, whether they were our military's or those of a government agency. They placed safeguards against the abuse of power by any one man or group of men. The War of Northern Aggression proved their fears were well founded.

A quick reading of the rest of the amendments will reveal what happened. The radical Northern majority removed the founding fathers' tight restrictions on government power. A prostrate South lay powerless to resist, her armies dead or starved. Her cities were in ruins. Her white population was largely forbidden its most basic American right, the right to vote. The means was oppression. The end was the new American Empire. The rebirth dragged Southerners, kicking and screaming, from freedom and independence into bondage and tyranny.

The empire retains enough of the surface trappings of the old republic to provide the illusion of legitimacy. Many settled in to make the best of their circumstances. Still, Southerners were not all fooled. We call these wise ones "unreconstructed Confederates." Many of them rode at night to restore some semblance of the public order. A poplar song of the 1870s illustrated the attitude of a prostrate, helpless, but still defiant people. "I'm a Good Ole Rebel," written by Major Innes Randolph, C.S.A., was an overnight success.[8] It was largely passed by word of mouth from artist to artist, because the Yankee occupation government controlled the printing presses that would have printed the sheet music. Southern musician Bobby Horton preserved the song on his first "Homespun Songs of the C.S.A." album. The song shocks the modern indoctrinated Southern mind, but once heard, it finds a familiar, haunted place in the Southern heart and memory. It fills the soul with a longing for that which we lost.

Paralleling the song's chilling message are the least publicized words ever spoken by Robert E. Lee. He uttered these words after a session in which former Confederate leaders were expected to express thanks for their maltreatment to a group of gloating Yankee officers. Lee's words left little doubt as to his true convictions.

> If I had foreseen the use those people designed to make of their victory, there would have been no surrender at Appomattox Courthouse; no, sir, not by me. Had I foreseen these results of subjugation, I would have preferred to die at Appomattox with my brave men, my sword in this right hand.[9]

Still, the people are not all fooled. The electoral revolution of November 1994 shows that the whole citizenry, not just the South, is waking. Their real awakening is yet to come. They will realize that they have merely traded big Democratic government for big Republican government. This is already beginning to show; another broken contract. Of course, those of us who are of Native-American descent should not be surprised. Broken contracts and treaties are nothing new to us.

How was our Constitution subverted? How was the original "Contract with America" broken? The Fourteenth Amendment is a prime example, an example that David Lawrence, then editor of *U.S. News and World Report* magazine, subjected to a two-page editorial in 1957. The magazine considered the subject so important that they reprinted the editorial in 1970. You can order a copy of this article from your local library. It is fittingly titled "The Worst Scandal In Our History." In his editorial, Mr. Lawrence clearly shows that the Fourteenth Amendment was never legally ratified. Southerners should know why.[10]

The war was over. From 1866 to March 2, 1867, the Southern states were back in the union. Again accorded the rights of statehood, their representatives and senators took their seats in congress. The states participated in the ratification of the Thirteenth Amendment, outlawing slavery. They also participated in the first consideration of the Fourteenth Amendment, which resulted in its rejection.

On March 2, 1867, congress openly violated Article V of the Constitution by passing the Reconstruction Act of 1867. This first Reconstruction Act ejected the Southern representatives and senators. President Andrew Johnson vetoed the act and congress overrode his veto the same day.[11]

This first of the Reconstruction Acts also abolished all civil government in the South and subjected the Southern states to government by military occupation forces. Because of the abuses committed by these troops, federal law now prohibits this peacetime use of federal troops against U.S. citizens under the *Posse Commitatus* Act. Remember that the war had been over for two years.[12]

The Reconstruction Acts declared the Southern states to be outside the union. That is absurd. The North spent the lives of more than 300,000 of its troops in the argument that the South could not leave the Union. The military occupation governments then disenfranchised all white citizens who had supported the Confederate government or who had served in its military. This violated the prohibition against *ex post facto* laws in Article I, Section 9 of the U.S. Constitution.

The federal government then required the occupied states to ratify the Fourteenth Amendment before they would be allowed back into the union. This measure forced ratification. It not only violated constitutional law, it was a breach of both civil and common law known as coercion.

Since the military had installed its own legislatures, why did ratification not continue and the states rejoin the union? There was still much wealth left to plunder before the Northern radicals would allow Southerners relief. For a decade, the plunder continued. It did not relent until the Southern states' treasuries were as barren as their war-ravaged land. In the meantime, the states of New Jersey, Ohio, and Oregon rescinded their ratification of the Fourteenth Amendment.

An example of the corruption present in the radical Northern legislatures was Oregon's first ratification vote. Two of the Oregon legislators opposed to ratification were abducted to prevent them from voting. Impostors supporting ratification took their place.

The ratification barely passed, with the impostors' votes playing a vital part in its passing.[13] When the dust settled, the outraged citizens of Oregon insisted on a new vote.

The U.S. Secretary of State refused to accept the three states' recall of their ratification. He counted New Jersey, Ohio, and Oregon as voting for ratification of the Fourteenth Amendment. He did so over the objection and without the consent of the three state legislatures.

This brings us back to consent, the principle justification of all government. Where is our consent? Did we consent to the destruction of the old republic? Did we consent to the invasion of our beloved Southland? Did we consent to our repeated reconstruction? Of course, we did not.

THE HIND TIT

Did you ever wonder? Why do hard times always hit hardest in the South? Where, for instance, is the Northern version of the "Dust Bowl"? With all the fabled economic prosperity of the Sun Belt, with all our native talents and natural wealth, why can't our people live the American dream?

The states of the former Confederacy are the armpit of the stagnant American Empire. Why is this? Our region is rich in natural resources. We have the richest farmland and the most productive grazing land in the world. We have an ample supply of labor and talent. The want ads in our newspapers prove there are plenty of opportunities for those who are willing. In the 1980s, financiers proclaimed Little Rock, Arkansas as the new Wall Street of the West. We have great natural wealth in our region. So, where is our share of the prosperity? Why are we kept the poorest section of the empire?

At one time, we were the richest section of the Old American republic. The Confederates of the 1860s had every reason to be optimistic. If you examine the South of that time as a separate nation, your findings do not jibe with the official myth of history. As of 1860, the South would have been the third-most-prosperous nation on earth. Remember that this was mainly due to agriculture. The South had one-third of the country's railroad mileage, and invested heavily in new agricultural technology. However, the industrial base of the South was geared more toward food production and the support of agriculture. The flour mills of Richmond, Virginia are good examples. With a few exceptions—like the iron works of northern Alabama—most Southern industries were cottage industries. These operations were geared toward local consumption. The South was not an industrial super-power in 1860.[14]

The North and England were richer because of their mix of agriculture and highly developed industry. Their devotion to trade and heavy investments in shipping played an even larger role. The North also had a government-enforced tariff designed to milk the Southern section of its wealth. The trade and industrial development that would have been necessary upon independence could possibly have made the South the richest nation on earth.

What happened? The resources are still here. Our industrial development is complete. We still have a large agricultural base. We have plenty of willing and talented workers. We have everything a nation needs to succeed. Where is all the prosperity? The answer: In a precious few pockets, pockets that reside elsewhere.

During reconstruction, Northern speculators seeking bargains chartered special trains. Destined South, they bought more than 50 million acres of virgin forest for mere pocket change. The speculators razed those lost forests to further build the North, not to rebuild the South. The profits from that sale went back north, along with the carpetbagger and the rest of the South's wealth.[15]

During the Great Depression, we again lost much more of our natural wealth. Small subsistence farmers inhabited much of the Ozarks, the Appalachian region, and northern Mississippi. Most of them lost their land to delinquent taxes and mortgages, or moved to cities to find work. Many of these lost lands are now known as national forests.[16] Beneath these government holdings are the South's richest mineral reserves. The Department of the Interior parcels out our lost wealth to developers and exploiters. News services expressed alarm at the recent exposure of a foreign company that bought mining rights to land holding an estimated $10 billion worth of gold for $5 per acre. The company applied a little-known, but often used law, the General Mining Law of 1872. This was just an instance the emperor allowed us to hear about, because he wants to change the law and raise the price of any future sales.[17]

Currently the U.S. Forest Service is planning to swap 50,000 acres of the Ouachita National Forest for more than 100,000 acres of land owned by the Weyerhauser Corporation. This would appear a wise trade, until you look below the surface. Weyerhauser will keep all oil, gas, and mining rights to its traded 100,000 acres. This acreage has suffered years of exploitation and is of questionable economic or recreational value. Where accessible, Weyerhauser converted its parcel to commercial pine plantations. Weyerhauser could presumably retain harvest rights to this timber.[18]

The public parcel is mostly native hardwood. Preserved largely through the efforts of local environmentalists, it retains its natural ecosystem. It is very accessible to logging, because our taxes paid to build access roads for fire protection. Supposedly, the Empire protects any public land from exploitation that would adversely affect the environment. All of this is subject to change with the swap. According to environmentalist Bruce McMath, "Public land swaps clearly present a great potential for private profiteering through the exploitation of preserved public resources."[19]

The swaps would also give the U.S. Forest Service the commercial pine plantations they have coveted for so long. Courts forbade the Forest Service to develop these plantations on their own. This resulted from settling a lawsuit that made public the Forest Service's aerial spraying of Agent Orange. The spraying aided their wholesale conversion of native hardwood acreage into pine plantations. The court found this conversion was in progress all over the South.[20]

The loss of family-owned land due to financial hardship caused all of this. That is how the large timber conglomerates and the Federal Empire came to own most of the land in the South. For those die-hards who saved their land, a different fate waited.

The battle cry of the 1970s was "Save the family farm!" All the protectionist scheming and lawmaking was mainly a show. At the same time as the "Great Tractorcades" of the Carter years, agricultural policy shifted to favor corporate farms and the large operations—like the ones Carter family owns. Still, the problems of the Southern farmer started long before the 1970s. Early, the moneylenders encouraged us to borrow federal money to overproduce. Large numbers took the bait and sold their independence. Was it any wonder that they found themselves in trouble? For many this started an endless chain of borrow and refinance, until the final default. We should have known better. Twelve Southerners known as the Fugitive Agrarians warned us in the 1930 treatise, *I'll Take My Stand.* As Fugitive Andrew Lytle cautioned, "A farm is not a place to grow wealthy; it is a place to grow corn."[21]

The 1970s were the result of more than one hundred years of agricultural discrimination by the Empire. In a political climate of such oppression, the Southerner was, and still is, left the hind tit. Again, Southrons must appeal to the mercy of their current emperor, because all the warnings came true. Just the Fugitives said, the industrial revolution failed. It did not restore our former prosperity. The industries that now employ most Southrons depend on owners and financiers outside the South. The profits of business do not remain here. They are deposited in outside banks and distributed to outside financiers. In turn the big-money interests erect barriers to prevent competition from any would-be Southern industrialists. Even conglomerates with their headquarters in the South depend on outside and foreign capital.

Although Southern industries are extremely successful and productive, they are notorious for their pay and working conditions. The sweatshop of legend and reality finds its home in the South. Exploiters find a pool of cheap labor. The same Northern companies gravitate to our lower standards that are devised to attract industry. If problems or resistance in the work force arises, the company simply moves. This keeps costs down by threat. There is no sane reason a man or woman in Georgia or Oklahoma, working under the same union and doing the same job, should not receive the same wage as they would if they worked in Illinois or New Jersey. Still, the census of 1990 shows that the Southern worker still makes 20 percent less than his Northeastern counterpart. This might be one reason that 40 percent of Americans on food stamps, and 41 percent of all Americans living below the poverty level, live in the South. These Southern poor are another visible reminder of the Empire's campaign of economic oppression. [22]

Yes, the South is still the land of the sweatshop. This is a fact many of us learn the hard way. I did. My first industrial job was spreading fabric for a clothing manufacturer. After working my way up to full pay in 1984, I earned $4.65/hour. My Yankee counterpart in the same manufacturer's Milwaukee, Wisconsin plant not only earned 320 percent more, but also had a lower production standard.

Another example of the industrial espionage directed at the South is the much-publicized Saturn auto plant in Spring Hill, Tennessee. When then-Tennessee Governor Lamar Alexander persuaded General Motors to build its Saturn plant in the tiny community of Spring Hill, the citizens rejoiced. The original deal was that local workers would make up the bulk of the labor force. After Alexander lost to Democrat Ned McWherter, the deal changed instantly. While the locals still wait for their jobs, GM placed hiring preference on present United Auto Workers employees. This created a mass migration from places like Detroit and Pontiac, Michigan. Despite the immediate and futile uproar from jilted Tennesseans, Saturn hired workers by U.A.W. seniority, where no U.A.W. local had ever existed. The citizens of Spring Hill sift through the scraps. While local employers laid people off, Saturn hired from out of town. Saturn also paid to have prospective employees and their families flown South to view the opportunities that awaited them.[23]

Saturn's appearance placed the Maury County residents in even more desperate straits. The already under-employed locals bear the burden of the new population growth. Sales and property taxes rose drastically to provide education for the 1,500 transplanted Yankee children. The locals also face skyrocketing rent, utilities, and taxes with no increase in income, all due to their new neighbors from the North.[24]

The problems cut deeper in the form of an increased crime rate. Also, there are now reports of gang activity, where it was never a concern before Saturn. The tiny Spring Hill Police Department and the Maury County Sheriff's Office have neither the budget nor the staff to handle *their* increase of business. The unexpected social problems that accompany a mass influx of people who neither respect nor care for the local culture became a plague. Now Saturn pressures local businesses to hire the spouses of Saturn employees before the locals. Middle-Tennessee's golden dream is now a cheap tin nightmare.

Meanwhile, forty minutes' drive away, Nissan built a new plant in Smyrna, Tennessee and kept its promises. Nissan hired local workers to staff its new plant. The population welcomed the Japanese automaker. This is mainly because the Japanese gave them none of the trauma associated with inviting a Northern corporation into the community.[25]

The Empire will not allow equal Southern business competition. This competition might draw away the empire's sacred profits to boost Southern economies. So, the balance of economic power, one of the chief causes of the original War For Southern Independence, still milks the South of its wealth. As the elite suppress Southern agriculture and industry, they also suppress the achievement of the individual Southron. The empire brushed aside the constitutional prohibition against direct levies upon the people with an arrogant and vengeful disdain. Our oppressive tax system drains the middle class of its productivity. Like most citizens, we do not mind paying our fair share. Still, we wonder: What is our fair share?

By stifling middle-class workers, the elite use our tribute to create an underclass ensnared in the welfare web. The very existence of the welfare system in its present form is an insult to the taxpayer. When closely examined, we find it is merely a colorful scheme for buying votes. Even the lowest dog, though he will not hunt or work, will not bite the hand that feeds him. The Empire's social engineering has shown its stupidity and serves no real purpose but to further degrade society. Like most government-contrived insults, we foot the bill for our own abuse. Whether we look at it as insult or abuse, it continues because we have never known things to be any other way.

The Empire never misses a chance to wage its campaign of unlimited economic warfare against the South. This conflict is designed to keep us an economic colony of the Empire. Ever subservient and beaten into line, the Southron works to enrich the elite of his and other regions. Even those who opt for "the easy way out" are cheated. Those entangled in the Southern version of the welfare web find their payments 47 percent lower than in other states.[26]

Along with the Empire's economic campaign, another hidden assault slowly begins to show its effect. The war on the Southern environment has the potential to harm as many innocent victims than the most terrible war waged against men. Today we can see many chemical time bombs surfacing across the South. Like the other oppressions that befall us, the ruling class will try to shift the blame for this tragedy to us. However, this disaster is entirely a creation of twentieth-century corporate greed.

The industrial exploitation of the South goes on with traditional Yankee recklessness. Our masters give no thought to the cost. They have no concern for tomorrow. The very standards that we relaxed to invite outside industry could mean our death. Every Southern paper mill, chemical plant, and refinery has its "blue lagoon." Government requires these holding areas as treatment facilities for waste and toxic by-products. Most are inefficient and release tons of waste products into our environment. Usually, the result of EPA wrist-slapping only accounts as operating costs. The big polluters have plenty of money to keep on running.

While the big boys keep up their depredations, the EPA contrives to harass the public. Many counties and small towns feel the effects. Bureaucrats force counties to close their landfills for technical violations and spend millions to replace rural dumpsters with private trash pickup. The same bureaucrats force cities to change water sources at a whim, while the industrialists are given a free hand. Meanwhile, federal judges ensure that the South continues to be the Empire's dumping ground. Southern states and communities face court orders to accept garbage, contaminated soil, and other toxic wastes from outside areas. The latest outrage is the dumping of low-level radioactive wastes. No matter what the container, it eventually leaks. What *they* dump today, *we* drink tomorrow. Such repeated abuse of the Mississippi River gave its lower valley its name, "The Cancer Corridor." The finger, of course, always points to blame the South. Does no one north of Memphis ever dump his waste into the river? Of course they do. All the North's agricultural and industrial deadly brew does not stay up North. It flows South, where Washington forces us to drink it. It is just one more example of the Empire's legacy of death and destruction.

The South is by design the poorest section of the Empire. Without internal funds, it is much harder to lash out against our oppressor. We are nothing more than an economic colony of the American Empire. The Empire siphons off our natural wealth for the benefit of its privileged few. We scrape together just enough leavings to keep us producing for our masters. How do we break this chain? Placing our faith in elected officials is not the answer. They value the Empire's thirty pieces of silver too much. Instead we must place our faith in ourselves and pursue our independence.

THE LEPER COLONY

In our corner of the world, there is an uncontrollable idea at work. It is a dangerous idea. More of a heresy, its followers show fanatical devotion. No men's beliefs are sacred to them, save their own. They stop at nothing. Using all the tools of the modern era, they spread their imperial un-gospel. Their arsenal includes the typical run of tyrant's weapons, from media to mind control, but they favor violence. It is multiculturalism, a perverse version of secular humanism. Even its name, multiculturalism, is a lie.

Sharing the wealth of ideas from other cultures is not evil. Southerners have done it for several centuries. Multiculturalism, however, is an evil. Multiculturalism is a mask concealing the death of culture. Tolerance and the brotherhood of man are just a front. This doctrine censors and destroys certain cultures while substituting one universal non-culture. Multiculturalism assumes that certain cultures are good and virtuous. Naturally, all others are inherently evil. The American Empire's ruling elite proclaim that Yankee and pseudo-African cultures are profound, the height of virtue. Of course, that leaves the opposite, Southern culture and its Confederate heritage, as the ultimate evil.

Southrons know this to be absurd. The South itself is a wonderful mix of cultures, each precious and complementary. This blend of Gaelic, Hispanic, French, and African influences is what gives the South its special air. The South was the first true cosmopolitan community of the New World. This is our unique and priceless legacy. It is almost absurd for Southrons to think of the threats of New England. Led by Massachusetts in 1803, the birthplace of the American Revolution showed its unique brand of tolerance by threatening to secede over the Louisiana Purchase, then again during the War of 1812 and over Louisiana's planned statehood. Massachusetts's bluebloods and puritans felt themselves too good to associate with a land of Creoles and Acadians. They especially dreaded Louisiana's large population of free men of color. The Southern fold welcomed this same rich blend of cultures.[27]

Again in 1845, New England threatened secession over the annexation of the Republic of Texas.[28] This time one of their chief grievances was Texas's many Hispanic Catholics. Sixteen years later, Massachusetts and the other New England states changed their minds. They sent thousands of troops to enforce their continued association with Louisiana, Texas, and the other states of the Confederacy. What a heartwarming gesture it was.

Multiculturalism is simply a tidy word for cultural genocide. It is an intellectual version of ethnic cleansing. The sad part is that you pay taxes to fund your own demise. The cultural elite who propagate these ideas are too lazy to work and too scared to steal. They live comfortably on the government payroll, hiding in bureaus and public universities. There, they are secure from the crime and social turmoil that afflicts real people. There, your tax dollars are at work.

Social engineering is not new to the South. It is the fate of our unsuccessful defense of liberty and constitutional government, our lost War for Independence. Reconstruction followed and continues. Our self-destructive association with the Yankee Empire seals our fate as the scapegoat. What we see today is nothing. Judging from the past, we can easily forecast what tomorrow holds. Such social engineering dooms itself to failure because human nature is not a bridge or a mathematical calculation. Humans are not rivers for the Army Corps of Engineers to turn or channel. True, the South has many social problems today, but few of them are of our own making. It is not coincidental that all the establishment's solutions only lead to more decay. While the American Empire claims it is concerned about the state of society, why does it constantly attack the family, the very root of society? We have an Emperor who laments for family values one minute yet, the next he signs dubious legislation that destroys families.

The welfare web is a prime example. Still, the central government will fight ruthlessly to keep the system in place. By keeping those who choose life in the web dependent, the establishment, in effect, buys their votes. The Empire also gives the leech a pay raise for breeding even more out-of-wedlock dependents into the trap. All the while, our taxes go for *free* child care, *free* medical care, *free* housing, etc., all to keep the welfare experience convenient.

Why does the Empire provide advantages to those who chose immoral and deviant lifestyles? Surely, there is no great public virtue in homosexuality. Due to their *choice* to live in immorality, these people are special. They all have the same rights as every other citizen but, because of their political value, the Yankee Empire grants them extra protection and privileges. People receive bribes for their lifestyles as well as their ethnicity.

Why does the central government manufacture racism? Human nature already salts itself with preferences. Why should government magnify it into hatred by policy? Human nature is ingrained, unconquerable. Human nature ensures that if one class or race is seen as favored, others will resent it. That resentment is returned as it is felt. Add a few social programs to kindle further resentment, linked with the work of the Empire's propaganda machine, and you have a constant state of racial and ethnic turmoil. This is the true goal of programs such as affirmative action, minority set-asides, and empowerment. None of these programs ever solved a single social or racial ill. They only magnify resentment and envy into hatred. These programs aim to do just that. Why else should the American Empire seek to propagate the very problems it says it wants to end?

Why do our so-called leaders refuse to halt illegal immigration?

They direct much rhetoric at the problem, but no effort. There is no enforcement of existing laws. One reason is that illegal immigrants water down the traditional Southern populace. Eventually all these illegal immigrants gain citizenship and the vote. For whom will they vote? Will they support their neighbors, who didn't openly welcome them into their community, or will they support the Empire? Of course, they will support that same Empire that provided them with free education, health care, and a steady monthly welfare check. These are not the honest people who wait patiently while the bureaucrats process their papers to begin their search for a new life. Illegal aliens are just that, illegal. This makes them criminals. Usually, their criminal disdain for our immigration laws is just the beginning. They welcome the chance for a windfall by breaking other laws.

Why does the tide from below the Rio Grande continue unchecked? If it were the problem of Ohio or Pennsylvania, then the illegal immigration crisis would be top priority. Instead, it is a Southern problem. As a Southern problem, it furthers the aims of the Empire. What would be the result of putting these criminals, these illegal aliens in prison? It would be the same as incarcerating any other felon. They would spend a minimum of time behind bars, pampered by the federal judiciary before their early release.

Punishment is just not what it used to be. Authorized by the questionable Fourteenth Amendment, federal judges have made sure it is not. The state can actually do little to punish an offender within the rigid guidelines set by federal courts. Consequently, courts force the states to give convicted criminals better living conditions than many of the state's law-abiding citizens. With little or no forced labor, a convicted criminal has little to do except enjoy the facilities provided by our money. In most cases, this includes weight training and recreational programs superior to most health clubs. We furnish them large law libraries, to better plan appeals and frivolous lawsuits against the state and its prison staff. In addition, many convicts enjoy the ability to earn a college degree free of charge. While sometimes fewer than 50 percent of a state's law-abiding citizens have access to cable television, almost 100 percent of prison inmates do. Many have in-cell televisions furnished by the taxpayer. Pornographic programs on cable or satellite are popular viewing fare. Keep in mind that courts hold that this is the prisoner's right, and our obligation to provide this service.

Today, prisons consider themselves centers for counseling and rehabilitation. Contrast this with the prison's old yet effective role as a center for punishment. There was a time when our prisons were self-sufficient. Convicts worked to earn their keep. Many prisons actually turned a profit, primarily through farming and contract work. Now, prisons devour fortunes in tax moneys with little result. It is little wonder the crime rate soars under these conditions. There was once a time when a felon left a prison only upon paying his debt to society, not after achieving early release. In that day, few that graduated from the penal system ever considered doing anything that would risk their return for further "education." That is the sure sign of rehabilitation.

Parallel the millions wasted on prisons with the millions wasted by our public education system. Don't even consider all the money spent to bus students away from their own neighborhoods. That is nothing. A look at the real educational crisis shows that no matter how much money the central government funnels into public education, the results only get worse. How could this happen? It is primarily the result of control by the educational establishment's experts. These experts are always willing to experiment on someone else's children using someone else's money. They assure us they always know what is best for our children. In the meantime, their children go to exclusive private schools. Seated with their admiring followers around them, the elite never quite realize that they are mere mortals like us. Put simply, the educational crisis is another way of furthering the Empire's goals. Fewer and fewer high school graduates know how to read, write, and do simple arithmetic. The obvious question is, "How could they graduate?" This is a good question. Especially since the three R's are the basis of all education. Several, several years ago, such students would not have graduated.

One educator noted that the quality of American education has declined one grade level each decade since the turn of the century. That means that a high school diploma today is the equivalent of a sixth grade education in the 1940s. A college degree earned today is the equivalent of a sixth-grade education at the turn of the century. When compared against the rest of the world in 1991, American students ranked fourteenth in math. The once proud American intellect that placed men on the moon now positions itself somewhere between the level of Spain and Jordan. America's public education system is definitely on the skids. However, we know it is not for lack of money being thrown at the problem.[29]

Emphasis in modern education strays farther away from the basics, and more toward computers and social science. This amazes many of us. What is the apparent need of children for computer skills if they cannot read a computer's output? Also of dubious value is the ability of any small child to lecture on the oppressed Muslim masses in Bosnia-Herzegovina. Most of these same kids can't even spell the word "oppressed." Could it be that the same system that forbids even the mention of God in public schools has some use for uneducated masses of people?

When Thomas Jefferson promoted the idea of public education, he did so for two reasons. First, he assumed that any public schools would be locally controlled. Second, he knew that education is the best insurance policy for liberty. Through the years, we see what become of local control. There is no such animal. Unless of course you have a federal judge stationed nearby.[30]

The national teachers' union has their hand in the mess as much as any body of the empire. I cannot think of any rural Southern school district that would be warped enough to declare October to be "National Gay-Lesbian Month" in our schools. Still, the National Education Association did so for all American schools in its 1995 convention. Their resolution B-9 requires plans to teach about homosexuals throughout history, diverse sexual orientation, and the celebration of "Lesbian and Gay History Month." More than likely these deviants would not get a single day from a rural Southern school board, let alone a whole month.[31]

As for Jefferson's second reason, he felt it was the most important. He felt that the success of the American secession from British rule depended largely upon the intellect of the colonists. Why was Jefferson so concerned about education when our current leaders obviously are not? Because Jefferson saw the real cost of education. He saw not the cost of teachers and schools, but of the lack of them. For two centuries, thirteen colonies of uneducated European immigrants had no choice. They had to accept the English crown as their ultimate authority.

It was only after the colonies developed a literate middle class that people began to question the "Divine Right of Kings." Jefferson knew well that knowledge is the most effective tool for gaining and preserving liberty. Tyrants and despots feed off ignorance. Without a large, literate middle class, few could have read Thomas Paine's

Common Sense, or *The American Crisis.* Those two statements of reason transformed indifferent British colonists into Americans. Jefferson knew that tyranny does not sit long with an educated people. He also knew that an illiterate people had no choice but to swallow any argument thrust upon them. It mattered little whether that argument came from a king, a pope, or a president.

Whenever a people lack education, they are doomed to follow blindly. This is a prime reason that we see the failure of modern public education. The American Empire does not need educated men and women. It has its ruling class already. It does not need dissent. What the American Empire needs is followers. It needs followers who don't question the ruling class. That is why Johnny can't read. The Empire does not want Johnny to read. If he could read, Johnny might learn to think. For this reason, his classroom teems with hooligans, to disrupt his education. The teacher is not allowed to keep order, so Johnny can't learn basic skills. Meanwhile, educators remove the emphasis from the fundamental subjects and concentrate on social sciences. What is the main diet of the social science that schools feed our children? Of course, it is multiculturalism. Multiculturalism destroys the historic distinction of cultural groups, creating an easily controlled mongrel mass. Though our children want to learn to read and write, they will instead receive the mush the establishment wants programmed into them. It is easy to see it happening around us. We only need to look. Too many of us freely accept blinders along with our shackles. What does it all mean? Where does it all lead? Do we have to accept our own demise?

We must not make it easy for those who seek to control us. We can ensure that those convicted felons, illegal aliens, perverts, and social deviants have no more rights than productive citizens. They have no claim on the fruit of our labors. Along the same lines, we must not submit to our own disarmament because someone else claims it is for our own protection.

FORTY YEARS IN THE WILDERNESS

To find a moral basis for our separation from the rest of the American Empire, all we have to do is examine our surroundings. The events taking place around us are enough to make your blood boil. The moral plight of the American Empire is its greatest threat to the people it holds captive. We will feel the result of our captivity not only in this life but the one that comes after. It is amazing to see how much we allow, condone, and even finance in the name of so-called responsible government. A central question we must ask ourselves is "What do we worship today?"

We like to answer, "God," but if we open our eyes, we find the true answers. The Empire accepts and proliferates many false gods. The American Empire expects a good citizen to give his all to the pursuit of money. Still, who needs a god vulnerable to economic whims or even a match? The lust for power is the driving force of many of our self-styled masters. The power that they pursue still cannot conquer death. Many of these same status-seekers tell us that our best hope lies in science and progress. They too, are false messiahs that crumble before judgment and reason. Yet, all of these are jealous gods who will have no other god, or even God, before them.

The ignorant and the blind preach these earthly pursuits with passion and force—much like the gnosis warned of by the apostle Paul. These false prophets gnaw at the soul of our people, and convert many. Their irreligion is the road to ruin for all to share equally. Fittingly, the only true equality among men shall be found in the fires of hell. Only its duration determines whether their hell is the supernatural version or a man-made hell on earth. In view of all that takes place around us today, we must ask ourselves "Where does God reside?"

You could believe Friedrich Nietzsche and the ultimate blasphemy with his declaration, "God Is dead." Nietzsche developed quite a following. Some of his most ardent followers were Benito Mussolini, Joseph Stalin, and Adolf Hitler.[32] Of course, there is no peace and comfort in Nietzsche's kind of logic. If you believe such a heresy as his, then all freedom, liberty, and struggle on earth is a waste.

The majority of Southrons are raised according to the same Judeo-Christian ethic that America was founded upon. The typical Southron, even if he is not the media's stereotypical Southern religious fanatic, still adheres to the basics of his native faith. He knows where God resides. God lives in Heaven and in the heart of the believer. He manifests His presence in nature. That way we can see God around us daily. He shows himself in everything natural, beautiful, and holy that man has not managed to vandalize. The majority of Southrons know God lives because we have talked talk to Him. Sometimes, we are smart enough to listen when He answers. More believers bless the South than any other region of the American Empire. Our devotion has earned us the derisive name

"The Bible Belt." Yes, we have an abundance of Bibles. Could the West Coast ever wear our label? In any event, our title is one we should wear with pride.

Still, for all our fierce devotion, we fall short. Just look at what we allow. Nowhere in our constitution do the founding fathers mention the mythical separation of church and state. It is a later idea taken out of context from a letter Thomas Jefferson wrote to the Danbury Baptist Association of Connecticut. Jefferson did not even attend the constitutional convention. He was overseas as the ambassador to France at the time. The separation of church and state has no root in law. Presidents write many letters, but this one is the only letter taken as constitutional law.[33] Yet, we allow anyone armed with this lie to beat us into submission. The media denounces any possible influence of politics by religion. Therefore, we purge God and His influence from government, which is where we need it most. We remove God from all public places and gatherings. We forbid God to enter our schools. God is our Creator. It is absurd to restrict His access to His creation. If we remove God, guess who shows up? Then we get Jonesboro, Pearl, Paducah, and Littleton for a result.

The guilt for all of this rests equally with all of us. It is not necessarily because we knowingly cooperated. We didn't. Still, the guilt rightly rests with us. Why? We allowed it. We had the power to prevent it and did not. For knowing better, we are guiltier than those who orchestrated our spiritual sabotage. Our indifference set the wheels in motion. We unleashed the pattern of our own persecution by holding the cloaks of those who cast the stones. We made it easy for them. So, now our children go to school and they leave God at the gate. The people we trust with one-third of our children's time forbid them to mention or discuss God. They discourage prayer, and many schools consider prayer unruly behavior. We must also realize the urge to conform that peer pressure puts on our children. I know. I served time in a modern public school.

It is the height of treason to our Higher Authority that we even allow a government to dictate special conditions for prayer before our children's school events. Activist federal judges constantly attack invocations before graduations, sporting events, or any other school activities. The result of our children's isolation from God shows in them more every day. Taught that they descended from animals, they naturally behave as beasts. Now, our schools are shooting galleries. Remember also that if the Empire declares there is no God, then in the Empire's eyes there are no God-given rights. Millions for metal detectors, but not one penny for the Creator.

Corporate America, in its lust for profits, bans God from the workplace, also. As in our public schools, the mere discussion of religion can be grounds for suspension or dismissal. These same industries enforce Sabbath-breaking by shift work. To overproduce, they must run twenty-four hours a day, seven days a week. Of course, the boss will gladly tell you that you may have Sunday off, if you work someplace else. You could challenge this and maybe win in court if you have more money for lawyers than your employer. It would accomplish little, though. In the workplace, as in the school, the establishment uses peer pressure to whip the believer into line.

In public, we face censorship of a different manner. The establishment's elite call it being "politically correct." This practice is the institutional use of misinformation to induce a feeling of guilt. The Empire manipulates this feeling of guilt so we act only as our masters desire. A prime example is the Southern Baptist Convention's recent issue of an apology for past racism and the institution of slavery.[34] Their logic defies me. There is little sense in an apology one hundred or so years too late, for something that wasn't illegal. Especially since first the English and then later the North forced slavery upon Southerners. This part is what their history books neglect to tell. Virginia tried to abolish the slave trade constitutionally in 1789. The North refused.[35]

Political correctness is simply another form of peer pressure the Empire uses to whip us into line. It serves them well to hobble any protest that might offend a given group. In the politically correct doctrine, it is a cardinal sin to offend a protected group. They are valuable, the Empire's special children. They have rights. You do not. You are fair game. Persecution is alive and healthy today. What excuse did Washington give for the tragedy at Waco? The response was almost the same as the Nazis' reason for reducing Warsaw, Poland's Jewish ghetto. Both regimes claimed that their victims were evil religious groups who performed revolting sexual rituals on young children. The coincidences did not stop there. The BATF wore black uniforms and coal-scuttle helmets, just like the Nazi SS did fifty years earlier. The Star of David adorned the smoking ruins of both places. The reason given for both attacks was to protect the very children incinerated in the result. Well, Ms. Reno, if the jack-boot fits, wear it.[36]

The aftermath of both was a media circus of justification. One network news anchor declared that this is only the beginning.[37] This is the same American Empire that pets street gangs. This same authority coddles militant, anti-Semitic black groups, while leveling charges of intolerance and racism at the South. It makes you wonder. Is this only the beginning? Who is next? I can think of only one group that has already published an admission of guilt. Is your church government approved?

If you think that a man's home is still his castle, the Empire is preparing to prove you wrong. The bureaus and agencies swarm with eager agents. They want to convince you that they know more about how to raise your children than you do. Thus, the Empire can defeat the last stand of sanity in society. This conquest completes their invasion of every aspect of our lives. While child welfare is a noble cause, it is also a dangerous principle when abused. Unrestricted warfare on parents is the result of faceless bureaucrats abusing the system. Why do they do it? Because they can.

Returning to the case of Waco, allegations of child abuse supposedly prompted the final federal assault. The media and the government overlooked one tiny problem—he jurisdiction of federal law enforcement only covers violations of federal law. Child abuse is a state, not a federal, crime. Accordingly, the federal government was out of bounds trying to enforce laws against child abuse. It mattered little that the charges of abuse were not federal, just as it did not matter that the state of Texas investigated and cleared the Davidians three times on the same charges. Rightfully, the charges were in Texas's jurisdiction, and the state of Texas had the right to use force to prevent the incineration of the allegedly abused children and their parents. That right and jurisdiction often pales next to an opportunity to flex imperial muscle and perhaps set a precedent.

A gray area appears when the protection of parents' rights is in question. Historically, a parent not only has the right but the responsibility to discipline an unruly child. When laws and moral responsibility collide, the result is always outrageous. The case of one woman in Woodstock, Georgia is a classic example of this conflict.

A checker at the local grocery store squealed on this mom. As she shopped for groceries, she had little idea that Big Brother's little sister was watching and waiting. When she committed her crime against the establishment, the checker summoned the police, who arrested the mother in the checkout line. Her offense was disciplining her nine-year-old son in public by the Biblically mandated practice of spanking. The charges read cruelty to children, a felony in Georgia. Cuffed and stuffed, her bond was set at $22,050.[38]

This mother's case is another tragic example of the Empire's parental abuse. The Yankee Empire's experts claim to know better than God, Solomon, or you how to handle your children. So they will prosecute or persecute you to the fullest extent of the law. How many actual child abusers and molesters went free because the Empire busied itself depleting the finances of this poor woman, we shall never know.

We can prevent the encroachment into our homes on the state and national level now. What about in our future? All it takes to make the "Great Imperial Nanny" a permanent fixture in your home is a treaty. In 1994, the senate did not to ratify one such radical treaty from the United Nations Committee on Child Welfare. What about this year? Next year? Any treaty entered into by our emperor, with ratification by the Senate, becomes the law of the land, equal to or superseding the Constitution. What remains of our Constitution clearly outlines this process in Article VI. Noncompliance with the worldview of child rearing would be a breach of not only federal but also international law. Meanwhile, there is no UN Committee for Parental Rights.

Similarly, the establishment's nobility denounces any try by state and local citizens to erect legal barriers protecting children from unwholesome influences. They scream, "You can't legislate morality!" This was the battle cry of 1960s left-wing radicals. Many of those hippie kids from Berkeley and other publicly funded socialist training centers are today's government leaders and bureaucrats. They love to cite the South's blue laws and many dry counties as an example of legislating morality. For once, they are at least half-right. We cannot legislate morality. That is why we legislate against immorality. No law on earth can make your love your neighbor. That is why we have laws against you murdering him. No law can make anyone tell the truth, so we have laws that punish perjury. A law can make no man honest, so we write laws to punish stealing. Laws are not supposed to be a code of moral conduct. Laws are a code against immoral conduct. If immoral and unethical behavior cannot be wiped out, we must at least make such behavior inconvenient. Therefore, we have dry counties, sodomy laws, and a host of other statutes designed to make such behavior not only inconvenient, but costly as well. We of the South learned from example what happens when government does not restrict immoral or unethical conduct. Historians called it Reconstruction. A better name is the "Southern Holocaust."

The very foundation of Western Civilization and its laws was an act of legislation against immorality. The Law of Moses stands the test of time as the premier example of a barrier against immorality. God gave Moses the Ten Commandments. His intent could hardly be plainer. God called them *Commandments*, not *Suggestions*. Strictly enforced, the commandments do more for society than all the Empire's volumes of laws. That is why the Ten Commandments adorn the walls of the chambers of the Supreme Court. Notice that it is now illegal to post those same commandments in our public schools, or even in a state judge's courtroom.[39]

Another area where the Yankee Empire fails miserably is its war on drugs. After spending billions, there is no end to the problem. The elite's experts tell our children to wear red ribbons and to just say "No." Meanwhile, judges refuse to take no for an answer and turn pushers back out on the streets. At the same time, the Empire busies itself erecting signs reading "Drug Free Zone" around our school campuses. A better solution would be the erection of those same signs at the state line. It will never happen, though. That would be practical. For that reason, a federal judge would decide it violated the criminal's constitutional right to sell dope. Besides, effective law enforcement might cut into the profitability of the elite's own smuggling operations, such as the long-rumored CIA-backed cocaine smuggling operation centered at the Mena, Arkansas Airport. The CIA recently admitted to conducting operations at Mena, and to hiring drug smuggler Barry Seals. When was the last time that you heard of the CIA admitting anything? Federal law prohibits the CIA from conducting operations inside the U.S. Still, most federal agencies have ways of getting around something as trivial as the law.[40]

The corruptive promise of easy money from drugs parallels another destructive lure, the casino. The areas that legalized casino gambling proved the warnings of those who opposed casinos. The Mississippi River is the new strip of vice and corruption. Louisiana citizens found that several important legislators took payoffs from the gambling lobby. In Greenville and Vicksburg, Mississippi, the promised prosperity fails to show itself. A new rise of crime, vice, and corruption links itself directly to the arrival of the casinos. The crime rate in Greenville jumped 19 percent the year the riverboats opened. Across the country, crime rates are almost double in communities were there is gambling.[41] The casino brings with it a legacy of broken lives, broken homes, and squandered fortunes. Voters should ask themselves one question: Could the casino stay in business if the games allowed the player to win? It is gambling from the player's point of view, but it is hardly a gamble from the casino's. Such should be expected if you emulate the Romans who cast lots for the meager possessions of Christ.

Still, casinos are not as widespread the most disruptive and destructive influence in our society, the national media. We cannot overestimate the media's influence on people, especially that of television. As Wayne LaPierre explained in *Guns, Crime, and Freedom*, the media is a driving force in manufacturing and manipulating public opinion.

> When the major news media, run by a tiny cohort, crank out a steady stream of distortions, ordinary citizens begin to feel isolated and disempowered, believing they're the only ones who feel differently from the news media. That is not accidental.[42]

Is there any doubt that not just the news, but all media portray a left-of-reality view? A survey in *Public Opinion* magazine shows why this is so. Based on interviews with 240 journalists and broadcasters, the magazine asked their religious outlook as well as their political and social views. The results were revealing.[43]

- 50 percent said they had no religious affiliation whatsoever.
- Only 8 percent said they attend a church or synagogue weekly.
- 86 percent said they seldom or never attend religious services.
- 54 percent said they are politically left of center.
- 76 percent said that homosexuality was not wrong.
- 90 percent said they favored abortion.

While this survey polled only news people, a later survey polled the entertainment industry. They asked the same questions of television's most influential writers, producers, and executives. This group showed themselves even worse off than the news media. Of this group, 93 percent said they seldom or never went to church. Another 80 percent said homosexuality is not wrong, and 97 percent favored abortion. A majority did not even regard adultery as wrong.[44] This is the character of the people controlling what you, and your children, see on television, at the movies, or read in the paper.

How did they get such power? There is at least one television in 98.3 percent of households in the U.S. In 1960, the average TV stayed on five hours and six minutes a day. By 1992, the average time rose to seven hours and four minutes per day.[45]

Who watches the most television? Our children do. The TV often serves as an electronic babysitter. The most easily influenced persons in our society, during their most susceptible years, receive the most exposure to the people mentioned in the survey. You would shudder to associate with these same people, but through television and other media, they use sophisticated techniques to change our attitudes toward bizarre behavior. When media introduces the outlandish, the natural first reaction is shock, especially if the media portrays the behavior as widespread. With repeated exposure, shock becomes indifference. We adopt an attitude of "It's their business, not mine." As the bizarre behavior becomes more accepted through repeated exposure, media increasingly portrays it as normal, and it actually does become widespread. At the same moment, media brands those who oppose such behavior as dangerous, intolerant radicals, extremists, and religious fanatics. Media uses any sound bite or buzzword that will cast the normal in a bad light. Usually, that and other even more sophisticated techniques are how the establishment decides what you will think, whom you will vote for, and what car you drive around the Yankee Empire today. There is, however, more to this policy than that.

Recent revelations show that television is a much more persuasive propaganda tool than previously thought. This is something media and government officials already knew, but never disclosed to the public. Clinical studies show that watching television induces a light hypnotic effect, known as an "Alpha" state of consciousness. In the Alpha state, the brain releases morphine-like compounds called endorphins. The body craves endorphins. The more endorphins the body gets, the more it wants. While endorphins are released during exercise also, the body wants them the easiest way possible. The easiest way is through further exposure to television. The tendency explains the country's many couch potatoes. Other studies showed that 80 percent or more of the population is susceptible to trance-like states, with vulnerability for all increasing with

repeated exposure. While in an Alpha state the brain is most susceptible to outside influences, just as when under hypnosis. The
Alpha state slows your thought, while you allow someone else to
think for you.[46]

This study and others also found that there is no way to participate in such activity without suffering its effects. You cannot resist.
That is why companies pay millions for television advertising. It is
effective. None of this discussion includes the whole textbook of
subliminal and neuro-linguistic techniques. While frightening, all
these practices are also legal. The question is not "if," but "how
much" we open ourselves to the control of others. What does television show as normal and desirable while we sit in our trance? What
does it give legitimacy? Media portrays abortion on demand as a
right. Television shows homosexual, interracial, and extramarital
sex as normal and desirable. A common TV theme is a dysfunc-
tional family, with arrogant, bratty kids rebelling against their backward parents. Meanwhile, there is no shame in living a life of
dependency, trapped in the welfare web. This is what TV hypnoti-
cally suggests to you every day. Worse, this is what the Empire suggests to your children.

The American Empire and all its influences have their effects on
us. It teaches us to live a life of materialism. We find ourselves in an
endless quest to buy happiness with more consumer trinkets in a
search for that great contradiction in terms, instant gratification. In
our material quest for fulfillment, we even come to see religion as
suspect. Its practitioners appear abnormal, fanatical, backwards.
Still, without God there is no fulfillment. We doom ourselves to the
life of the modern mass-man, no man at all, with even less room for
an individual. In our modern existence, nothing has value anymore, especially life.

It all adds up to the destruction of our people's vision. As they
only live day to day, is it really living? There is no thought of the
consequences. There is no goal for tomorrow, or eternity.
Everything but the moment is beyond the scope of our thought.
Where no is plan for life, there is no vision. As the Bible tells us,
"Where there is no vision, the people perish."[47]

The Yankee Empire's goal is not Bacon's *New Atlantis*. Even with
all its social justice programs, the empire will not create Utopia. As

we can readily tell, the Empire's goal is definitely not the New Jerusalem. The Southerner must listen to his own reason. He must fight back using his common sense.

Did we consent to our rule by federal judges? Their control of our schools? Busing for racial balance? An enforced Northern/socialist/homosexual-slanted school curriculum? Did we consent to the emasculation of our state and local governments? Did we consent to minority set-asides? Affirmative Action? Reverse discrimination?

Legal scholars and bureaucrats tell us that we give our consent by participating in this government. That argument does not wash. It is plain. Our participation is not wanted. If one uses their logic, then all the great atrocities of recent history are justified. Because they voted and sent members to Parliament in the past, did the Irish give their consent to be terrorized and shot down by the Black and Tans? Because they participated in the 1930s, did the Jews of Germany consent to be sent to the gas chambers of Auschwitz? Because they voted in their one-candidate elections for all those years, I suppose the citizens of the Soviet Union also gave their consent. This line of logic does not make sense. Who would try to believe such erroneous ideas except the mental slaves of the ruling class?

Did we consent to give one-third of our wages, our property, to pay the way for those who will not work? To pay them to breed? Did we consent that our prisons should become colleges and health spas? Did we consent to banish God from our schools and civil governments? Will we consent to one more broken contract?

If our people go to Hell in a hand basket, the fires will be no less hot for those of us who could have prevented it. Our future generations will pay for our neglect. The fight of our sons, daughters, and grandchildren will be much worse than ours would have been. The Bible tells us:

> When a righteous man doth turn from his righteousness and commits iniquity, and I lay a stumbling-block before him, he shall die: because thou hast not given him warning, he shall die in his sin, and his righteousness which he hath done shall not be remembered; but his blood will I require at thine hand.[48]

Whose blood will coat our hands? Will it be our neighbors? Surely, it will be our children's blood, but what about their children's? Will it be the blood of our whole Southern nation? We can cleanse our hands and souls of their blood before it stains them.

Our plight has a remedy. Our demise is preventable. We cannot wait for someone to do it for us. No one will. We must do it for ourselves. We have never been in a better position. Our development is sufficient to assure our economic independence as well as our political independence. Independence is the only guarantee that our livelihood stays home where it belongs.

CHAPTER IV

The Birth of a Nation

It is true that we are completely under the saddle of Massachusetts and Connecticut, and that they ride us very hard, cruelly insulting our feelings, as well as exhausting our strength and subsistence. Their natural friends, the three other Eastern States join them from a sort of family pride, and they have the art to divide certain other parts of the Union, so as to make use of them to govern the whole. This is not new, it is the old practice of despots; to use a part of the people to keep the rest in order.   Thomas Jefferson[1]

I have talked extensively about the South as a nation of its own, held captive within the American Empire. Many people dismiss this idea out of hand. They think of the United States as a nation. The founding fathers never intended it to be. At the Constitutional Convention, the founding fathers expressly disavowed the suggestion that they create a national government.

If the United States is not a nation, then what is? Perhaps it would be best just to define the word "nation" and see. A nation is usually considered a group with common heritage and culture inhabiting a common homeland, a politically independent state, or a group with a desire to have and maintain their own state.[2] When you read this definition, notice the recurring word, "state." Up until 1865, a state was never defined as an administrative sub-unit of a country. When the word is used correctly, it still means a sovereign, self-governing body. Why do you think that the founding fathers called their alliance the United States and not the United Provinces? Also, note that any definition of nation that you might look up will exclude empires from its definition. Empires are not nations. They are receptacles for holding nations, usually against their will. All this brings to mind principle Number two: "The South is by definition a nation of its own, with its own unique language, culture, history, philosophy, and icons."

We can see our uniqueness any time we contrast ourselves against the rest of the American Empire. Our language is the much-maligned and endangered Southern dialect of the English language. Our culture is also at odds with the Empire. We are the heirs of the same Western civilization that Yankee liberals take such great pains to reject. Of course, we also have our own Southern history that the Empire enjoys rewriting to fit its latest social whim. The Southerner's philosophy finds its roots in our religion and the practical side of our nature. Our icons are wholly different from the Empire's. The battle flag, Robert E. Lee, Jeff Davis, and Stonewall Jackson, among other symbols, inspire no reverence up there. Our very being is at odds with the Empire. That is not a coincidence. There is a good reason why we do not get along now, why have never gotten along, and probably never will. The reason is that we are not of the same nationality.

From the initial colonization of the New World, two different groups with different outlooks settled North and South. The Puritans and radical religious dissenters of England and northern Europe settled New England. The Scots-Irish and the English settled the South. Most of them were conservative Protestants and Anglicans.[3]

From the beginning, two different nations emerged. New England concerned itself with industry and shipping. The South geared itself towards building the best features of rural English society through agriculture. Religious experimentation characterized the New Englander's philosophy. Most of their experiments were heresies in the eyes of orthodox and evangelical Southerners. In the beginning, the only goal the colonies shared was our commitment to get the King out of our homes and pockets.

Unified temporarily under the Articles of Confederation, we clung together long enough to win the Revolution. When the colonies won, England recognized the independence of the colonies and listed them separately. Each was now an independent sovereign state. After the Revolution, the Articles proved to be an ineffective instrument of government between the new states. The states had too loose of a compact to ensure their peaceful coexistence. Territorial disputes were common. In the summer of 1871,

New York troops actually invaded Vermont. The Vermont militia repulsed the attack, discouraging a similar threatened invasion by New Hampshire. Congress found it had no authority to intervene in such disputes. In an act of desperation, the states scrapped the articles, along with their "Perpetual Union."[4]

In drawing up a new instrument of government, two camps of philosophy emerged. The Federalists were predominantly Northerners and merchants. They wanted a loosely interpreted document with a strong central government. The anti-Federalists were primarily Southerners. They remembered their experience under a strong central government just a few months earlier. In the end, the Constitution and Bill of Rights was a compromise. Each state retained its sovereignty, while allowing the central government to defend and execute certain government functions for the whole. The Constitution, from the start, was a compact, not a national government. The convention and the ratifying states understood that if the union proved to be unhappy, they could leave anytime. Otherwise, there would have been no ratification. Just in case, New York, Rhode Island, and Virginia put a secession clause in their ratification documents.[5]

As a wedding of different nationalities, the United States was a stormy relationship from the start. During the convention, Virginia tried to outlaw the slave trade. The New England states refused. They were making too much money bringing slaves into the country. Northern-authored history texts neglect to tell this story. Northerners imported the very slaves that they always hold over the heads of Southerners. Their live cargo began as captives sold on the coast by other Africans. New England traders usually bought them for a little rum or a few trinkets. The slaves crossed the Atlantic Ocean on New England-owned ships. When they made their destination, they were sold for the profit of New Englanders. Only 8 percent of slaves were lucky enough to come to the South. Traders sold the others in the Caribbean or Brazil. In those climates, under excruciating toil, the slaves lived short lives.[6]

When it dawned on Northerners that slavery was not profitable to practice up north, New England found other ways to profit from it. In the 1820s, New Englanders suddenly took a moral fever over slavery. New England shipping magnates converted their millions into industrial investments or more carefully hid what their cargo manifests read. This way they kept an air of respectability. So it is that many New England family fortunes (some of the names are still very familiar today) were born on the back of the black man.

With the acquisition of the new territory west of the original colonies, Northerners opposed further expansion. Early on, Northern politicians favored ceding the Mississippi River to Spain. This way, they could maintain their monopoly on shipping by the East Coast. Later, for the same reason, they opposed the Louisiana Purchase. In fact, Northern opposition to the Louisiana Purchase was so heated that in 1803, New England almost withdrew from the union. Senator Timothy Pickering of Massachusetts wrote:

> I rather anticipate a new confederacy exempt from the corrupt influence of the aristocratic Democrats of the South. . . . The British provinces (of Canada), even with the consent of Great Britain, will become members of the Northern confederacy.[7]

During the War of 1812, Northern states again rose in opposition. Though British aggression against Northern shipping provoked the war, the North soon wanted none of the responsibility. The representatives of five New England states (Massachusetts, Connecticut, Rhode Island, Vermont, and New Hampshire) met in a secret convention in December 1814. There, at Hartford, Connecticut, they held sessions for three weeks and discussed their options. The delegates developed a list of demands for Congress and seven constitutional amendments. To begin with, they demanded an immediate end to the war. They also desired that the political balance of power forever shift toward New England. Additionally, the Northerners wanted to limit westward expansion. Most of all, the delegates recommended secession. The irony is that as they met, the United States won the war. The United States and Great Britain signed the Treaty of Ghent while they convened. At the same time, General Andrew Jackson's army of frontiersmen, pirates, and free men of color won the Battle of New Orleans.[8]

The Hartford Convention was not the end of Northern secession fever. In 1845, Congress debated statehood for Texas. Former president John Quincy Adams opposed Texas statehood. He opposed it so much that Adams openly urged the New England states to dissolve the union. He delivered his recommendation only fifteen years before the South seceded.[9]

Outside its preoccupation with leaving the union, the North also showed its preoccupation with rewriting the Constitution it so recently helped ratify. Congress passed the Alien and Sedition Acts during the presidential administration of John Adams in 1798. These were four laws passed for internal security as a war with France threatened. The first three acts primarily restricted the activities of immigrants, but the fourth put limits on the freedom of the press. What many considered reasonable laws soon saw misuse. Adams, a closet monarchist, used the full force of the federal government to silence all of his political opposition. The Kentucky and Virginia legislatures responded by passing resolutions written by Thomas Jefferson and James Madison. The Kentucky and Virginia Resolutions, as history knows them, declared the Alien and Sedition Acts to be unconstitutional, and therefore invalid. It was the beginning of nullification, a practice used effectively by both North and South.

The North still tried to read new rights into the Constitution. This is something that Northern liberals continue to do today. Their next project was getting the central government to fund internal improvements to aid its industry. Many also accepted this as reasonable. Congress agreed to fund the improvements the same way they paid for the rest of government—by customs duties. Over time, the North became more demanding. What began as customs duties matured into a protective tariff. In various forms, it is still with us today. It reached its most oppressive form in 1828, in what was known as the "Tariff of Abominations." This measure forced the South to foot the bill for further developing the North.

At the time, John C. Calhoun of South Carolina was vice president under Andrew Jackson. Calhoun resigned to enter the Senate and fight the issue. He quickly became the champion of the South. As many of his fellow Southrons, Calhoun believed the tariff was nothing more than tribute levied against the South, a tribute the North levied to benefit New England industrialists. In a paper entitled "The South Carolina Exposition," Calhoun urged the South Carolina legislature to declare the tariff unconstitutional.[10] The South Carolina Legislature listened. They adopted the "Exposition" and nullified the tariff. Still, Jackson insisted on enforcing the tariff. It was a Southern state's turn to talk of bowing from the union. Even as Washington blew smoke and threatened a military expedition to bring back Calhoun's head, South Carolina held fast. Contrary to the impression your high school history text gave, Congress backed down. It reduced the tariff.

The coming of the abolitionists was another challenge leveled at the South. As of 1826, there were 250 anti-slavery societies in the United States. All but 38 of them were in the South.[11] This new brand of radical abolitionism was a political game, and nothing more. Historians have well documented the struggle against the radical abolitionists and the war they caused, though seldom from the Southern point of view. It is too complex a subject for this chapter. Instead, I refer you to Francis Springer's *War For What?* and John Tilley's *The Coming of the Glory.* These are two of the best-handled treatments of the subject from the South's viewpoint.

From the very first breaths of the founding fathers, the relationship known as the United States of America was stormy. Until 1850, the two nations, North and South, sweated together and worked out their differences. Calhoun always defended the South. Daniel Webster of Massachusetts, though a centralist to the core, tried to bring sanity to the North. Meanwhile, Henry Clay of Kentucky often substituted as a marriage counselor. The balance of power shifted as the radical element rose to power in the North. Calhoun passed away in 1850. As he lay dying, among his last words were, "The South! The poor South! God knows what will become of her!"[12]

Webster and Clay were on the way out, too. With the rise of the radical, a stranger plowed the common ground that held the union together. The stormy marriage of two nations as different as Israel and Egypt reached its end. It was the battered lady, the South, who could take it no more and filed for divorce. Unfortunately, it was a contested filing. The North chose war. Angels wept as Abe Lincoln snuffed out the life of one-twelfth of the continent. You know the story, at least the Yankee version of it. Anyway, we lost. Still, it did not wipe out our Southern Nation. It just means we are still married. In this case, we are still married to hypocrites.

The years following the war found most Southrons occupied with the job of putting their shattered lives back together. It was an insurmountable task, but this did not mean the end of Southern resistance to Northern domination. Occupation caused resistance to Yankee rule to shift from individuals to actions taken within community institutions. The South mainly had two civic institutions left intact after the war. To these, Southerners gave their time, even in the turmoil of rebuilding civilization. The church and the Masonic Lodge were the only semblance of order and social structure left for most communities.

While religion always was and still is the backbone of Southern culture, the church could offer no effective framework for continued resistance. It did give the inspiration, but many of the church roll-members were dead, buried beneath battlefields from Arizona to Pennsylvania. The war also destroyed many of the South's churches. Others were in disrepair. In addition, occupation troops attended worship services as censors or they halted worship altogether. Despite all these disadvantages, religion still played an important role in the fight against Yankee domination. Southern churches still managed to inspire the faithful and strengthen weary souls to fight oppression.

The Masonic Lodge, on the other hand, was not an open public institution. Masons had little to fear, because they met behind closed doors. From the misty depths of time, Masons had met on hilltops, in secluded woods, and old out-of-the-way buildings to preserve secrecy. It was simple for them to do so again. In many cases, the war had destroyed their lodges anyway. The war also did much to spread Freemasonry, in both North and South. As was traditional in the British and Continental Armies, both the Confederate and Federal Armies had what Masons commonly called "Military" or "War Lodges." These were lodges within each unit, from regimental down to company level. These war lodges readily made new Masons from their units and held memorials for fallen brothers of both sides after battle. Recognition of Masonic distress signs and other symbols spared more than a few homes from the torch, and saved even more lives. Masons on both sides often preferred to render the laws of war subservient to the Golden Rule.

Freemasonry has three watchwords that do not sit well with any tyrant or would-be oppressor, be he Yankee or Nazi. Those words are liberty, fraternity, and equality. These words became a foundation of Masonic thought in the 1700s, espoused by brethren like Voltaire, Benjamin Franklin, and George Washington. While it is true that Masonry forbids lodges to meddle in political affairs, unofficial actions often occurred throughout American history. Saint Andrew's Lodge of Boston undertook an important project on the eve of the Revolution. It became known as the Boston Tea Party. Among that lodge's members were Paul Revere, Samuel Adams, John Hancock, James Otis, and Joseph Warren. Many say that Saint Andrew's Lodge was the birthplace of American independence.[13]

Most Southern lodges inherited the same spirit. Most leaders of the Confederacy, most of its general officers, and more than 10 percent of its troops were Masons. Contrast this with the Yankee government of the 1860s. Its government and military leaders, with a few notable exceptions, were not Masons. However, about 10 percent of Northern soldiers were Masons, like their Southern counterparts. In the areas of the South that came under martial law, which included most of the South after 1866, one of the occupation troops' first tasks was to close the local lodge halls. This was the same tactic used by the British in occupied areas during the Revolution. The tactic did not work in 1776 or in 1866. Masons continued to meet in barns, homes, and isolated patches of woods. The Masonic role in the Southern Resistance bought the Southern people time to form other avenues and organizations in the later 1860s. This development freed the lodge to return to its role as a community-building, philosophical fraternity.

Still, the forces of Yankeedom had one more blow to receive from Freemasonry. Albert Pike, Confederate general and Indian commissioner, philosopher, and statesman, would rise and deliver that assault. Pike was the Sovereign Grand Master of a branch of higher Masonic degrees known as the Scottish Rite. Pike was a highly respected man in legal as well as Masonic circles. In 1871, he published an explanation of the thirty-two Scottish Rite degrees entitled *Morals and Dogma*. Until recently, lodges gave the book to every Scottish Rite Mason upon the receipt of his thirty-second degree. This made it one of American history's most widely distributed books. Written in the fragrant style of the nineteenth century, it is not light reading. It contains many references to classical mythology, familiar in the 1800s, but easily misinterpreted today. Modern education, devoid of the study of the classics, makes many of Pike's illustrations unintelligible today. Still, there are many gems of philosophy, political science, and beautiful prose to glean from Pike's 861 pages. Also tucked neatly within his explanation of the first three degrees are some of the age's most piercing attacks on the Yankee Empire.

> A war for a great principle ennobles a nation. A war for commercial supremacy, upon some shallow pretext, is despicable, and more aught than else demonstrates to what immeasurable depths of baseness men and nations can descend. Commercial greed values the lives of men no more than it values the lives of ants. The slave trade is acceptable to a people

enthralled by that greed, as the trade in ivory or spices, if the profits are as large. It will by-and-by endeavor to compound with God and quiet its own conscience, by compelling those to whom it sold the slaves it bought or stole, to set them free, and slaughtering them by hecatombs if they refuse to obey the edicts of its philanthropy.[14]

Remember, though now *Morals and Dogma* is hard to find and often neglected, it was one of America's most widely read and distributed books (both North and South). Many had a chance to read the fiercest of the Southern apologists. We should also note that Albert Pike was not a native Southerner. He was born, raised, and educated in Massachusetts.

As events freed Masons of the burden of Southern Resistance, a more suitable and effective vehicle arose from the ashes of the reconstructed South. In early 1866, six young Confederate veterans formed what started as a recreational fraternal society in Pulaski, Tennessee. They named it the Ku Klux Klan, an abuse of the Greek word *kuklos,* meaning circle. They held their meetings in what local folklore claimed was a haunted house. The local Negroes, used as voting pawns by the Reconstruction forces, grew frightened by the strange happenings. Soon, it dawned that the superstition of the Negroes was a more powerful weapon than any that the Yankee government had at its disposal. As disenfranchised Southrons realized the Klan's effectiveness against Yankee domination, its membership bloomed overnight. The organization soon needed a leader of vast experience and energy to combine and control the efforts of the various Klans and enforce discipline. It was a position tailor-made for General Nathan Bedford Forrest.

After the war, Forrest had tried hard to make peace work. A Confederate hero, he was easily the most respected man in western Tennessee and northern Mississippi. In his work for a peaceful coexistence, he even took in seven former Yankee officers, renting them farms. He went so far as to make one a business partner. His efforts failed shortly.[15] His destiny and that of his neighbors changed with Reconstruction and carpetbag rule. Martial law became amnesty for crimes that occupation troops were yet to commit. Lawlessness and oppression reigned. Nathan Bedford Forrest was not the kind of man who would sit still while anyone tried to oppress him.

Recognizing the Klan's potential, Forrest journeyed to Nashville,

Tennessee, where he met with John W. Morton, his former chief of artillery. Morton was the leader or "Grand Cyclops" of the Nashville den. He gave Forrest the preliminary Klan oath in the woods outside town. Later that night, in room ten of the famous Maxwell House Hotel (where the brand of coffee originated), the Nashville den initiated Nathan Bedford Forrest into the Ku Klux Klan. In April of 1867, at a secret convention held in Nashville, the Klans proclaimed Forrest the Grand Wizard of the Invisible Empire.[16]

Forrest was the perfect choice for the head of the empire, which consisted of several similar Klan-type groups. Forrest traveled extensively in his business dealings and often communicated with his old comrades. Coincidentally, everywhere he went, Yankee occupation troops found that a new Klan den arose to fight Northern oppression. Of the character of the men involved and their motives, Forrest told a Senate committee in 1871 that the Klans only admitted:

> worthy men who belonged to the Southern army; the others are not to be trusted; they would not fight when the war was on them, and of course they would not do anything when it was over. . . . they admitted no man who was not a gentleman and a man who could be relied upon to act discreetly; not men who were in the habit of drinking, boisterous men, or men liable to commit error or wrong, or anything of that sort; . . . By all people, my object was to keep the peace.[17]

Unquestionably, the Klan involved itself in some violent acts. Such acts were mainly retaliation for atrocities committed by occupation troops, carpetbaggers, scalawags, and Reconstruction militia. Occasionally, they carried out a preemptive strike before retaliation was necessary. In spite of the bad press, records show that the occupation troops and militia committed more violence than could ever be pinned on the Klan and in most cases, violence was not necessary to achieve the ends the Klans desired. Many a sound-sleeping scalawag or carpetbagger found himself awakened by the thundering hooves of horses. Hooded and robed riders suddenly surrounded him in the moonlight. A spokesman usually issued an oral warning and stated that a return visit would not be nearly as pleasant. The first visit was usually enough. By such means, the Klan defeated Reconstruction and returned a vestige of order and peace to the South.

Despite its effectiveness, the Klan's weakness was that anyone could don a bedsheet and tarnish their reputation. Brigands and even the carpetbaggers themselves began to disguise as Klansmen and commit even more atrocities. To prevent this, late in 1869 Forrest ordered the Klan disbanded. The dens were to destroy all documents, records, and regalia. The discretion of local commanders decided the rest of the campaign against Yankee rule.

Carpetbag rule finally collapsed in the 1870s. As the chains of occupation loosened, a rather informal truce existed between North and South. The South began repairing the damage wrought by war and Reconstruction. Southrons did their best to rebuild Southern civilization from the ashes. In spite of Southerners' best efforts, many scalawags and carpetbaggers remained in positions of authority. Thus, they retained enough power to keep the ban on Southern symbols, such as the display of the Confederate battle flag, in place.

Additionally, most of the Southern educational system lay in ruins. With a few exceptions, the only schools still operating were those that the North established for the education of the freedmen. These schools were more for the propagation of Northern ideology and political control than for education. Unfavorable conditions forced the Southern schools that still managed to stay open to use Yankee teachers or texts printed up North. There was little chance of improving Southern education without money, and money was something that Southerners universally lacked. Impoverished, with plenty of room for improvement but no hope to improve, the Southern man faced many obstacles. As Frank Lawrence Owsley wrote, the North

> commenced a second war of conquest, the conquest of the Southern mind, calculated to remake every Southern opinion, to impose the Northern way of life and thought upon the South, write "error" across the pages of Southern history which were out of keeping with the Northern legend, and set the rising and unborn generations upon stools of everlasting repentance.[18]

When the Yankee legions departed, the Northern schoolmaster, robber baron, banker, and railroad continued where previous carpetbaggers left off. Men such as Jesse and Frank James became folk heroes in this kind of environment. Former Confederate leaders became apologists for the cause. Jefferson Davis, Alexander Stephens, and others published their memoirs in the hope that they would inspire future generations to pick up the fallen Southern standard. Instead, the result was a lost, uneducated, and hopeless generation, many of which simply went west.

As the influence of the carpetbagger faded, the South again managed to stand on its own. In the 1890s, the ban on Southern symbols was finally relaxed. Confederate veterans groups began to organize to offer mutual aid to stricken comrades, their widows, and orphans. While the Empire forced Southern states to contribute to the pensions of Yankee soldiers, the federal government refused all aid to Southern veterans. This was the final slap in the face. It caused the South to organize again.

The first major movement to arise was the United Confederate Veterans. It was a confederation of earlier veterans' associations, and was organized in 1889 at New Orleans. As stated in their constitution, the organization was "strictly social, literary, historical, and benevolent." General John B. Gordon of Georgia was the first commander in chief. He quickly set the UCV about its mission:

> to gather authentic data for an impartial history of the war between the States; to preserve relics or mementos of the same; to cherish the ties of friendship that should exist among men who have shared common dangers, common sufferings and privations; to care for the disabled and extend a helping hand to the needy; to protect the widows and the orphans, and to make and preserve a record of the services of every member, and, as far as possible, of those of our comrades who have preceded us in eternity.[19]

Within ten years, the UCV grew from a few hundred members to a powerful organization of many thousands, organized into 1250 chapters called "camps." The UCV published a monthly magazine known as the *Confederate Veteran,* under the supervision of S.A. Cunningham. Their annual reunions, held throughout the South, grew into political and cultural extravaganzas. This helped fill the void of the "lost generation's" cultural handicaps. The reunions also renewed the lost spirit of Southern nationhood. Though now white-haired with age, the former soldiers of the Southland returned with renewed vigor to the cause of unifying the Southern people. Their newfound political influence defeated the last vestiges of occupation rule. Their growing influence finally forced Washington into making political concessions to the South, the first of which was the return of most captured Confederate battle flags to their home states. Confederate soldiers' homes rose in every Southern state, while the states managed to start their own Confederate pension systems. The UCV was a force for all politicians and robber barons to fear.

Time, however, accomplished what Grant and Sherman never could. The thinning ranks of aged veterans grew thinner still. Then there were no more. The old veterans could pass to the land beyond with clear conscience. They had made a dent in Yankee domination. In doing so, they rallied a new generation and passed the torch of Southern nationhood.

The first of the spin-off groups formed because of the UCV was the United Daughters of the Confederacy. An association of female descendants of Confederate veterans and government officials, the UDC organized at Nashville on September 10, 1894. Within six years, the UDC grew to more than 362 chapters, with more than 17,000 members. The Daughters' goals were similar to those of their parent organization. The United Daughters of the Confederacy quickly proved they were not just a Southern sewing circle. The Daughters wasted no time in setting about their mission: "ridding our schools of text-books that falsified history, that poisoned the minds of our youths by instilling a doubt of the virtue, sincerity, and honour of those who upheld the Confederate cause."[20]

The Daughters were untiring in their work. They established and cared for cemeteries, decorated graves, established hospitals and museums, and erected a forest of Confederate monuments throughout the South. The Daughters did valuable work in publishing histories of Southern notables and many memorial volumes. Though women did not yet have the right of suffrage, no politician would dare be foolhardy enough to tangle with the UDC of the early twentieth century. Through their perseverance and militancy (though their militancy is diminished today), the Daughters changed many of the policies toward the captive Southern states. They never wasted a chance to strike a blow for Southern nationhood. Under their leadership, monuments to the Confederate soldier appeared on most Southern court squares, along with the occasional artillery piece and a perpetually flying Confederate battle flag.

Organized two years after the Daughters, the Sons of Confederate Veterans likewise spread quickly throughout the South. The SCV opened its membership to all male descendants of those serving in the Confederate Army, Navy, or Marine Corps. Organized along the same structure as the UCV, the Sons rapidly grew to more than one thousand camps and many thousands of members. While the SCV espoused similar aims to the Daughters, the Sons also inherited a higher purpose. The UCV assigned the Sons a specific mission at their founding at Richmond, Virginia in 1896. General Stephen D. Lee issued their charge: "To you the Sons of Confederate Veterans, we submit the vindication of the Cause for which we fought . . ."[21]

The Sons immediately went to work at these and their other duties. While the SCV never quite achieved the strength of the Daughters, they still got results. Membership rolls lagged slightly behind the ladies' lead, but the SCV still did great service erecting monuments, establishing museums, and preserving Southern shrines. All these tasks they did well, but their greatest focus was that of their charge—vindicating the Southern cause.

During World War I, the imperial government drafted Southerners in higher proportions than men from other states (a practice the empire has followed in every war since, also). Washington's propaganda apparatus, known as the Committee for Public Information, filtered and delivered the war news reaching the public. All information that found its way to the public came from CPI press releases. Washington discredited and shut down any news organization that chose to circumvent the CPI. During the war years, CPI press releases blasted the Kaiser and his Huns. Often CPI reported distorted and even more often manufactured news of German atrocities and Allied victories. Eighty years later, scholars are just beginning to separate history from CPI's fiction.[22]

After the war, CPI found a new reason to exist. It applied its propaganda to putting down a new resurgence of Southern pride and Southern nationalism. D.W. Griffith's film epic, *The Birth of a Nation*, swept the South with a nationalist revival. In fact, the Southron reaction to Griffith's masterpiece was much the same as the Scots' reaction to Mel Gibson's movie, *Braveheart*. Both movies awakened what the ruling empires claimed to be a dead issue.

Non-Southern audiences acclimatized to CPI's coverage of Germany readily listened as Washington pointed out yet another enemy of mankind, the South. The bloody shirt waved on high. The South caught the blame for most of America's social ills. The war, racism, genocide, the national debt, anything CPI staffers could dream up, the blame for it fell South. There were even amazing similarities between supposed Confederate atrocities and those attributed to Germans just a few months earlier. Why not? The same propagandists wrote them on the same typewriters. One week the South was almost as bad as Germany. The next week, Germany was almost as bad as the South. It was only after the CPI propaganda caused race riots in Northern cities that Washington abolished the committee, but many of CPI's stereotypes still plague Southerners today.[23]

True their charge, the Sons of Confederate Veterans rose to vindicate the South. Their rebuttal was *The Gray Book*. Really more of a pamphlet than a book, it still served its purpose well. The SCV released *The Gray Book* in 1918 and distributed it all over the South. While the North and the West chewed lies, the South fed on truth. (The SCV re-released *The Gray Book* when needed in 1955 and 1986.)

Too many people belittle the great service done to the Southern people, by the veterans and descendancy organizations. From the 1880s to the 1930s, they spread a renewed pride and nationalism across the South. Theirs was an uphill fight against the armies of error and malevolence. Sadly, the progression of time still would not allow the Southern Nation its rebirth. As the ranks of gray-haired veterans thinned, so did the ranks of their children. With the loss of the Confederate warriors of old came the loss of their example. Through the years, the membership and influence of the UDC gradually diminished. The SCV almost lapsed into extinction. But the efforts of these pioneers were just the beginning. They laid the groundwork for a new class of Southern soldier, the agrarian and Populist reformers of the 1930s.

During the prosperous times of the 1920s, the shaky truce between North and South almost resumed. The Yankee's propaganda attacks turned mainly to importing and enforcing the Northern way of life on what they claimed was a poor benighted South. In truth, Northern leaders saw the South as a vast pool of cheap labor and natural resources to exploit. They wasted no time in launching their campaign of "progress." It was a version of progress guaranteed to make Northern men rich off Southern backs. Their progress would pull the Southerner into the factory and out of the field. Reduced competition would ease the burden on the Midwestern farmer, who always remained intensely loyal to Washington. The Northern idea of progress ultimately would pit black against white neighbors. The project hoped to provide black votes to support a new class of carpetbagger. It was a Yankee version of progress in which Southerners of both races had little interest. Of course, it was a Yankee plan designed so Yankees could profit. Their scheme almost worked. The actions of the same Yankee bankers and industrialists, who planned the New England-ization of the South, led to the stock market crash of 1928 and the Great Depression that followed.

We should have expected it. Southerners were warned. A courageous and innovative young group of Southrons had preached the dangers of industrialization long before the crash. Centered on Vanderbilt University, they were poets, historians, and men of vision. Southerners know them as the "Fugitive Agrarians" or simply the "Fugitives." Their works are some of the finest of Southern literature. The fugitives were all respected men of letters, including several Pulitzer Prize winners. They contributed the backbone of the Southern literary renaissance. William Faulkner, Tennessee Williams, T.S. Elliot, James Dickey, and Winston Groom all drank from the cup of Fugitive influence.

The twelve Fugitives had diverse backgrounds. They had varying sources of education, from the one-room schoolhouse to the Ivy League. Some were born poor, but one or two were independently wealthy. Some were revolutionaries. Others were conservative social critics. Still they were, to a man, common to the Southern ideal of oneness with the soil.

Stark Young, born in Como, Mississippi, was the son of a doctor. He was to become a teacher, as well as a playwright and novelist. Art enthralled him, but he devoted his life to the Southern ideal.

John Crowe Ransom was the son of a Methodist minister from Pulaski, Tennessee. He was a Rhodes scholar at Vanderbilt and soon became an acclaimed poet and social critic. As an artist, he refused to be a passive spectator to the world.

Henry Blue Klein was a massive, energetic Tennesseean. After a stint as a teacher, he held posts with the Civil Works Administration, the Tennessee Valley Authority, and the Atomic Energy Commission. One writer described him as a rebel against anything comfortable or conventional.

Frank Lawrence Owsley was from Montgomery County, Alabama. He was the son of a farmer and teacher. Educated in history at Auburn University and the University of Chicago, he later taught at Vanderbilt. He specialized in scholarly historical works, and thrived on challenging the Yankee establishment's mythological history.

Herman Clarence Nixon was the son of a country storeowner in Merrellton, Alabama. His education began in a one-room schoolhouse. Later, he taught history and political science at Louisiana State University, the University of Missouri, and at Vanderbilt. Nixon was no mere reactionary or nonconformist. He served on the Wilson Peace Commission in France, among other projects. He did, however, strictly reject the false gods of industrialism.

Alan Tate of Winchester, Kentucky became a biographer and one of America's most celebrated poets. Tate devoted himself to classical education and literature. He made a stand for absolute standards in art and education, as well as life. His life was a crusade against applied science without the moral restraint of philosophy.

Lyle Lanier of Madison County, Tennessee was the son of a small farmer. He too began his education in a one-room schoolhouse, but went on to become a devoted student of philosophy. He was soon a respected scholar, with his most prestigious work being done in the field of psychology. Lanier constantly defied social scientists, whom he considered charlatans.

Andrew Lytle was a farmer, teacher, and editor from Murfreesboro, Tennessee. His education was varied, ranging from military school to the Yale School of Drama. He loved farm life most, but won his fame as a novelist and historian. The themes of his work always feature the family as the pivotal unit of society and express the redemptive power of the Christian heritage.

John Gould Fletcher was born in Little Rock, Arkansas, the son of a Confederate Army colonel and Arkansas politician. He grew in up the mansion that Albert Pike abandoned in order to pursue the frontier life. Fletcher then quit school when he was a senior at Harvard, and spent his youth roaming Europe. There, he saw the effects of World War I on the people of the continent and became involved in the Fabian socialist movement. He returned to Arkansas in the 1930s, and championed the cause of folk art. A complex man, Fletcher scorned pure democracy and was "A lone hand battling against the tide of modernity."

John Wade was the son of a doctor from Marshallville, Georgia. He studied at Vanderbilt, Harvard, and Columbia, and was a renowned biographer and a teacher of English. Wade observed that the chief proponents of progress mainly had their own material progress in mind.

Robert Penn Warren was from Guthrie, Kentucky. As a child, he saw his neighboring tobacco farmers suffer under martial law. He was a Rhodes scholar, and taught at LSU and later, at Yale. He won fame as a social critic and novelist. His works issued a moral challenge to the reader, portrayed through raw and realistic violence. His most popular novel was *All the King's Men.*

Donald Davidson, born at Campbellsville, Tennessee, was perhaps the least well known of the Fugitives. He was a son of teachers. Davidson served in France during World War I as an Army lieutenant. Davidson studied and later taught history at Vanderbilt, and was a skilled editor and poet. Davidson's war experiences led him to prefer poetry as a weapon. In his hands, it was a potent weapon indeed. Most historians recognize Davidson as the leader of the Fugitive movement.[24]

For all their differences, the Fugitives shared a common concern for preserving Southern agrarian civilization. They revered man's relationship with nature as only Southerners could. That reverence spilled over into their writings on religion, philosophy, politics, and economics. Theirs was a view that embraced all that warms the heart of traditional Southerners. Their view also related well to the rising Western Agrarian movement.

As a group, the Fugitives' most visible work was their 1930 symposium, *I'll Take My Stand.* This monument of Southern philosophy and political thought is even more relevant today than it was in the thirties. The decay and tragedy the fugitives warned of visited its full force on our nation. All their predictions came true. Of great importance is the benchmark the Fugitives' observations provide. Modern scholars reflect on the 1930s as if they were the Dark Ages. In truth, ours is the barbaric age.

Fletcher's contribution, which focused on education, stated that the public school system of the early 1900s was a failure. His reason was that students of the thirties entered college unprepared. They needed two semesters of English composition to gain the grasp of our language they would have needed to enter college in earlier years.[25] Had he lived long enough, Fletcher would see his forecasts fall short. (He drowned in a pond near Little Rock's Central High School in 1950.) In a society where children never achieve the educational competence of their great-grandparents, education is merely a government frame of mind.

It is tragic that the world chose to ignore the Fugitives. Otherwise, we would have avoided so much pain and suffering. Theirs was a wake-up call for a society losing its relationship with nature and the soil. The soil, God's appointed giver of life, cannot be forsaken. People as well as plants must have a place to sink their roots. Neglect of the soil is fatal for any civilization, from Mesopotamia to the Soviet Union. Without the soil's nourishment, life withers, from grape to raisin, plum to prune.

Like later Southern reformers, the Fugitives made a strategic error in their second attack on industrial society. They tried to create a larger movement by appealing to a countrywide audience. This dissipated energies that would have best been spent in their regional crusade. As a result, the second symposium, *Who Owns America?*, drowned in a sea of dime novels and mass-produced fodder. The Fugitives would have been better off best saving their energy and staying in the South.[26]

Two of the fugitives, Donald Davidson and John Gould Fletcher, initiated a Southern student movement that predated the student activism of the 1960s. Their group was known as the "Gray Jackets." As one of their goals, the students planned the removal of the marble forest of memorials erected to Yankee invaders. These monuments still litter the South. The students judged one particular obelisk, near Nashville, especially offensive. They set out to destroy it at all costs. It was the assignment of the Vanderbilt chapter, known as the "Phalanx." The Great Depression defused the Gray Jacket movement more effectively than the ruling class ever could have done. An obligation to stay home and feed the family kept recruits away, through economic necessity. The New Deal sewed socialist lace on the sow's ear economy until the outbreak of World War II. This silenced Southern dissent. Except in academic circles, few ever realized the extent of the socialist revolution that Franklin Delano Roosevelt led. We still pay dearly for this ignorance.[27]

World war again caused Southrons to put aside their dreams of nationalism. WWII probably caused more damage to the Southern nationalist cause than the War of Northern Aggression. Our fight for survival probably united North and South more than at any other time, including 1776. The war also caused a new social phenomenon, the 100 percent American generation. While Southern veterans have every right to feel proud of their sacrifices during WWII, too many accepted blinders along with their draft notices. As in WWI, the Empire drafted Southerners wholesale, in numbers far out of proportion to the rest of the states. This, plus the treatment given the South in the post-war generation, should have forever

removed those blinders. Still, the "My country, right or wrong" attitude prevails in the war generation. This is amazing considering the
American Empire's constant attempts to prove to them that this is
not their country.

The post-war boom almost quieted Southern sectionalism for a
time. As in all periods of prosperity, people are less likely to complain. In good times, they are even less likely to look for an alternative system of government. During this period, the SCV almost fell
into extinction. There were few of the aging Confederates around
to remind us of our lost nation. Still, the South was a land apart,
with different ideals and moral values.

As with all times of peace, there is always someone standing
around, just waiting to muck things up. True to form, the next blow
fell from Northern hands. In 1948, the Democratic Party adopted
the platform of "civil rights." This was mainly due to the party's
infiltration by numerous socialists during the Roosevelt years.
Southerners naturally objected to their own party adopting the tac-
tics that the Radical Republicans used during reconstruction. The
Northern Democrats hoped to lure black voters away from the
Republicans with promises of federally enforced reform in
Southern states. Southerners split from the party to form the State's
Rights Party, the "Dixiecrats." The weakening split resulted in a
Republican president in 1952. Later, that president, Dwight D.
Eisenhower, dispatched the 101st Airborne Division to Little Rock.
The South's second reconstruction began.

The Dixecrats denounced the North's planned cure-all for the
supposed sins of Southern society. They knew that it mattered little.
Then, as now, that racism finds its most fertile soil in Northern fields.
The bloody shirt waved anew. Every finger we could point North
found five more pointing back. For every one of those Northern fin-
gers, there was a rifle, bayonet fixed, ready to subdue any Southern
resistance. The Southern congressmen issued a powerful statement
of principles denouncing the federal government's actions that tram-
pled the Tenth Amendment. It became known as *The Southern
Manifesto*. (See Appendix A.) Virtually every Southern senator and
representative signed the resolution except Senator Al Gore, Sr., of
Tennessee. He sold out then and every other time until the day he
died. In the end, his neglect of Southern principles cost him his seat
in the Senate.

I have seen and heard the opinion voiced often: "Why didn't

Arkansans just unite and resist? Why didn't they all just pull their kids out of school?"

The answers to those questions are simple. The American Empire met every avenue of resistance with fixed bayonets and the promise of bloodshed. It was the same in Tuscaloosa, Baton Rouge, and Oxford. In fact, it was the worst at Oxford. Agents of the empire forced Mississippians indoors. A reign of terror followed. Agents of the Empire beat innocent men, women, and children, all in the name of brotherhood. All across the South, the casualties mounted, black as well as white. All of this was because Washington needed the black man to resume his Reconstruction role as a political pawn.[28]

James J. Meredith was the first black man to attend Ole Miss through forced integration. He was wounded in the attempt. His thoughts in recent years reveal the wisdom he gained from experience. In a 1990 *Southern Partisan* magazine interview, he plainly expressed the view that white liberals had concocted the civil rights movement to create a second class of citizenship for black men. He felt that white liberals and the black elite had deluded and re-enslaved the black man as their servants in a quest for power and money.[29]

Times and attitudes change. If history teaches anything about Reconstruction and the civil rights fallacy, it is that it is better to let time do the changing, not federal occupation forces. Force only leads to violence, and violence to hatred. Older Southerners remember how much better the races got along before Washington tried to force us to get along.

If the 1930s were the Dark Ages that Northern scholars suppose, then the 1950s, 60s, and 70s naturally must be the Renaissance. However, do not confuse this Northern version of renaissance with some gilded age. It was a uniquely Northern phenomenon, occurring only so that the Northern elite could be legends in their own minds. It was a Yankee renaissance, complete with savage political intrigue and no-win wars. It was an attempt to finally destroy the last vestiges of traditional Southern nationhood. It failed. Southerners rejected the revolution that occurred around them. Steadfast in our traditions, we resisted the erosion of society. While beatniks, and later hippies, polluted the rest of the country, here their social trends never quite caught hold. Every town, of course, had its token hippie, but here we called them the village idiot. Some, with names like Clinton and Gore, sought greener pastures. Freedom riders in Mississippi, Alabama, and Georgia ran out of gas.

The only part of the whole campaign that really caught on was "The Great Society." Of course, that was, and still is, nothing more than a grand scheme of wealth redistribution. It steals from the middle class so the nobility can buy votes using our money. This is what Yankees consider "great."

In 1968, the ruling class again delivered Southerners notice that America was no longer their country. The Democratic Party ejected all Southern conservatives. Strom Thurmond was out. Abbie Hoffman and company were in.[30] George Wallace rose to the occasion to lead the Southern act of defiance. Wallace ran for president on a platform of law and order. He won every Southern state, ensuring popular Republican Richard Nixon a trip to the White House. When Wallace ran again in 1972, it appeared he might win. Shots fired in a Baltimore shopping center made sure he did not. Instead of law and order, we got Watergate.

In 1318, the blood of William Wallace nurtured a Scottish rebirth. Four hundred years later, the blood of George Wallace ushered a new Gaelic revolt. This new Southern spirit festered as discontent for a while, before emerging as a full-blown movement. As always, the catalyst was the actions of outsiders.

The new Yankee renaissance failed. The rift left a huge crater in the middle of America. The void grew into an abyss as the trendy libertine society of the west and upper east coasts grew steadily more decadent. The trendsetters tried every new and novel method of socialist ideology to fill the void. American society slid down the slippery slope toward decay and spiritual abandon. Nature abhors a vacuum. Vacuum is the creature of only deep space and the laboratory. Working according to natural law (pre-ordained instructions from God), Nature always fills a vacuum. It is the law of Nature that ordered systems decay into chaos. However, the same knowledge of good and evil that exiled man from the garden also forbids man to coexist with chaos. The vacuum created by the collapse of materialist Yankee culture (itself a vacuum) will fill, even if with the shreds of its existence. It is out of the collapse of unsuccessful systems that truly successful societies emerge. From the failure of the Yankee renaissance, we see the rise of Southern renewal, our "Southern Renaissance."

If one dated the beginning of the Southern Renaissance, it would have to be around 1984. Orwell's famous year was when things really started to happen. Many Southrons began to question the motives of the American Empire as scandal after scandal began to surface from the pasts of both major political parties. Later in 1988, *Southern by the Grace of God,* by Michael Grissom, was published. This was the first book since *Gone with the Wind* that allowed Southerners to feel good about themselves and their culture. Grissom showed us that the road to fulfillment is not the nearest interstate leading north or west. Instead, it is a Southern country road, without a name, number, or even pavement.

Coincidental with this period was the rebirth of the SCV. Under skilled leadership, the SCV grew from near-extinction to over twenty thousand members in just a few years. The rebirth featured hands-on management, complete with an aggressive recruiting campaign. It also involved public relations efforts gleaned straight from the culture of Madison Avenue. Perhaps the most important factor of the SCV's rebirth was that the camps did not sit around daydreaming. Instead, they got out and did something. The success of the SCV, and many of its heritage preservation spinoffs, was mainly due to its re-adherence to the original mission, that of vindicating the Southern cause.

The SCV has several weaknesses preventing it from taking a full leadership role in Southern renewal. Foremost is its tax-exempt status as a non profit organization. Remember that the power to tax is the power to destroy. If the SCV took an active role in politics, the IRS would tax them to oblivion. A sudden reduction in income would leave the heritage organizations without funds for the work they do well, already. This precludes a new and expanded role in Southern renewal. The "bottom line" is often the final line, so such organizations wisely guard their tax-exempt status.

Another prohibition is the diverse membership of the SCV. Because of this, the character of individual camps reflects the attitude of its members or its chosen leadership. This varies from location to location. Some camps are filled with the most fire-eating Southern nationalists. Others only indulge in an air of Southern Shinto ancestor worship. In other locations, a Southern nationalist might find his way to leadership, only have himself hobbled by respected and influential members, who prefer to avoid controversy. This conflict of goals is even apparent in the upper level of SCV leadership. As a respected figure could rise in government while disguising his agenda, so it is with most organizations. This became more than a worry in the early 1990s. A leadership clique tried to cleanse the SCV of its Southern nationalists and members of several other prominent pro-South organizations.[31] Since the SCV has such weaknesses, it was necessary to find another vehicle to promote Southern nationalism. In some cases, the SCV's weaknesses even prevent it from fulfilling its primary mission of vindicating the cause. Because of this, several spin-off or accessory groups organized to do what the SCV could not.

The first was the Heritage Preservation Association. While still centered mainly in the East, and with limited membership, the HPA still proved it could pack a punch. The HPA proved the effectiveness of small group and individual efforts. Their successes in defending the symbols and traditions of Southern life are too numerous to mention here, but one effort stands out above the rest.

Georgia Governor Zell Miller showed his willingness to pander to liberal portions of his electorate. He vowed to remove the Confederate Battle Flag from the Georgia State Flag. The HPA swung into action. HPA refuted the liberal propaganda of the establishment press. Only the skin of his teeth, and an endorsement from the National Rifle Association, kept Miller in office against an awakened electorate. Even the execution-style murder of one of its most outspoken members by black militants did not deter the HPA. It continues to be a leader in the preservation of Southern culture.[32]

Next to emerge was the League of the South (originally known as the Southern League). The league drew its inspiration from Italy's Lega Nord (the Northern League of Pandania, Italy), which remodeled Italian politics. Formed in June 1994 at Tuscaloosa, Alabama, the league shows great potential. In its first year, the league boasted over one thousand members in Virginia, alone. Paramount to its success is its goal: "to advance the cultural, social, economic, and political independence of the Southern people by all honorable and peaceful means."[33]

One possible key to the league's success is its leadership. The league swarms with some of the South's greatest thinkers. It revels in the likes of Grady McWhiney, Don Kennedy, Ron Kennedy, Clyde Wilson, Thomas Fleming, and Michael Hill. This union of the intellectual and the middle class is an important factor, one that was missing from past Southern political movements. Under such inspiring leadership, the league has pioneered many new avenues of activism. The league was the original pro-South organization on the Internet. This innovation not only helps educate young Southerners to be effective in the fight for Southern nationalism, it also alerts the world to the cause. *The League of the South Papers* are an excellent collection of pro-South writing, which are also available on the Internet. The League of the South also played a crucial role in replacing a scalawag Alabama governor for a time with a Southern patriot, Fob James. Although the league has a large audience, it still flexes most of its muscle east of the Mississippi. It still shows considerable potential as a major vehicle of Southern nationhood.

Farther west, the Confederate Society of America is gradually building its strength. The CSA formed in Monroe, Louisiana in June 1992. Backed by Southern patriots from fourteen states, the CSA declared its intention to be the action arm of the Confederate movement. Their chosen method was "diligently working for a return to moral, constitutional government, with its inherent guarantees of personal freedom."[34] The CSA never got the fast start that the League of the South did. Despite a few early organizational problems, they have managed to attract a respectable following west of the Mississippi and a scattering back East. The CSA continues to show promise, and could reach its full potential with wise leadership and an aggressive recruiting campaign.

Another influential organization is the Council of Conservative Citizens. Although not exclusively Southern, the CC of C's membership is greatest south of the Ohio. The council promotes conservative middle-class political dialogue and a traditional European-American worldview. This includes a sympathy to the Southern cause. The council is particularly active in the South, and could become a vital influence on policy affecting middle America. Its membership includes many notables, such as columnist Samuel Francis, Michael Masters, John Vinson, Gordon L. Baum, and Senate Majority Leader Trent Lott of Mississippi. One of the council's important features is its quarterly mouthpiece, the *Citizens Informer*. The *Informer* is an excellent publication and a marvelous pool of conservative thought.

Of course, the rise of the Confederate movement swiftly attracted the attention of the establishment. We knew it would. That is a sign our efforts work. Several liberal spokesmen, who called themselves Southerners, recently belittled our movement as just another phenomenon of multiculturalism. This naturally enraged many real Southerners. We know that there is no place for us in the Yankee, multicultural scheme of disorder. The Southern response was the first Confederate summit, held at New Albany, Mississippi, in October of 1996. Representatives from virtually every major Southern heritage organization met to discuss topics important to Southern heritage and Southern nationalism. After considerable discussion, the delegates reached a unanimous conclusion.

> Southerners are a distinctive Christian people, related by blood as well as shared culture, with a continued right to exist as such. All future political activities must support that principle.[35]

Confirming that Southerners have a right to exist as a distinct people is a decided turn of strategy in modern Southern nationalism. It also is the same strategy used in Quebec and Scotland. A sense of self-identity and a right to honorable means of self-defense is crucial to the new direction of our people. To further affirm this right, the delegates issued a powerful statement of principles, called the "New Albany Declaration." (See Appendix B) The Declaration restates the natural rights of a free people, if one can still term Southerners as free. It emphasizes our oppression by the American Empire. It also stresses our dispossession by the Empire and how much we lost. More importantly, the New Albany Declaration explains the direction we must take to reclaim our lost inheritance of freedom. The document also puts to rest another area of controversy. It defines just who is a Southerner. This important document will prove the beginning of a new world to the Southern man.

Therefore, we see that the Southern cause has many friends. It doesn't quite sound like a dead issue yet, does it? Outside the organizations already listed, there are more pro-South organizations than you could ever follow. There has even been an effort to establish a Southern nationalist political party, the Southern Party. Furthermore, the newly formed Confederate Alliance promises to be an important coalition of pro-South groups, designed to better coordinate our efforts.

The American Empire goes to great lengths to keep us in our place. Southrons and the other peoples of the Empire have never thought the same. We never worshipped the same. We do not talk the same, and we do not live or breathe the same. There is of course, a good reason for this. We are of different nationalities. Because of this, we do not get along, and we probably never will. Now, more than any other time since 1861, we have the will, the means, and the direction to better our condition. The New Albany

Declaration of 1996 will guide our people just as the Philadelphia Declaration of 1776. We must simply pursue our dream and make it a reality.

Before you form the opinion that you can sit back while someone else does all the work, think again. We still have far to go. Sure, we have a good start. But we still have much to learn. There are coalitions to form, campaigns to win, a people to educate and revitalize. Nobody ever said it would be easy. Freedom is never a cakewalk.

CHAPTER V

The Southern Phoenix

I have often heard gentlemen, who were thoroughly loyal to the Union, speak of what a splendid fight the South had made and successfully continued for four years before yielding, with their twelve million of people against our twenty, and of the twelve four being colored slaves, non-combatants. I will add to their argument. . . . In the South no opposition was allowed to the government which had been set up and which would have become real and respected if the rebellion had been successful.

Ulysses S. Grant[1]

No one can accuse Grant of just using his hindsight. He pursued a vindictive campaign against the Southern people until he rode its crest to the lofty perch of being America's first full-fledged emperor. Grant's administration wrote new chapters of cruelty and corruption in American history. He, and his protégé Sherman, knew what they were doing when they waged their war to destroy Southern civilization. Jealousy of their Southern acquaintances and the desire for power overshadowed what sense of honesty they might have once concealed. In a fit of greed, they destroyed what they knew was the best possible future for both nations involved. We know that is how they felt. They wrote it down in their memoirs in later years, as they tried to justify their actions. Grant, like the other members of the Yankee nation, knew what a crime they were committing against the Southern people. At least, in his later years he expressed a basic understanding of what he had done, even if he refused to show remorse.

Many Southrons know the truth, too. The South had and still has a much better future in store living separate of the Empire. Some of us are not shy about saying it. Hank Williams, Jr. popularized a song called "If the South Would Have Won." He probably says it as good or better than anyone does. His daddy probably would have agreed with him. Hank Williams, Sr. lived and died in a Southern generation lost to war and social turmoil. While Hank Junior's anthem was recorded with a bent on humor, his message is still worth considering. The popularity of his song shows that, like Hank, there are still plenty of people who feel stuck in a foreign land with Dixie on their mind. These people, whether they know it or not, have a working knowledge of Southern principle number three: "Southern Nationhood is practical as well as possible. The South will be better off as a free and independent nation."

What would it be like? A nation of our own? Could we exist independent of our neighboring states? Could we make it economically? Socially? Politically? Militarily? The prophets of doom all answer a resounding "No!"

Take heart. Such answers are the only type available to people who take the "Prophet of Doom" career choice. They are harmless as people (or prophets) go. The only damage they cause with their negative opinions is when someone actually listens. Assuming we examine the arguments of the Empire's paid spokesmen, what would an independent Southland be like? Could we make it on our own? Would it be a land flowing with milk and honey, or would it be Hell on earth? As with all complex questions, there is a complex answer. As usual, there is also good news and there is bad news. Since it is best to get bitter medicine out of the way, we will take the bad news first.

The bad news is that we will have problems. There will be social problems dealing with race, poverty, education, and just about anything else we could care to place a label on. There will be turmoil as we establish, replace, or abolish institutions. There will be complex issues best handled by the most competent and best-qualified members of our society. Some of our problems will require the attention and talents of all our society. Economics and preferences would dictate our markets. Our Southern society would remold itself with each new advance of technology. We would either flounder or triumph with each new day. Hard times would always lurk over the horizon, even in the best of times.

It is scary, isn't it? It sounds a lot like what the skeptics predict anytime someone mentions the idea of Southern independence. No one ever suggested that freedom means freedom from worry. It does not mean freedom from responsibility, or freedom from work.

It is a difficult road. That is why so many people shy away from the job of pioneering our future. That is the bad news. That's it, the bitter pill. It is not as bad as you might think. If you are ready to throw up your hands and quit, don't. At least, do not quit until you look at the other side of Southern nationhood.

Here is a challenge. Get one week's worth of any major newspaper from anywhere, any city, any country. If there is even a hint of the freedom of the press in the area of your source, you will learn something interesting. Ninety-nine times out of a hundred you will find that the "bad news," described two paragraphs back, is the common state of affairs everywhere from Australia, all the way around the world, and back again. If you chose a paper from inside the American Empire, you will find that it is the common state of affairs in the good old U. S. of A., also. Of course, we will have problems. The remarkable thing is that at any spot you can pick on the globe, they also have the same set of problems. Most have even worse problems. We have these same problems already. We will continue to have those same problems whether we are independent or not. The bad news is not nearly the perpetually impending doom that the Empire's paid mercenaries always make it sound. Every problem is an opportunity in rough form. Every challenge is an invitation to win. Our independence is the best chance to solve our problems. So much for the bad news.

Now, get ready for the good news. Be forewarned. There will be some boasting, because we have plenty of good news. It even feels strange referring to it as good news, because what I boast about is actually closer to 135 years of missed and forbidden opportunity. I take issue with the gentleman who first proclaimed, "Opportunity only knocks once." He was no gentleman. He was a scoundrel and a liar. Opportunity not only knocks; it beats on the door. It kicks and screams until someone finally listens and lets it in. This is especially true in our case. What is our great opportunity? It is something that other nations can only dream of. We can be almost totally self-sufficient. We can be economically independent, almost unassailable by world standards. That is a position almost any nation would envy.

Agriculturally, we are especially blessed. The Mississippi Delta region is arguably some of the most productive farmland on earth. Our farmers also till most of the South's other non-mountainous areas. We produce an ample portion of the vegetables grown in North America, with plenty for export. We have sugar from

Louisiana and citrus fruits from Florida and Texas. The South's production of corn, wheat, other grains, and soybeans surpass our need even in the worst years. We also have a virtual monopoly on modern rice and cotton production. Don't forget that despite the Empire's efforts the demand for tobacco is still high. Almost every crop we need is grown in the South, except for coffee, bananas, and cocoa. Our longer Southern growing season is indeed a blessing.

Meat is no problem, either. The South is the center of poultry production, especially in areas where row crops are not an option. Likewise, pork has always been a Southern staple. Our new industry of fish farming is thriving. Even our Gulf Coastal Plain is arguably the most productive grazing land in the world. Typically, it supports one to three cow/calf units per acre on improved pastures. Additionally, there is still abundant land in Texas and Oklahoma for free-range grazing at lesser levels. We have dairy farms mothballed all across the South since the Yankee Empire discouraged production in favor of imports. Southern civilization sprang from the riches of our soil. It shall rise again. The soil's humble treasure is the only true form of wealth.

Below the soil, we are equally blessed with natural resources and raw material. The mid-South is a focal point of petroleum and natural gas production. The coalfields of Tennessee and Kentucky can again prosper. Alabama can again increase its steel production to feed a hungry young nation's industries. The salt domes of Louisiana will supply our needs for several centuries. Additionally, our aluminum, tin, and lead industries are throttled back to favor Northern and foreign mills. They can again thrive. Even our large underground salt-water reservoirs are a gold mine in the hands of our chemical industry. There are a few resources that we lack, such as uranium, but we are still in the most favorable position, considering what we do have, of any nation in history.

While the Southern states were not an industrial superpower in 1861, we do not have that problem today. In their search for a source of cheap labor, the industrialists took care of that for us. We now have the means of our industrial, as well as our political, independence. Our industrial development is a winner in the global marketplace. As manufacturing goes, we are better off than most nations. We can build it all here, from automobiles to electronics. We have clothing and textile mills crying for a rebirth, with more jobs leaving our nation, destined for the Third World, every day. We even have a start in the computer industry. Who knows? The next Silicon Valley might be in North Carolina or Mississippi.

We always have our renewable staple resource of privately owned timber. Our timber products industry is the world's finest, especially in paper production. The petroleum industry located most of North America's refineries in the South. The by-products of both our timber and petroleum industries created a flourishing chemical industry. We already have our own steel and aluminum mills, which any industrial nation finds essential. Even the space program centers itself in the South.

Perhaps no other nation of the earth has a more advantageous transportation network than our Southern Nation. While our highways are crumbling from neglect, we have the basis of a system in place that is all we require to efficiently move our goods. The largest trucking firms in the U.S. had the good sense to make their headquarters in the South because of our agreeable climate. We already have established airports and the world's most efficient airfreight business. We have a network of railways that connects all our Southern centers of production. In fact, our industrialist sages are dismantling many of our railroads as excess mileage. In addition, just as in Mark Twain's day, we have our rivers. Our network of inland waterways and ports readily provides inexpensive and convenient transport for both our raw materials and manufactured goods. This network is the envy of the world.

Our separation from the rest of the country would also have a positive impact in areas besides economics. Our differing moral perspectives have long caused friction between us and the rest of the Empire. The imperial view of the South's traditional moral and conservative outlook is to label us backward and intolerant. For Southerners it is difficult to see what is forward or progressive about the moral decay so evident in New England and on the West Coast. Still, that does not stop the imperials from force-feeding us their corrupt and trendy fads. Because of this, there is inevitable conflict. They cannot even keep up with their own absurd dictates. How can we expect to satisfy their demands? Our separation would spare both our nations from continued association and conflict. Then, we would be free to follow our own traditions and conscience in relative peace.

This would go along way toward repairing the damage the American Empire has already inflicted on our society. One area that would show almost immediate improvement is that of crime. Under almost any form of conservative Southern government, the state would be free to administer quick and effective justice. Criminals are not big fans of the Southern version of justice, because it involves swift and sure punishment. Couple this with the traditional Southern view that punishment should fit the crime and that punishment should not be a pleasant experience. This is the effective deterrent to crime, one the Empire refuses to let us exercise. Career criminals would either move to easier hunting grounds or find safer occupations.

A similar improvement would occur in the South's social situation. A free South means schools free from the dictates of non-elected federal judges. It also gives our schools an escape from the latest hare-brained schemes of the Empire's dogma mills. Since the old math is not broken, there is no need to fix it with "New Math." Our schools could again educate instead of indoctrinate. Even the task of educating our kids would be easier, since they would not have to wake at 5 A.M. to ride a bus seventy miles. That's something Southerners, both black and white, can agree on. Agreement would be easier on other issues without Washington to manufacture incidents that provoke artificial hatred and envy between our races. All over the South, there are communities with racial and social harmony despite Washington's help. On the other hand, there are many communities across the Empire where racial tensions run hot, due only to Washington's meddling.

The heart of Southern life is our traditions and our social institutions. A free South would be a celebration of tradition. It would definitely be a land "where old times are not forgotten." Tradition and history are a nation's heritage, the basic fabric of its existence. There are plenty of old Southern traditions to observe, and we have many more to develop. The sense of time and place, which a nation's heritage gives, is essential to man's mental health. Our culture is the glue that binds strong families and communities. In other regions, cultures clash. In the South, they compliment.

A free South would be an icon on the world stage, an embodiment of the Biblical principle of liberty tempered with personal responsibility. Because of our self-fulfilling economy, our livelihood would depend less on the actions of foreign leaders. Thus, we would end the need for the entangling alliances that have spilled so much Southern blood in senseless foreign wars. With a military patterned after the Swiss model, we would need only a small standing army. Still, with even just such a singularly defensive force, we could be as unassailable as Moscow in winter. Such a system would blessed us with both peace and security.

As an independent nation, we could again base our politics upon tradition, law, and common sense. It is easy to see how differently Southerners would govern themselves. Just look at the voting records of our congressmen over the last thirty years. We will look at just a few specific instances. It is eye-opening just how different our condition would be if we had the right to rule ourselves.

If you imagined the South were an independent nation and observed the voting of Southern congressmen as a separate group over the last thirty years, you would find that they voted exactly the opposite of the rest of the U.S. on almost every critical issue. (1965-1995). Once more, this confirms the deep differences between the South and the rest of the country. It is an illustration of the South's character through its elected representation. This also shows the "tyranny of the majority" that John Calhoun warned us of in the 1840s. For instance, Southern representatives and senators usually vote to curb immigration. Against our consent, the rest of the U.S. jams immigration down our throats. The Immigration Reform Act of 1965 opened the country to massive Third World immigration. The Immigration Reform Act of 1986 granted amnesty to *illegal* aliens. The Immigration Act of 1990 increased immigration by over 40 percent. All these acts passed the whole assemblies, but Southern statesmen always opposed them by nearly two-thirds.[2]

In the area of crime control, Southern lawmakers show that they are the ones with their heads on straight. In 1991, Southerners in the House voted by almost two-thirds to limit the federal appeals process on cases that had already had "full and fair hearing" at the state level. The rest disagreed, allowing frivolous appeals that bog down our legal system. When the Brady Bill passed the House in 1994, Southerner congressmen opposed it by 58 percent. When the "Assault Weapons Ban" passed the House, they again opposed it by 66 percent.[3]

There is more. In an independent South, we would have an amendment protecting school prayer, although Southrons see no need to protect what common sense allows. There would be an amendment returning abortion decisions to the states. We would have a balanced budget amendment. Southern senators voted in favor of such an amendment by an incredible 80 percent margin. Southern senators would bar federal judges from hearing cases involving public schools. There would still be a law against women in combat.[4] Our president would have had the line item veto as a constitutional amendment, instead of a statute that a federal judge is sure to throw out. The list goes on and on. The great truth is that Southern statesmen, just as in 1861, still steer our course closer to the original intent of the founding fathers. The Empire's most pronounced political weaknesses almost make the case for our separation from the rest of the country. Though they constantly hint that we are the ball and chain, we actually prop up the union politically, socially, and morally. Still, economics strikes the final blow that vindicates the practicality of Southern independence.

How would the South perform as an independent economic power, compared to the other nations of the world? We would be in a lot better position than most of us think. We can tell by comparing our Gross Domestic Product (GDP) against that of other nations. The GDP is a measure of the total value of a nation's goods and services produced in a year. When we compare the production of the Southern Nation to our neighbors, we see that our future is indeed bright.

First let's see how we stand against the rest of the U.S. We will define the South as the *Congressional Quarterly* does. That is the original eleven states of the Confederacy plus Kentucky and Oklahoma. This region is that most typically thought of as the South, and it best describes us politically. (For those of you in Missouri, this is the *Congressional Quarterly* talking, not me.) The South as described by the *Congressional Quarterly* is not exactly the backward and barefoot land Washington makes us out to be. We make up 31.5 percent of the U.S. population, roughly equivalent to the population of unified Germany. In addition, we produce 28.5 percent of the goods and services of the United States.[5] The *Congressional Quarterly* South is more populous and out-produces every other region of the U.S. Remember that we also do this for less pay than workers in the rest of the Empire. Even a South made up of the original eleven Confederate States compares well. An eleven-state South would have 28.8 percent of the U.S. population, still close to the population of Germany. We would still produce 26.2 percent of the goods and services in the U.S. This is roughly equivalent to the Northeast, but still much more than the Midwest and West. Now, let's see how we would compare to the world.[6]

An independent South, as the census bureau defines it (the original eleven states plus Maryland, Delaware, West Virginia, Kentucky, Oklahoma, and the District of Columbia) would be the world's third most-prosperous nation. We would have a GDP behind the U.S. and Japan, but still ahead of Germany, France, Italy, and the United Kingdom. That would be powerful, but it is unrealistic because of the political differences such a coalition would involve. The more realistic and better-defined *Congressional Quarterly* South would rank fourth, between Germany and France. An eleven-state South would fall in the same place. Even a ten-state South, without Texas, would be the sixth most-prosperous nation on earth. That would rank just behind Italy, but ahead of the United Kingdom, the Russian Federation, Canada, Spain, Brazil, and China.[7] For a better idea of how we stack up, see Table 1.

Doesn't quite sound like what they told you in high school, does it? You surely remember when your history teacher gave you the official line on how we should be grateful that we lost the war. What they never could explain was just why we should be grateful. They still can't.

Had the South won, we would have been even more prosperous. We would have avoided the destruction of Reconstruction. Instead, we provide almost one-third of the goods and services produced in the American Empire for only two-thirds of the pay. Pardon me, but it doesn't sound like we won by losing. Instead, we lost our right to self-government. We lost our right to prosperity. We lost our right not to participate in Korea and Vietnam. We lost the right to be our own masters, steer our own ship. Also somewhere along the way, the Empire made sure that we lost our selves.

TABLE 1

SOUTHERN PRODUCTIVITY COMPARED TO OTHER NATIONS

Rank	Country	GDP (1990 data, in millions of US Dollars)	Rank	The Southern Nation	GDP
1	United States	5,464,795			
(1)	(US-CB South)	(3,713,036)			
(1)	(US-CQ South)	(3,906,004)			
(1)	(US-11 State South)	(4,029,512)			
2	Japan	2,932,088			
3	Unified Germany	1,641,908	3	Census Bureau South	1,751,759
4	France	1,192,217	4	Congressional Quarterly South	1,558,794
5	Italy	1,094,765	5	Eleven State Confederate South	1,435,283
6	United Kingdom	979,121	6	Ten State South (minus Texas)	1,063,295
7	Russian Federation	940,390			
8	Canada	566,680	8	Nine State South (Minus Tex. & Fla.)	818,671
9	Spain	491,761			
10	Brazil	473,697			
11	China	369,439	11	Five States of the Deep South	401,680
12	India	303, 282			
13	Australia	296,317			
14	The Netherlands	283,552			
15	Ukraine	247,447			
16	Mexico	244,047			
17	South Korea	244,043			
18	Sweden	227,900			
19	Switzerland	226,022			
20	Belgium	192, 303			

Source: William Lamar Cawthorn, Jr., "The South As Its Own Nation," The League of the South Papers, 1995. The League of the South, P.O. Box 40910, Tuscaloosa, Alabama 35404-0910, 1 (800) 888-3163.

CHAPTER VI

The Irresistible
Gray Force of Freedom

An invasion of armies can be resisted, but not an idea whose
time has come.   Victor Hugo[1]

History proves that no tyrant, no army, no regime can stand
against a people who seize the moral high ground and refuse to
yield. There is no ground higher than man's unalienable right of
freedom and self-determination. History also proves, especially in
the modern era, that it is not necessary to shed blood to win nationhood. The modern arsenal of freedom is not stocked with guns and
bombs. It swells with neurons and electrons.

Once captive people think of themselves as a nation, they can see
the better future that awaits them. At that point, they automatically
try to better themselves. It does not matter what force tries to stop
them. The promise of a brighter day coaxes that people down the
path of freedom. This is the mechanism behind Southern principle
number four: "As a nation, it is our duty and obligation to practice
our God-given right of self-determination. Once Southerners determine to free themselves, no force on earth can stop them."

History celebrates the tales of underdogs who succeed against
insurmountable odds. Their stories make for good reading and
entertaining movies. Everyone loves it when the underdog triumphs. Beating the odds is heroic. It is admired. People want to see
Forrest Gump succeed. No one goes to a movie to see Sherman pillage the defenseless women and children of Georgia.

The little guy who overcomes the odds becomes a part of legend
and a center point of history. The Greeks heroically faced the odds
at Thermopylae and Marathon. Everyone studies them. Nobody
cares about the multitudes of Persia, unless they are from Persia. It
is the same in all cultures and throughout history.

- Everyone watches John Wayne or Fess Parker fight at the Alamo. Have you ever seen a movie about Santa Anna?
- The name of the Apache war chief, Geronimo, is still a household word after more than a hundred years. Can you name the general responsible for subduing him?
- In the winter of 1939-40, the world admired the few courageous Finnlanders who fought hordes of Russian invaders to a standstill.
- Only other Arabs or the anti-Semitic hoped the Arabs would beat tiny Israel during the Six-Day War or the Yom Kippur War.

It is the same here. The South held out against the North for four agonizing years. When our forefathers laid down their arms, the American Empire cheated them and us out of the peace they promised. Later, Southern leaders saw the folly of surrender. Some, such as General P. G. T. Beauregard, proposed counter-revolution and the first large-scale guerrilla war. Even the model Southron, Robert E. Lee, expressed his sorrow at having quit. After sampling the Yankee version of peace, he stated that he would rather have died with his sword in hand.[2]

As a nation, we have plenty of role models to guide us in our struggle against imperial rule. Many nations won their freedom and independence against worse odds than we face. The key to our future is to learn from their experience and imitate their success. We must not stop at just reading about them in a chapter of a book like this. Southerners must study the fundamentals of their experience. We must apply their methods to fit our needs.

English treachery first subjugated Scotland in 1291. The pope lent legitimacy to English domination by declaring Scotland to be an English possession. Supposedly, this was sort of a property deed from God. With their papal authority in hand, the English soon proved to be cruel masters. The crown never missed a chance to suppress its Scottish subjects. The English nobles considered the Gaelic Scots to be less than human and more like dogs. To keep their unruly captive nation in line, the crown targeted every vestige of the Scots' heritage as a free people. The English outlawed the assembly of the clans. They outlawed the wearing of kilts. The Scot's conquerors even imposed the death penalty for the playing of bagpipes. Not content even with that, English nobles tried to "improve" the Scot bloodline by demanding the first fruits of the marriage bed.

The Scots realized that their life as English subjects would never get better; it could only get worse. No man has a right to rule another against his will, no matter what a particular pope says. The Scots drew their claymores on moral principle. Under the leadership of men like William Wallace and Robert the Bruce, the Scots defeated their oppressors and won back their independence. They kept it for 380 years. It was only after a shady royal wedding in 1707 that Scotland became part of the United Kingdom. If recent events in the UK are any indication, Scotland will soon be independent again.[3]

The lesson of the Scots: *Seize the moral high ground and refuse to yield.*

The Irish became English subjects in a manner similar to the Scots. The only difference was that the pope issued the deed before the conquest. As with the Scots, the English tried to eradicate all traces of Irish nationality. The English imposed laws against wearing green, speaking the Gaelic language, and even went so far as to outlaw the shamrock. As their efforts failed, the English attempted to water down the Irish population by immigration. This did not work either. The English crown soon described its transplants as "more Irish than the Irish." Finally, in one of history's worst crimes against humanity, the English systematically starved the Irish population during the Potato Famine of the 1840s.

Still, the fabled luck of the Irish would not sit idle. The Irish had several things in their favor. First, they had a rich cultural heritage, which they jealously guarded. Second, the Irish practically invented guerrilla warfare, although it often produced tragic results. Third, and most of all, the Irish were persistent. Throughout all 750 years of their English domination, the Irish never quit. Irish history became a series of revolts and guerrilla campaigns. Until 1921, failure and the inevitable brutal English retaliation marked their efforts. After the disastrous Battle of Tara ended the 1798 rebellion, the English impaled the surviving Irish troops on their own pikes. This punishment was not enough to suit the English, so Redcoats roamed the countryside with mobile gallows. They hanged any Irishman that they thought too impudent (or that they just plain found in many cases). The British poured flaming pitch over the heads of other victims. The arrogance and brutality of their English masters only strengthened the Irish resolve to overcome.

The Irish finally realized that they could never defeat the British Empire on the conventional field, whether they armed themselves with axes, pikes, or cannon, depending on the particular century.

Instead, the Irish found that they could make British rule such an inconvenient and worrisome job that their captors would eventually give up and go home.[4]

The Irish lesson: *Never quit. Make your oppressor quit instead.*

At the beginning of World War I, the Ottoman Turks had occupied and ruled over the Middle-Eastern Arabs for more than four hundred years. Turkish rule was oppressive, but not particularly disagreeable with the Arabs. The peoples had a lot in common. Ottoman rule lasted because the various Arab tribes never put aside their Turk-fostered feuds and united long enough to kick out the invaders. In local affairs, the hereditary sheiks and sharifs still had some leeway, but as centuries of Ottoman rule dragged on, the Turks began to meddle and assume more control, beginning with an effort to eliminate the Arabic language. Eventually, the Turks forced the Arabs to adopt the Ottoman legal system. Turkish law, though harsh by today's Western standards, was much too liberal for Arab tastes. As orthodox Moslems, they preferred the even harsher and stricter Islamic code of their ancestors. The Arabs considered the Turkish law to be a degenerate farce.

Still, Arabs viewed Turkish rule as an annoyance that they had to bear. This changed when the Turks pushed too hard and the Arabs began to see themselves as a unique people with a common heritage and as a distinct nation. The Arabs and their hereditary leaders began to view their future differently than did their Turkish masters. The Arabs formed secret groups that spread the message of Arab nationalism. The result was the Arab Revolt during World War I. T.E. Lawrence, the famous Lawrence of Arabia, advised and chronicled the Arab struggle. He watched as the Arabs forged a national unity, then fought beside the Allies in the Middle East. Together, they drove out the Turks, and the Arabs won their freedom.[5]

The Arab lesson: *Any people who are discontent can learn to see themselves as a nation. Then they can be free.*

The story of India and its struggle for independence is well known. Less known and even less studied are the attitudes and techniques that made India free. The turn of the century saw riots and bloodshed in India. The people grew tired of both the caste system and British rule. Violence, the historical response to oppression, appalled Mohandas Gandhi. His great service to the world was to show people how to win their freedom without warfare and violence. The principle he taught was simple: Indians would simply no longer participate in British rule, no matter what the British did to force them to conform. Even if it were something for India's benefit, Indians would just not take part. In Christian terms, they turned the other cheek. The British troops beat the Indians until they were too tired to beat anymore. Gandhi's followers did not resist. Finally, the common British soldier refused to beat or shoot the defenseless. A tired British lion left to find game that would fight by it's rules. The British were powerless against those who would not draw a sword.[6]

India's lesson: *Violence is not necessary to achieve freedom.*

More recently, we all watched as the people of Poland won their fight for freedom. The communist takeover of Poland did not create Karl Marx's dreamland. Instead, shortages and hunger plagued the nation. Polish workers unionized and struck in defiance of Soviet policy. The Polish riot police (ZOMO) attacked and overwhelmed the unarmed laborers. The police killed several workers, but the Poles refused to quit. The brutal tactics ZOMO used turned world opinion against the Warsaw regime. Further attempts to disband the union, now named Solidarity, proved bloody and futile.

In an attempt to pacify the laborers, the Polish puppet regime granted the workers a few token concessions. It did not work. Encouraged by the win, Solidarity grew explosively and became more than just a labor union. An electrical worker, Lech Walesa, appeared as an innovative leader and a new hero on the world stage. To bring the Poles to heel, the Communists installed a hardliner, General Wojciech Jaruzelski. He failed to restore Moscow's brand of order. His token concessions, meant to pacify the Poles, only emboldened them. The Poles realized that they could reclaim their nation. The world watched in color as Soviet domination crumbled. Lech Walesa became president. It was the first Polish ballot with more than one candidate since WWII. Why did Moscow let Poland go? Because the world was watching.[7]

The Poles' lesson: *Grab the world's attention and sympathy.*

Poland was the beginning. The rest of the captive Eastern Bloc states finished the Soviet Empire. Latvians, Estonians, Lithuanians, East Germans, and the rest saw their opportunity. They went out and made freedom happen. These nations could have demanded and probably have gotten reform, even within the security of their empire. They did not. They knew that if change were to last, their nations were their own best security. So, they followed Poland's lead and went it alone. The Soviets stacked all the cards against them. Fifty years of Communist rule had almost eradicated their native cultures, languages, and traditions. In addition, the Soviets were their only trading partners. All of their future was a gamble. Their gamble paid off. The Soviet empire could hold them no longer. Freedom was their reward.[8]

Their lesson: *Freedom is worth the risk of losing security.*

Closer to home, thirteen colonies decided that a foreign monarchy more than two thousand miles away had no right to abuse them any longer. Years of political and economic discrimination blended with Parliament and the king's arrogance. It came to a head on Lexington green. Shots were fired. The colonial militiamen ran to save their skins and fight another day. The colonists tweaked the nose of the most powerful military machine on earth.

The colonial patriots had many demoralizing obstacles to overcome. Their effort easily could have derailed before it got started. They were at war. They had no army. They had no navy. Worse, they had no money. Even more discouraging, the patriots could not muster the support of even 10 percent of their fellow colonists. Even after Thomas Paine's famous public opinion campaign, they never held a majority of the other colonists' support. John Adams observed that even in the closing months of the North American colonies' war for independence, only about one-third of colonists supported the revolution. One-third supported the Crown, and the other third simply couldn't care less, one way or the other. We know how the story ended. We won, but it took more than six years of sacrifice.[9]

Their lesson: *A majority or even a large following is not necessary to win freedom.*

These examples are important. Captive nations, who triumph against the odds, have many important traits. In all cases, they did the best they could with the very limited resources they had at hand. There is always the importance of holding to a high moral principle. Ideally, the most important element for success against all odds is a stubborn refusal to quit. Still, we have one other meaningful lesson to learn.

We know that children need positive role models. So do nations. The Scots served as a role model to the Irish. The North American colonies served as a role model to South America's Spanish colonies. In addition, the American colonies' War for Independence provided the inspiration for the Texas Revolution and the War for

Southern Independence. When Ireland finally freed itself of the British crown, their win inspired India to try freedom (using different methods). India served as the role model for the Polish. Poland was the role model for the rest of the Soviet empire. This same former-Soviet wasteland is the role model for Quebec.

Lesson number eight: *Every nation that achieves independence and freedom serves as a role model for others.*

Who should be our example? All of them should be. The winners, and even the losers, provide us with lessons to learn. These examples are the building blocks of our future. They also teach that as man progresses, freedom is bought less with blood and more with will. There is no more reason for a foreign power across the Potomac to rule us than there was for a foreign power across the Atlantic to do so. Winning freedom is a big responsibility. The free nations of the world all learned their lessons from others. Now, let's learn from them. Who knows who may be watching and learning from us?

With knowledge comes the responsibility for using that knowledge. The citizens of a nation not only have a right, but a duty of self-determination. This principle was firmly re-established by our own Declaration of Independence. Jefferson wrote the sacred principles of freedom into our original American republic's founding document just as he learned them from John Locke and other philosophers of freedom who came before him. Locke merely restated what Western civilization has long recognized as the unalienable rights of man. Our rights are unalienable because government cannot take our rights from us. Our Creator granted man his natural rights. They existed long before any human attempts at legislation. The recognition and classification of these unalienable rights—namely life, liberty, and property—were not the brainchild of John Locke. They descended to us from the Old Testament, the classical Greek thinkers, and from later Christian philosophers like Saint Augustine and Saint Thomas Aquinas. It is clear that all man's other rights derive from his basic unalienable rights of life, liberty, and property.

Since man has an unalienable right to life, liberty, and property, it is only natural that he be able to defend those rights. Thus, man has a natural right to lawful self-defense. Both natural and common law define lawful self-defense as what force any reasonable person would use if confronted by the same threat under the same conditions.

It is a given that man has a predatory nature to take what he wants when he thinks he can get away with it. Because man has a natural right to lawful self-defense, it follows that he must have the means to defend his life, liberty, and property from other, predatory men. Therefore, from this natural right we derive the natural right to keep and bear arms. Following from this train of logic, we derive what is best defined as the right to be let alone. This right is so that we may enjoy life, liberty, and property as we see fit, as long as our method of enjoyment does not violate the rights of others.

From the definition of lawful self-defense, we also derive the natural right to due process. This applies whenever man is in civilized company. Because lawful self-defense is defined as what force any reasonable person would use when confronted with the same threat under the same circumstances, it is assumed that someone other than those involved in the original dispute must decide just what is reasonable. Due process insures that a man only forfeits his rights when he has caused unjust injury to others, and that his forfeiture is only in proportion to his offense. In most areas, the right to due process equates to a right to a speedy trial by a jury of one's peers.

Why does man have an unalienable natural right to property? Property is necessary for his security and his means of production. Man uses his property to provide the necessities of life for himself and his family. As the Apostle Paul tells us:

> If any provide not for his own, and specially for those of his own house, he hath denied the faith, and is worse than an infidel.[10]

When man and his family are well provided for, they are generally considered content or happy. Thus, we have the natural right to the pursuit of happiness that Jefferson mentioned in the Declaration of Independence. Since the worship of God is always necessary for true happiness, man also has a natural right to freely exercise his religion. Because God granted man his rights, it follows that the worship that man renders must only apply to the one real God and not false fad gods and idols dreamt up by man.

Man can only sustain his life through labor. The labor I refer to is the production of food or goods to trade for food. Without a doubt, man has a natural right to the fruit of his own labor. For most of us today, this means a right to collect the bulk of our earned wages. Related to this natural right is the freedom of economic choice to trade with those we desire. We are free to get the best deal or seek the highest return on our labor. We are also free to refuse to trade with those who would cheat or otherwise injure us. Likewise, we do not want to sell a spear to someone whom we feel would likely turn it against us later.

Along the same lines, and deriving from a similar logic, is the natural right best known as freedom of association. Everyone knows that associating with the wrong crowd is harmful to our families and ourselves. Thus, the freedom of association derives also from our natural right of lawful self-defense. In the same manner that we are free to avoid harmful or demeaning people, we are free to associate with those people who are beneficial to our families and ourselves. We are similarly free to band together with people of like concerns for our economic benefit, our comfort, or to better defend our rights.

Some "post-modern" philosophers and political scientists deny the existence of natural law and natural rights. Their stance defies reason. The statements of these public-provided philosophers are not only dangerous; they are blasphemous. Theirs is a pagan concept and assumes the absence of a Creator. Their logic is an extension of the "Might makes right" principle that shut out the light and began the Dark Ages. If we look to the Bible, in the third chapter of Genesis we find that the original sin that banished man from the garden was a crime against property. (The fruit of the tree of the knowledge of good and evil belonged to God, not the state.) A chapter later, we see that Cain violated Abel's right to life. Jumping to the twentieth chapter of Exodus, we encounter the Decalogue that God gave to Moses. The first four commandments concern man's duty to God. Commandments five through ten concern our duty to our fellow man. This is the first written codification of life, liberty, and property. Remember that the commandments did not come from the mind of Moses. They were direct from God. Moses just carried them down the mountain. We see that natural law and natural rights have easily been around for 16,000 years or more. Those who criticize natural law and natural rights can scarce claim a hundred years.

Because men are by instinct lazy creatures, they fulfill their needs by the easiest means possible. This often means that those lacking in moral guidance prey upon those weaker than themselves. This inherent trait of man as a fallen creature caused men to band together to defend their life, liberty, and property. There is, of course, safety in numbers. As a group men could more easily defend against wandering predators, whether two- or four-legged. This necessity was the origin of government. First, men gathered as families, then later as clans, tribes, etc.

Once men assemble for their common defense and economic benefit, they bind themselves to the other members of their society. With this protection and benefit comes a new responsibility toward the whole. In 1651, Thomas Hobbes termed this responsibility the "Social Contract." The contract need not be a conscious arrangement. Often it is understood, as in a family. All members of a society delegate certain individual rights to the whole of society. We exchange these rights for the benefits of association with that society. Whether the society's form of government is a patriarchy, monarchy, aristocracy, or democracy, the individual delegates a portion of his individual sovereignty to the whole. This delegated sovereignty resides with society at the donor's consent. If the individual is not happy with the arrangement, he can always go it alone. This delegated power was the origin of states.[11] Because of the state's dependence upon the delegated power of individuals, it exists only by the consent of its citizens.

In 1690, after the death of Hobbes and England's "Glorious Revolution of 1688," John Locke took the social contract and refined it, rectifying it more fully with natural law and Christian philosophy. Locke's teaching is most notably condensed in the second paragraph of our Declaration of Independence.

Locke observed that with rights come responsibilities. He also declared that the social contract binds not only the citizen but also his rulers. Locke reasoned that since the consent of the governed gives rulers their power, the citizen has the right of revolution. Citizens can recall the powers they delegate to government if that government violates the people's trust. Mere rule by law is not enough. Rule must be just.[12] Even Joseph Stalin applied his laws consistently. No one claims he ruled justly.

A government has responsibilities toward the citizens it serves. They give the government its power. Of course, the citizen also has responsibilities in relation to his government. Since the citizen is the source of all governmental power, with him rests the responsibility to see that government's power is used correctly. The customary and written laws of nations hold that the ultimate responsibility for a government's actions rests with its citizens. Nowhere was this concept more thoroughly endorsed than at Nuremberg, Germany after World War II. The nations and empires of the world held the German citizen responsible for the atrocities of the Nazi regime. One after another, German military and civilian leaders pleaded that they were only following orders. Their excuse did not wash the blood from their hands. All civilized nations recognize that illegal orders are the same as unjust laws, which are not recognized as laws at all.

It was the same with the individual German citizen. He could plead ignorance, saying, "We never knew." Still, the lesson of Nuremberg is clear. The citizen has a duty to know the actions of his government. If those actions are unjust, his government is unjust. In such a case, the citizen's duty is clear. He must fight his government's actions. If necessary, he must exercise his right and duty of revolution to dissolve and replace that government with a new one that will rule justly. In the thirties and forties, German citizens shirked this responsibility. Despite their excuses, the Allies held them responsible for their leaders' actions. Because they neglected their most basic human duty, German civilians reaped the whirlwind of their leaders' crimes. The Allies partitioned and occupied Germany for more than fifty years.

Remember the previously mentioned examples of captive nations pursuing their nationhood? In each of these cases, the citizens did their duty according to natural law, natural rights, and the accepted usage of nations. There were no Nuremberg trials for the people of India or Poland. Nor was the secession of the original thirteen colonies from the British Empire a criminal act. Likewise, the thirteen states of the Confederate States of America were innocent before the international laws. Likewise, Quebec is free to leave Canada at any time. Australia and Scotland are free to secede from the British Empire. It is their right. If their empires are harmful to their citizens' well being, it is the citizens' duty to correct the condition. Although the odds might be against us, the Southerner's responsibility is the same.

It sounds simple enough. This is the great mystical secret that was never really a secret. All the winners know. Now that you know, you are saddled with the responsibility for your nation. It is especially important that you decide soon. Now you are the one who knows the goal is within your grasp. Which team do you want to be on? What do you want your children and grandchildren to think? Do you want them to thank you for being a winner, or curse you as a loser who never tried? Well, it is your choice. Do you want to be free? Do you want to be a loser, or do you want to win?

THE EIGHT PRINCIPLES OF GAINING FREEDOM

1. Seize the moral high ground and refuse to yield.
2. Never quit. Make your oppressor quit instead.
3. Any people who are discontent can learn to see themselves as a nation. Then they can be free.
4. Violence is not necessary to achieve freedom.
5. Grab the world's attention and sympathy.
6. Freedom is worth the risk of losing security.
7. A majority or even a large following is not necessary to win freedom.
8. Every nation that achieves independence and freedom serves as a role model for others.

CHAPTER VII

The Personal Quest for Freedom

Rebellion to tyrants is obedience to God.

Benjamin Franklin[1]

The great value of heritage is that we can borrow from our past to build our future. Our Southern heritage is not just the legacy of the old Confederacy. It reaches back to our Gaelic and Anglo-Saxon beginnings. Our heritage descends even further into the mists of time, rooting itself in the Old Testament of the Bible. Using our entire heritage, including our most ancient roots, we can map our path to personal freedom. What we aim for is freedom from error, freedom from spiritual darkness, and freedom from oppression.

Just as we learn from our recent past, we can learn from our most ancient relatives. We learn the most not necessarily just from their triumphs, but from their mistakes. Using our ancient cousins the nation of Israel as an example, we find that their triumphs came when they applied their faith and believed. We also find that their failures resulted when they lost sight of God, or when they shrank from their duty in fear. Because of their apathy, God scattered them to the four corners of the earth.

Personal development and growth is the strategy that will set us free of the Empire. In truth, our ability to learn and grow is the trait that separates humans from the beasts. Unfortunately, growth, reflection, and learning are a forgotten part of society today. This is why many residents of our inner cities could be best described as the "feral man" of some post-modern Sodom. They revert to savagery, and, like wild dogs, they prey upon the old and weak. When the sun goes down, our cities become steel and asphalt jungles. Feral is the right word to describe these nocturnal predators, but

Hollywood chooses to celebrate them. They are the Empire's authentic people, giving up their claim to civilization in favor of the law of the jungle. This is the true product of science's preoccupation with evolution. They are nothing more than man-apes armed with modern clubs and stones.

To elevate ourselves above the primal state, the rest of us need to set sail on a voyage of discovery. We could better call it a voyage of rediscovery. Southrons must re-learn the traits that define and enhance their lives. We must return to leading an ordered existence laced with the blessings of peace, fulfillment, and liberty. Our reeducation as a people, instead of imperial citizens, is not as difficult as one would think. All it requires is faith, an open mind, and a receptive heart. If you apply yourself, the lessons you learn will transform your life into one of meaning. God created man for a purpose. He intended that man live a life that meant something.

To improve ourselves, we must first make a conscious commitment to do so. Commitment is the first step. Still, if you keep a commitment to yourself, it is too easy to neglect its obligations. A promise to no one is no promise at all. To illustrate the idea of conscious commitment, we shall use an allegory, an illustration. In this case our illustration is Biblical. Our example is the Nazarite of ancient Israel.

A Nazarite was a person who made a sacred vow of service to God. In ancient times, the vow of a Nazarite was a consecration for a holy purpose. By imposing certain limitations on the physical self, the Nazarite kept his spiritual being away from those things that were profane. The vow itself lasted anywhere from a month to a lifetime. The Nazarite's vow was a special enhancement for holy purposes. It was a conscious commitment before God. It was a commitment intended as an example to the Nazarite's fellow man.

Mosaic law set strict procedures governing the conduct of Nazarites. The law prohibited Nazarites the use of wine or strong drink. Neither could Nazarites eat any other product of the grape. Nazarites did not cut their hair for the duration of their vow. The law also forbade them to touch or go near a dead body, even that of a family member. In addition, the Nazarites were naturally required to keep the rest of God's law, as given to Moses. These requirements set Nazarites apart from the rest of Israel. It kept them clean and fit for the Lord's work.[2]

The Bible and history give several examples of Nazarites, including two men who were consecrated from birth. One of the most detailed was that of Samson, the famous strongman and judge of Israel. Samson's downfall came when he ignored the strict code of his responsibility. We also find that John the Baptist was consecrated from birth. Unlike Samson, John kept the law. Even the apostle Paul took similar vows, as an example to Christian Jews that they should continue to observe the covenant of Mosaic Law.[3]

Throughout history, other religions and nations followed similar practices for similar purposes. Monastic vows, beginning with the Essenes, drew their origins from this custom. It was the same with the chivalry. The various orders of knighthood, from the middle ages to the present, derive from this ancient practice. So do the initiation ceremonies of most fraternal organizations.

In the trying times of today, we can learn much from those who built our past. It was not the vow, or the keeping of the law, that set the Nazarite apart from Israel and the world. Their commitment was what consecrated them. Fear of commitment is what so often separates modern man from God's assistance. Commitment is the most important ingredient of success, whether in business, marriage, or any of life's other activities. In most of man's undertakings, failure is already assured without this vital component. Commitment furnishes the example. Commitment wins the struggle. Commitment sets men free. A lack of commitment keeps our shackles locked today. We do not lack leaders. We do not need the hearts and minds of the masses. We need a few, a precious few, committed to do what is necessary so that our people may again breathe the air of liberty. What we need, what we must have, is a new Southern patriot fired by commitment, a New Nazarite.

What is commitment? It is a conscious mental, physical, and spiritual effort. It is all of this, along with a firm goal in mind. The goal you set is not a goal you think you might attain. It is a goal you know you will attain. It is not a goal easily attained, but one that requires dedication, perseverance, and faith. When you set that goal in the presence of God and man, you commit yourself. When you strive toward that goal, you demonstrate your commitment. Your commitment sets the example for others. As you read this, it should be obvious what a Southron's commitment is. Our commitment is the vindication and revival of our Southern Nation. A committed few can raise a county, a state, or even a nation from defeat and despair into freedom and prosperity. All we have to do is start.

Our faith and commitment will carry us down the road of our future. Whether as free Southrons or as imperial servants, we will still travel this road. You might as well cast off your chains and walk with men.

To travel as dedicated Southrons, we must rebuild our Southern selves from the unnatural condition of imperial mass-man into living, thinking beings. To do this, we just have to commit to a few simple routines. First, we must all learn to shun the Empire's vices and toys. This protects our gains and removes the Empire's destructive influences, so harmful to our families and ourselves. Second, we must educate ourselves with a curriculum based on truth. This gives us knowledge. Third, we must unify our families. This allows us to share our blessings with those we love. Fourth, we must pursue individual growth. This grants us new abilities. Fifth, we must rediscover our true heritage, culture, and pride. This gives us a sense of direction. Finally, we must pursue personal peace through Biblically founded spiritual development.

In this phase of Southron renewal, we commit to our individual improvement. This not only benefits us personally; our families and our Southern Nation benefit as well. We can reduce our personal quest for freedom to a simple formula. For clarity and convenience, remember it by the time-proven military method of an acronym. By following these six simple steps, we can remold ourselves into a strong unified people. We will rise from the ashes of our defeat systematically. Our acronym is R-E-B-E-L-S.

R—RENOUNCE: Renounce the corrupt influences of modern materialist society.

E—EDUCATE: Educate yourself and your family based on truth instead of imperial propaganda.

B—BOND: Bond with your family and peers to become the tight social unit God and nature intended.

E—EXPERIENCE: Experience life and grow into the person you always longed to be.

L—LEARN: Learn from your rich Southern legacy.

S—SEEK: Seek spiritual growth and renewal.

This simple program helps us develop the character and qualities a true Southron desires and that our nation needs. There is no one among us no, matter how good he is, who could not improve. As we improve our families and ourselves, we strengthen our nation. We reverse the effects of propaganda and media. We rise above the common mass of low jungle brutes. Using this program, you reverse the effects of oppression and Reconstruction. By committing to God and the Southern cause, you transform yourself, inspiring your family and friends.

In the spirit of the Nazarite, we set ourselves apart. Safe from the empire's influence, Southerners find room to grow. Our growth causes us to expand over the void left by the Empire's philosophy of error. It is this void, this emptiness and blackness, which threatens our very existence. Once our culture, our heritage, our nation, our souls, all slip away into this void, there is no return. We might not be able to fill the void left by Yankee imperialism, but we can bridge it. That would be a real bridge to the twenty-first century.

Renounce

Renouncing the corrupt influences of modern society means that we have to learn to do without a few things. The League of the South refers to it as abjuring the realm.[4] What this means is that we must forgo the corrupt, destructive influences of the American Empire's proud non-society. This is an old idea. The apostle Paul recommended the practice to his young friend, Timothy.

> If any man teach otherwise, and consent not to wholesome words, even the words of our Lord Jesus Christ, and to the doctrine which is according to godliness; he is proud, knowing nothing, but doting about questions and strifes of words, whereof cometh envy, strife, railings, evil surmisings, perverse disputings of men of corrupt minds, and destitute of the truth, supposing that gain is godliness: from such withdraw thyself.[5]

I hope that very few of you would ever place a gun to your head and pull the trigger. The introduction of a high-velocity chunk of lead into your brain would be a seriously disruptive influence. We call it suicide. It is immoral. In addition, it is illegal in most states. If you would not break that law, then why do you ingest a daily dose of poison, just to keep up with your neighbor? Why do you constantly "pull the trigger" on an electron gun for your entertainment? Inviting in the ever-caustic influence of the Empire is the same as ingesting spiritual strychnine.

The Empire's false society has many social diseases. Most of them are contagious and easily spread by casual contact. Does the newspaper leave you depressed? Then, save fifty cents. Don't buy it. Does the nightly news force opinions on you that you do not think are right? Then, turn off the TV. No matter what you think, you have a decisive influence over your own environment. It is time that you use that influence.

I personally have never bought a copy of the *New York Times,* although I have ready access to that paper. Why? I am a firm believer in journalism's responsibility for reporting the truth. The *Times* runs headlines like the one that read, "God Is Dead." I know God personally. You should, too. Therefore, I have contrary evidence, and know the *Times'* statement to be a lie. Since a mouthpiece of the Empire would lie about something I know about, I am relatively sure they will at least color the truth in matters I know little about. I cannot trust the *New York Times,* so I do not read the *New York Times.* When we renounce or abjure the realm of the Empire's popular culture, we turn our backs on all its lies, myths, abominations, and destructive influences. On the other hand, if we embrace their version of culture, we invite and accept the destruction it brings. If you ask for it, eventually you will get it. You do not need an invitation, just participate.

Television is the top offender on the list of destructive influences. TV networks are the world's largest suppliers of propaganda and smut. Actions once taboo in any civilized society introduce themselves and become commonplace through television. Shortly thereafter, those actions become acceptable to society. People learn to accept the outrageous through repeated exposure. Even televised sports are degenerating rapidly into a festival of the obscene and ludicrous.

Lucy, John Wayne, and the Three Stooges are dead. Regardless of this fact, their natural deaths would not satisfy corporate greed. They recently suffered electronic resurrection as commercial pitchmen, while the entertainment industry confines their best work to cable and late-night television. Likewise, Bugs Bunny and the Roadrunner are under the microscope. Now, the ruling elite tell us that even the cherished cartoons of our childhood are too violent for us to watch. On the other hand, at any given time you can find 57+ channels of crime, slaughter, smut, and immoral behavior, all glorified and all in color. When it comes to television, view it selectively. Better yet, turn it off.

Popular music carries much the same (and in many cases worse) themes as television programming. Most of us spend our workday or our evening with a radio. That is usually several hours per day. This much time adds up to a powerful influence on you, whether you consciously realize it or not. That is why broadcasters call what you see on TV or hear on radio "programming." Even country music is fast on its way into the gutter. Country music rose in popularity because it was wholesome. Its themes related to real, live, working-class people. Now the common people's songwriters are turning to the lure of the non-culture. You will seldom hear a song now unless it somehow involves drinking, cheating, or leaving. Artists defend their work by saying that their art reflects popular society. Unfortunately, that is not the case. Society usually tries to emulate popular art. Again, be selective. While you are being selective, call the station and its advertisers. Tell them what you find offensive and why you are tuning out. It really does make an impact.

There is no end to the destructive influences of imperial captivity. People should instinctively realize the harm of alcohol, drugs, and pornography. Society never receives any benefit from them and we easily feel their harm. Stay away from these and all the Empire's protected degeneracy. They are leprosy for the soul. Under their influence, you will do things that you would never do otherwise. More than likely, what you do will have unforeseen, tragic consequences. Would you really want to hurt those around you just to increase some faceless shareholder's dividends? Those shareholders will have plenty of blood on their hands in the end. Don't add your blood to that of others.

In the spirit of the Nazarite, we must set ourselves apart from profane and destructive influences. We must buy only what we need, not what Madison Avenue says we need. As a very wise and plain-spoken old lady once told me, "If you play with crap, you are going to get some of it on you. The more you play, the more you'll stink."

Educate

Today, the truth is an elusive animal. Each evening, the news media indoctrinate us with only the information they select. Daily, teachers guide our children through lessons that the education establishment chooses for them. The overlords in Washington, or wherever, carefully screen our entire daily dose of information. They do this to achieve their desired public reaction. It is their version of education. Political scientists more commonly call it propaganda. It is the science of control, the practice of dictators.

Mention of the word *propaganda* brings to mind images of Nazi

Joseph Goebbels, or his Soviet Politburo counterpart, toying with the minds and emotions of their proletarian pawns. It is the same idea, just under a different flag. There is a reason the Nazis and Soviets were so successful at their propaganda. They learned the science from where it was perfected, the good old U. S. of A. Edward Bernays developed the science to its zenith during World War I. Bernays knew much more about practical psychology than his famous uncle, Sigmund Freud. After the war, Bernays cloaked his science in legitimacy and went into advertising. Bernays literally wrote the book on propaganda. In 1928, he observed that after the war ended, intelligent persons should naturally ask themselves whether it was not possible to apply the techniques of war to the problems of peace.[6]

After experiencing the most horrific war humanity had yet fought, what would Bernays possibly consider a problem of peace? He meant us. Southerners experienced a revival of Southern nationhood in the 1920s and the early 1930s. The empire used its newly perfected weapon to cure this problem of peace. Propaganda and indoctrination disguised as education proved to be the most formidable weapons in the Yankee arsenal.

Truth is the only weapon against propaganda. To be free, we must access the truth. To be truly free, we must be able to form our own opinions based on that truth, and to make our own choices without interference. For this reason, much of our daily dose of imperial information has little in common with useful information. It has even less in common with truth. Before we can free ourselves, we must free our minds from the chains our Yankee masters impose there. The road to freedom begins with education. The founding fathers knew the value of education in producing a free people. Jefferson especially struggled to advance the idea of free education for all citizens, but where do you get an unbiased education based in truth today? You have to go out and get it for yourself. Remember, "ye shall know the truth, and the truth shall make you free."[7]

A good start would be to relearn American history. I am not referring to the version taught in the establishment-controlled public schools. I refer to true history, especially that of our Southern Nation. The empire's goal since 1865 has been to remake its conquered colony in its own wretched image. Public education, which was once our best hope in keeping our children free, is instead a tool to hold them in bondage.

To break our chains, we must read books uncleansed by our masters in Washington. We must find our own history. Knowledge is the weapon most feared by the ruling class. That is why there is so much publicity about regulating the Internet. Of course, our rulers claim it is an effort to keep pornography out of the hands of children. Funny, that is something that never concerned them very much in the past. Besides, a ten-dollar program will screen porn from your computer more effectively than any bureaucrat ever will. However, that is not the issue. The rulers fear knowledge. In a free society, free exchange of information and ideas, even unpopular ideas, is the safeguard against tyranny and corruption. It does not make sense to protect a supposedly free people from the unfettered exchange of information. That is, unless there is something to hide. Could that something to hide be something as dangerous and volatile as the truth? After all, knowledge for the masses is the presumed goal of every educational program we finance for Washington.

All the wonders of technology and the Internet are impressive, but they are not for everyone. For low-tech people, like me, the book still provides the best way to go. Time-tested and proven, my books do not disintegrate with a power surge. I can relax and feel comfortable wrapped in the warm familiar pages of a book. I include a list of these warm, dear, and trusted friends along with several excellent periodicals in Appendix C. I strongly recommend them. They contain ideas and information that are among the most feared on earth. Unlike the Empire's version of education, all they contain is truth. Prepare yourself for the Nazarite's work. Open their pages and you will open your eyes to a world unseen. Open your mind and you shall set yourself free.

Bond

The strength of any nation is the unity and well being of the families elemental to that nation. Our families are the bricks that form the wall insulating us from the evils of the outside world. Their wall provides shelter for everything good about our nation. Luckily, we of the conquered Southern Nation retain more of our traditional family unity than the rest of the Yankee Empire. This is one of our greatest strengths. Unfortunately, the Empire particularly targets this strength for destruction.

Our family unity, the South's traditional strength, erodes with each new advertising campaign. The modern mass-man has no time for family. His is a world without purpose, except to produce and consume. It is a world without light. Modern men deny the human spirit for the sake of profits and accumulation. Each 12-hour shift deprives us of our family, the reason for our labor. Our families gain nothing from soul-less accumulation. They gain nothing from material investment. The only investment that profits the family is the investment of time. Once we deprive our family of our time, we can never fill the void with consumer trinkets. Still, men will try. While trying, they sink deeper into the sickness that first caused their hunger. Man eventually tries to fill the void with alcohol, drugs, or more trinkets. Doing so, he creates an endless, destructive chain. Time is the tithe that Southrons must withhold from the Yankee's god of materialism.

Family is the only thing that matters. Your family is the main reason you work, anyway. The cure for the social disease of materialism is to place the family first. A good resource contrary to the teachings of the empire is the writings of Dr. James Dobson and his Focus on the Family ministry.[8] If the boss wants you to work late all the time, just say, "No." If the boss insists, maybe it is time to look for a better job.

Saving for your children's education is, of course, prudent and honorable. Still, instead of working two shifts, you can do a lot more by being there for them in person. Reading your child a book or helping them with their homework benefits them much more than a little extra money. Money will not help them if they do not know how to handle it, or if they cannot read, write, and do arithmetic. You can no longer trust modern education to furnish them those skills. There are other lessons they must learn, too. They can learn these life-lessons from you only. Not learning these lessons can lead them to tragedy, just like the Nazarite, Samson. There is no substitute for quality time spent with your family. Quality time is not that time we spend glued to a television. It is time spent together, with our eyes and ears open. Your spouse will appreciate your time and attention. So will your children. They will not only appreciate it; they will love you more for it.

Experience

A plant that does not grow withers and dies. It is the same with people. Growth keeps you alive in many ways. Never miss a chance for personal growth and development. Of course, as we grow, we should also consider those around us. Not only should we strive to grow in our own personal experience, we should also promote the growth of our family and friends. We are never too old to learn. Whether intellectually, physically, emotionally, or spiritually, our education ends only when we die. As Southerners, we can never be too intelligent, too healthy, too family-oriented, or too good at dealing with other people. As we grow and develop to our full potential, we gain more satisfaction from life. Traveling down life's path, we set the example for our family and peers. Like it or not, we influence the lives of many other people each day.

How many times have you avoided another person because you considered them vulgar, obnoxious, or depressing? We all do it. It is human nature. Likewise, if we are vulgar, obnoxious, or depressing, other people will avoid us. It is our duty to our family, our people, and ourselves to fulfill our potential. As Southerners, we should live our lives as a shining example, not as a black hole sucking all our energy and existence out of the lives of others. The Southron must be positive. He must achieve. He must live the Southern dream.

Success and personal fulfillment are not the result of fate or luck. Success and personal fulfillment are a conscious choice. They depend upon our attitude. There are no more powerful words in the English language than those contained in the simple two-word phrase, "I can." On the other hand, you form the most destructive phrase in our language simply by adding three more letters to form "I cannot."

If you want freedom, peace, success, and a strong family, you will have it. If you want to be a better person, you will be. All you have to do it is want it, and want it bad enough. If you want it enough, almost to the point of obsession, you will do what it takes to have it. The human will is one of God's most amazing gifts. The Nazarite's conduct proves that he is the model of commitment and will.

Learn

Perhaps the most difficult and absorbing task for the unreconstructed Southerner is that of rediscovering his or her culture. This task could best compare to a quest, like that for the Holy Grail. It brings us sorrow once we look back and see what we forfeited to the Yankee gospel of progress. Some cherished vestiges of our Southern heritage and culture remain, but for how long?

Before we can rediscover something, it has to be missing. In our case, we are fortunate. We are not searching for that which we lost as much as we are searching for that which hides. It is hiding, hiding deep within. It is a Southern gem waiting for its final cut and polish. Then our family jewel will shine for all to admire or fear, depending on their affections. Why does Southern culture hide today? For a start, our precious Southern heritage suffers the effects of receiving more than 130 years of bad press, along with the full concentration of the Empire's propaganda machine. The establishment is merciless in its desecration of any way of life that rebukes it. Twenty years from now, a few of us will be able to look back and say, "I was Southern when Southern wasn't cool."

What is our culture? It is the very identity of a people. Culture is a people's traditions, philosophy, art, and moral standards. It glues a society together. Culture is all that a people hold dear to their hearts. A nation's culture is its soul. What separates a life of order and contentment from one of barbarism? Culture and maybe the Mason-Dixon line. In short, culture is civilization.

Southern culture hides in the shadows, but it is still there. All we have to do is release it. This takes more effort with some of us than it does with others. It takes work to pry your seat off the "stool of everlasting repentance." One hundred-thirty years of imperial programming can be hard to overcome. That is why Southern pride and culture mostly remain hidden. Look hard enough and you will find them. They are there, but many of us look in the wrong places. This is a tragedy in itself. If you think you can find our cherished culture on television, or in a Burt Reynolds movie, perhaps you are too far gone. Maybe you should consider relocating to Southern California or even Fantasy Island, whichever is stationary at the moment.

Culture is our very reason for being. Culture is who we are. Without it a people is lost. They drift as a ship without a rudder, dependent on tides and currents for their grip on life. A people divorced from their culture is rootless and hopeless. An example that is near to my heart is that of the Native American. Once a proud and able people, the Indians ruled the continent. Theirs was at finely tuned culture, based on the needs of each tribal unit. Each tribe lived according to its own dictates, in a manner that time proved successful to them. Whether their focus was on farming, hunting, or warfare, sacred rituals governed each activity. It was culture in its truest, but least flexible form. The Indian held no fear for anything that he could find a way to explain.

When the Europeans came, worlds and cultures collided. The technology of the New World was no match for that of the Old. Some tribes, most notably the Cherokee, tried to adapt to the new ways and peacefully coexist. Instead, the empire subjugated them and marched them off to Ultima Thule.[9] The survivors suffered through re-education designed to make them good imperial citizens. The theory was that as long as the last trace of Indian culture remained, the tribes would never be pacified. Sound familiar? It was the same strategy empire builders used against Ireland, Scotland, the South, and many other places.

There is a parallel here. Drive through a reservation or drive through the South, and you will see it. Bars and liquor stores do a thriving business. The rulers promote immoral methods of raising revenue, such as gambling. Education declines. Crime increases. Children turn to gangs. Their parents turn to drugs and alcohol. Our masters mock and reject religion. Therefore, we as their subjects also lose respect for the Creator. These are traits of a conquered people, separated from their culture. Remember that nature abhors a vacuum and will always fill the empty space with something. If everything lying about is negative, then the void will fill with all the negatives it can suck inside. It is a tragedy that history reveals many times. Moral breakdown is the mark of a people in search of their historic self.

What we are searching for is not to be found in the outside world. It is buried deep within us. It takes serious study and reflection to renew. If you feel a surge well up within you when you hear "Dixie" or the "Bonnie Blue Flag," you are not alone. Grab that surge and hold it. Keep it and nurture it. That is a small piece of the object of your quest. Feed that small fragment and it will grow. Its diet is simple. Do what you know is right within your Southern heart. Learn from those Nazarites who came before you. Feel the essence of your roots, feed them, and let them sprout new growth. Do not fear who you really are.

Seek

If you turned to glance at the afore-mentioned list of suggested reading in Appendix C, you probably noticed the first book on the list. There is a good reason the Holy Bible should be the prime choice of your attention. A man's soul is his most valuable possession. It is the source of all his strength. If the soul is conflicted and in turmoil, the mind and the body naturally suffer too. Knowledge is ultimately useless without the guidance of values and inspiration. Christianity is the traditional Southerner's source of spiritual peace, since without spiritual peace, no individual's actions can reach their full potential. Before God was ejected from our schools, our children had moral guidance. They had divine example. Now, they have no example but the Empire, eight hours a day, nine months a year. All of the gall and rhetoric that politicians address to restoring family values can be answered in one simple declarative sentence. Family values are God's values.

Our road to spiritual renewal is simple. Attend an active, Bible-believing church. Read your Bible. Talk with God. Listen when He answers. Do what He says. It is that simple.

Christianity is an essential ingredient of Southern culture. However, traditional Southern Christianity is remote from the brand that is practiced up North. Our Southern faith is strongly influenced by the Old Testament. Learning from God's Word, we realize that the physical world is indeed the real world. There is always a right and always a wrong. We know that nothing is relative. Even the gray areas are made up of simple black and white dots. Southerners know that there are concrete truths.

Southerners also understand human nature. The Bible, as well as secular history, proves that human nature has changed little since our exile from the garden. Because of this, we know that our passions and feelings are real, whether for good or evil. Our religion bases its truths on the revealed Word of God, along with His gift of common sense. On moral issues, Southrons always take a traditional stance, because we know time does not modify God or His absolute truths.

On the other hand, the Northern version of religion is largely the culmination of their base fads and several hundred years of doctrinal experimentation. Theirs is a heresy of relativism. Unfortunately, their heresy seeps into and poisons many Southern pulpits today. Northern-influenced churches teach passive, unmanly values like fear and sensitivity. Their liberal theologians replace the Bible's natural order and hierarchy of man with a cult of total equality and New Age nonsense.[10] Such deluded people with no strong convictions are good imperial citizens and excellent cogs in the industrial machine. They are silent, productive, corporate clones.

True to our scriptural instruction, Southern Christians are not passive when confronted with evil. Christianity is the religion of manly men. Paul and Silas were not wimps. Neither were Martin Luther, John Calvin, or John Wesley. Likewise, devout believers such as Thomas "Stonewall" Jackson and Robert E. Lee did not shrink from battling evil. True, Jackson and Lee were not average Southern men. That does not, however, mean that they were exceptions to the traditional rule of Southern faith. This is why the Confederate army had an abundance of ministers who served as foot soldiers instead of chaplains. The Ninth Arkansas Infantry had so many that the unit was nicknamed "The Parsons' Regiment."[11]

By getting your spiritual house in order, you set the example for your family and your neighbors. If your example is good, a heavily reward awaits you at this life's end. If you set a poor example, the blood of your children, neighbors, and even your nation could coat your hands for eternity. Remember Stonewall Jackson's favorite verse of the Bible: "And we know that all things work together for good to them that love God, to them who are the called according to his purpose."[12]

Who is called according to God's purpose? All of us are. He has a purpose in store for all men. That is why we are here. God gifts each of us with unique challenges and talents. We are to use those gifts to His glory. Now that you know Jackson's favorite verse, here is mine: "What shall we then say to these things? If God be for us, who can be against us?"[13]

Like lawyers practice law, and doctors practice medicine, men practice their religion. We practice because we never quite get it right. A lawyer may heal your legal problems, an accountant may heal your bank account, and a doctor may heal your body, but only God can heal your soul. His healing power in other matters is also greater than that of those other three practitioners. Let Him heal your hurts. Our walk on earth is short. When we walk with God, we know our final destination. Then, ours is a pleasurable walk.

As we progress in the path of the Nazarite, we will notice other changes besides those we plan. These are not the harmful side effects people so often experience from even life-saving medication. In the case of our personal quest for freedom, these side effects are beneficial. They are just as valuable as the intended results of our program. This synergistic effect is one of the advantages we receive as a unique bonus from our personal growth.

As Southrons, we renounce the influences of modern materialist society to separate ourselves from its destructive effects. We also remove the base lures and temptations that the Empire so persuasively waves under our noses. Not only this, we abjure the petty, troublesome concerns that imperial society forces us to worry about daily. This reduces stress, something of which we all need less.

By educating our families and ourselves with knowledge based on truth, instead of imperial propaganda, we systematically remove the Empire's enforced patterns of thought. In addition, we remove the mental crutch our minds rely on in what were once trivial, autonomic decisions. Minus that crutch, we think for ourselves. It is scary it first, but soon thinking becomes a healthy, desirable habit.

When we bond into a tight cultural unit with our family and friends, we live as the social beings God intended. We also find vital support in our successes and even more importantly in our failures. With that support, we access love of a kind unknown to imperial subjects. We meet with the comfort and security that our ancestors found in their clans, tribes, and other family units. This is a very real cure to the many afflictions of modern imperial society.

By allowing yourself to experience life and grow into the person you long to be, you defy the empire at its heart. You become a person, a viable individual who grows and refuses to be put down. Media and government spare no effort to keep you a faceless statistic. Growth puts a name and a face on your number. As a free man, you know better than to listen to those who try to discourage you. You are the opposite of a good imperial citizen. You are free to achieve.

When you learn from your rich Southern legacy, you shake your fist in the face of the empire. You acknowledge that there is a whole different philosophy based on value and tradition. As you learn the philosophy of common sense, you open the door to a world that the ruling class refuses to even admit exists. You shake a fist in the face of our captors and say, "There is another way, a better way, the Southern way."

By seeking spiritual growth and renewal, you grow closer to the strong traditional faith of our fathers. Building a personal relationship with God, we come to know His infinite love. Each of us, no matter how far we fall, can rise again. Each of us, no matter how gross our imperfections, has value in the eyes of the Lord. We have creation's greatest proof of our value, the ultimate gift of salvation that God sent to each of us. Through His grace and the acceptance of His gift, we find peace. His peace surpasses anything that any man or government can offer.

Ours is a simple program, but it does require a conscious commitment. It requires effort. That is why so few try. That is why the lure of the Empire is so strong. Man is by nature a lazy creature. We often do not even resist as the Empire fastens our shackles in place. It takes work to break our chains. When we rise above the limits our masters impose, we are no longer passive, docile servants. When we think for ourselves, our minds are free. Where the mind goes, the body logically follows. We are no longer docile and easy to control, no longer mere subjects. Then, it is the imperial elite wallowing in the pigsty of mediocrity. No people will submit long to rule by those whom they see as their inferiors. Enough Southerners, applying these principles, would quickly rid us of our oppression. However, human nature is such that our deliverance will not happen that way. There is another step to Southern renewal.

A free Southern homeland will not be easy. It is not the work of individuals, no matter how numerous those individuals might be. No man is an island. If he stands alone, the Empire will assure that he falls alone. As New Southern Nazarites, we must follow the example of those nations who went this way before us. The work of freedom is the work of a team.

THE NEW NAZARITE

R-E-B-E-L-S.

R—RENOUNCE: Renounce the corrupt influences of modern materialist society.

E—EDUCATE: Educate yourself and your family based on truth instead of imperial propaganda.

B—BOND: Bond with your family and peers; become the tight social unit God and nature intended.

E—EXPERIENCE: Experience life and grow into the person you always longed to be.

L—LEARN: Learn from your rich Southern legacy.

S—SEEK: Seek spiritual growth and renewal.

CHAPTER VIII

The Community Quest

If you know the enemy and know yourself, you need not fear
the result of a hundred battles.   Sun Tzu[1]

At the head of every effort are the teams that do the actual work.
The military breaks its units down into teams. Our most popular
sports are all team sports. A candidate's campaign team leads every
political effort, from the national to the local level. Even business
makes use of the team concept. Japanese businesses thrive on teamwork. The concept also works well in our Southern brand of reform.

Teamwork gets the job done. Teams just work more efficiently
than individuals. The work is quicker and there is less stress.
Working in a team is naturally more enjoyable, because you have
others working along beside you. In addition, a natural synergistic
effect multiplies the power of work done by a team far above that
done by a group of individuals. Our Southern heritage battles
proved the value of the team concept. Teams won the struggles to
save flags, monuments, and other Southern cultural resources.
Teams of ordinary Southerners carefully planned and conducted
these campaigns, not mobs. Usually the winning teams were either
small, or a collection of even smaller teams. The heritage battles
proved that small groups of two to ten people, concentrating their
efforts locally and working toward specific, obtainable goals, could
achieve what hundreds could not.

Teams are also the core of every effort to achieve nationhood.
The American struggle for independence began with teams called
"Committees of Correspondence." The effort for Irish independence finally took the form of five-man teams. When South Africa
wrestled itself away from British control, the source of their success

was the Afrikaner Broederbond. History showed the Broederbond to be teams of three to five people, scattered widely across the country. The Broederbond did not spread violence. They spread an idea. The British thought that the Broederbond had close to a million members. Instead, they numbered a few more than six thousand. The idea the Broederbond spread was bulletproof. Their idea was nationhood.[2]

When foreign regimes conquer and rule a nation, a propaganda program is one of the first controls they impose. As time wears on, the people generally accept propaganda and indoctrination as truth. The ruling class portrays thoughts of nationhood as impractical and foolhardy. The people of the captive nation actually come to believe that they are better off as a colony of the regime. The propaganda machine makes sure of this. The propaganda machine usually consists of the courts, the news media, the entertainment industry, and a government-controlled education system.[3]

To preserve its power, an empire mentally incapacitates a subject people (as ours have been). There is only one remedy. That remedy is the free spread of ideas contrary to those of the regime. The people reject those ideas, at first. Sadly, many movements give up in disgust at this point. Instead of trying to change the world in one big effort, reformers must condition their people to accept the idea of freedom the same way their rulers conditioned them to the idea of captivity. The more we expose the Southern people to the idea of Southern nationalism the less the idea offends their sensibilities. The idea gradually becomes more common, a debatable issue. Then, the people gradually accept it. Later, they adopt and defend the idea as one of their own.

Of course, it is a tall order to change the attitude of a nation. Still, we must change our nation one attitude at a time, one community at a time, until our people see that the Empire deprives us of our nationality. This job is well suited to the team concept. The more teams we have, the quicker the change will take place. We can reduce the whole process to a simple fail-safe formula. Why is it fail-safe? First, the formula is simple. Second, the formula is adaptable to individual circumstances. One of the system's greatest strengths is that it affords privacy to those who carry out its principles. We can remember it easily by the use of another acronym: O-R-D-E-R.

O—ORGANIZE: Organize the Concerted Action Team.

R—REDUCE: Reduce our program to its simplest terms.

D—DELUDE: Delude the opponent.

E—EDUCATE: Educate team members and the public.

R—RECRUIT/REINFORCE: Recruit and reinforce education.

Order is what we hope to restore in our Southern Nation. Through order, Southrons will discover liberty, peace, and prosperity. This system will direct you in finding and creating other unreconstructed Southerners. These Southerners refuse to allow the American Empire to deprive them any longer of the blessings of our Southern nationality. These procedures are your weapon and your armor on the battlefield of the culture wars.

Organize

Your team of Southern nationalists should begin with a few close friends. This does not mean the fair-weather variety of friend. Instead, search for dependable people who think as you do. They need not be your closest acquaintances, but they should be trustworthy. Gathering such a group is not as easy as it sounds. It does take effort, and you might think it impossible. Take heart, though. The great movements and organizations of history all started in just this manner.

This will be your Concerted Action Team, your "CAT" team for short. The ideal size for such a team is between three and ten people. If you belong to a pro-South organization such as the League of the South, the Confederate Society of America, the Sons of Confederate Veterans, the United Daughters of the Confederacy, or one of the many others, gathering a team may be simple. If you have no such group in your area or no large collection of friends, try placing a carefully worded classified ad in the local paper. Sometimes this will lead you to people that you would never know otherwise. As you collect your team, encourage the members to follow the steps outlined in chapter seven. This will help refine them from raw material into the Southern nationals that we need.

The organizing phase is a growing and learning phase. It is best to organize your team without drawing unnecessary attention to yourselves. Do not waste time with rigid rules and structure, but develop a mutual trust and a good working relationship. Neither should you waste time on grandiose schemes: start small and build morale. It must be clear from the start that the Concerted Action Team is just that. As a team you must work together closely and ignore petty personal squabbles. The cause must be foremost in your minds. Focus on the cause. Let the cause absorb you.

During this stage, you should gather your resources. Access to a photocopier is a good start. A copy machine has unlimited use to our effort. It can cheaply print everything from newsletters to informational brochures to election campaign materials. Access to a personal computer and printer is also extremely helpful, if not necessary. No matter how much we despise modern conveniences, they do simplify many chores. A computer eases writing chores and gives professional-quality results. Personal experience proves that a simple combination word processor and office productivity package program, like the ones that now come with most new computers, yields space-age results from the most Neanderthal efforts.

Modern technology is at home with the reformer. With him, technology is a tool instead of an idol to worship. In the reformer's hands, technology reaps a bountiful harvest with an economy of force that even Nathan Bedford Forrest would envy. Desktop publishing and database management will prove to be skills essential to the final victory of the cause. Our fight is not one of bullets. Instead, it is a fight of electrons and neurons. The culture wars proved that an active campaign by a small, dedicated group, using the resources of technology and knowledge, is much more potent than any haphazard crusade by a large organization. In short, teams fight. Mobs flounder.

Reduce

To get the greatest effect from your efforts, you must reduce your program to its simplest terms. This is not only essential to algebra; it is essential to political and moral reform. Remember that complex plans are usually flawed plans. For an example of complexity in action (or complexity inaction) just look to our American Empire. The federal bureaucracy is positive proof of what happens when idle minds run amok.

Instead of imitating the imperials, the Concerted Action Team should strive for economy of action and economy of thought. Model yourself after the corporation that adopted the motto, K-I-S-S. This stands for "Keep it short and simple." The best-laid plans of mice and men come to naught, primarily because those who must carry out the plans need a Ph.D. in psychology to interpret them. Simplicity is the heart of the concerted action concept. A team progress toward a difficult, complex goal by concentrating its effort on simple, easily completed tasks. The team completes such small tasks easily. Give each task or series of tasks a mission name, like

"Gray Dog" or "Predator," anything descriptive or fun. When we manage goals wisely, we lessen the risk of team members growing discouraged. They enjoy their work. Saving a nation is difficult, but there is no reason it can't be fun.

Of course, we should plan our tasks well, but our planning should not rival that of the D-Day invasion. Ideal execution time for a task should be about one week, or two weeks at the most. Any longer duration breeds confusion and failure. If the task takes more than a week to complete, consider dividing it into two or more tasks. The tasks, by simple design, should ensure their own successful completion.

For one operation, place flyers on every public bulletin board in your county. The next week, follow with a telephone poll. Devote another week to mailings of an informational newsletter to rural box holders, complete with a free gray ribbon. Spend a week on writing letters to the editor of the local paper. Leave a stack of informative leaflets in a public place. Encourage citizens to abstain from pledging allegiance to the "Banner of Yankee Occupation." Put up signs. Deliver food to elderly and needy Southrons. Be creative. It may not be glamorous work, but these small efforts will be the decisive factor in our escape of the Empire.

Our main task is to create public opinion that is positive to the Southern cause. To do that, execute every task with the objective of focusing positive public opinion toward our Southern Nation. The establishment focuses its desired opinion every evening as you stare at the television. It is the way they whip us into line, electronically. However, our efforts are honest and straightforward. This gives us the moral edge.

Delude

There is strength and safety in numbers. This is a tired old cliché, but it is true. Superior numbers over time usurped our rightful government, the Southern Confederacy. On the other hand, in 1863 superior strength did little to help the raider, Streight, against the superior intellect of his pursuer, Forrest. General Forrest's theatrical displays in northern Georgia cowed the invader into unconditional surrender to a force one-third of his force's size.[4]

Likewise, "Prince John" Magruder's sideshow at Yorktown, Virginia, stalled McClellan's overwhelming invasion force on the James River Peninsula. Only severe chastisement from his superiors goaded McClellan to resume the offensive.[5] Looking further back in history, let us never forget that tiny band of Spartans that defended the pass of Thermopylae. There are lessons to learn from history. This is one of them. An illusion of overwhelming strength is often the same as having overwhelming strength. Take this lesson to heart. You see examples of it every day.

Here is just one example. At times, the National Association for the Advancement of Colored People has boasted of a membership of more than 6 million. In 1995, the NAACP also had more than $4 million in unsecured debt. With 6 million members, a mere 75¢ of each member's dues, plus a new focus on fiscal responsibility, would cover this debt and more. Why did they panic and restructure the entire organization a few years ago? The answer is simple. They do not have 6 million dues-paying members. It was an illusion of strength that enabled them to extort six-digit donations from American corporations to redeem their debt within a year. This same illusion allowed them $4 million dollars in unsecured credit. Get the idea? As the mismanagement became public, donations dwindled. Their illusion shattered. When the actual number of active members was found to be around 500,000, heads rolled in the national office.[6]

The tasks undertaken by the Concerted action team should embody the spirit of illusion. Like General Forrest, you should appear everywhere, at all places, at all times. Your work must be visible, though you are not. People must see it on the highways, in the city streets, in all public places. You must be present in the very den of your adversary. This places our nation's opposition constantly on the defensive, the position in which they are most vulnerable. Those who oppress the Southron soul are only comfortable with the offensive. The only strategy that works for them in the public arena is the offense. On the other hand, Southerners tend to stick to the defense. We defend flags. We defend monuments. We just defend. We allow our opposition to choose the objectives and we never seize the initiative. This is why our campaigns in defense of Southern heritage always look so futile.

To take the initiative away and keep it away, we must remain a pseudo-mysterious presence. The air of mystery and the illusion of strength will attract many Southerners that would support you. This is the "bandwagon" effect. No one will walk across the street to help ten people who are butting heads with the establishment. Instead, they will break down the door to stand beside a thousand winners. Draw a carefully selected few that have promise into the team and give them something to do. It will help curb fatigue among your members. Never discourage anyone from the cause of Southern nationhood, no matter how poor of material you think they might be.

We can easily produce our illusion, but it requires a little creative effort. Spread your campaign over the area of your county or parish. Plan your tasks for a saturation effect and execute them with attention to timing. Little details such as these help build our illusion. You will discover that a phenomenon springing from nowhere overnight arouses the public interest. People talk about what interests them. When they talk, occasionally they think. When they think, they are your audience, considering your message.

How do you know the campaign is taking effect? You look and listen. Telephone polls, the outrage of public officials and establishment support groups, any degree of press coverage, and especially the conversations you overhear in public are the indicators of the effect you desire. Watch for our common plague, the Empire and its establishment clones, to go over to the defensive. When they do, they are ours. The "bandwagon" effect will help by breeding copycats. Adults will begin to assert themselves in the coffee shop, in editorials, in the work place, and from the pulpit. All of this will begin while you comfortably remain anonymous and secure, retaining your privacy. Do not risk losing your momentum, now. Try new approaches. Visit the local computer bulletin boards. Print more flyers. Like a shadow, you will be everywhere by day, but you will own the night.

Educate

Our Southern education goes further than just the personal pursuit of knowledge outlined in chapter seven. Naturally, we encourage our team members and recruits to fulfill their personal quest for knowledge. However, education extends beyond our team members here. In this phase, we direct our efforts toward the public. Now we need to render our knowledge unto those who have little interest and motivation to learn about the cause on their own. This involves two stages: the preparatory stage and the animating stage.[7]

The preparatory stage is just what the name implies. It is like the indoctrination our children receive in the Empire's public schools. Preparatory education is the background information that controls the way their minds interpret the new information they receive. Our children react differently to outrageous behavior in public. This is because the Empire feeds them a steady diet of low-rent sit-coms, *Daddy's Roommate,* and *Heather Has Two Mommies.* This is the imperial version of preparatory education.

In the animating stage, we offer information that causes the public to express themselves in a particular manner. This result is the purpose of all that the Empire pretends is education today. No more mere reading, writing, and arithmetic. The goal of modern imperial education is to cause the public to react desirably to the actions of the current batch of carpetbaggers and scalawags. Remember that when you send your children to a public school that Washington controls, Washington controls them. Also, remember that through them, Washington controls you. This oversteps the boundaries of a free public education that the founders worked so hard to achieve. The result of this animating stimulus offered is directly proportional to the effectiveness of the Empire's preparatory groundwork.[8]

In our Southern preparatory phase, we must desensitize the public. We must remove the barriers and imposed norms of their public thought. For this to be effective, the individual must be vulnerable. It so happens that the individual Southerner is most vulnerable when in public, but isolated from the support of the masses. Given our limited resources, it is crucial that we use what we have wisely to reach our fellow Southerners.[9] The CAT team must shatter old mental alliances and offer desirable images contrary to those of the Empire's popular media. These images must offer more, more, more than imperial socialist dogma. The image Southrons put forth should be one of fulfillment and happiness, not through government intervention or popular culture, but through self-sufficiency and personal development. Ours is the image of our forefathers, the nobility of work, oneness with the soil, and oneness with nature. We must show that our reality offers more than mass production, mass consumption, and soul-less electronic trickery. Instead, we offer meaning, harmony, and family.

How is this done? Remember that the watchword of the team concept is simplicity. We deliver our message only by the simplest means. When our message is simple and delivered plainly, there is no confusion. People must understand it. In the past, movements succeeded or failed because of their message's delivery. The most successful movements used basic forms of delivery such as posters, songs, slogans, leaflets, and symbols. This proved more effective than the most complex and expensive media. The creativity of your team is the only limitation. "The South Was Right! Continue the Fight!" is an example of an effective slogan that you can include in any media for mass use. Do not limit yourself to the ideas of others. The Lord blessed all of us with talents and abilities. Develop and use them.

Posters are cheap and easy to produce in the modern age. Only your budget limits their size and color. Our Southern posters should present positive, feel-good images, using warm tones to bring on the desired emotions. Remember that a picture is worth a thousand words.

Symbols also summon elaborate thoughts and images from the depths of our minds. That is why symbols are so effective. When a person sees a swastika, images of blitzkrieg and concentration camps wash over their thoughts. The response is an instinctive revulsion at the evil of the Nazi symbol. Our experience embeds this response deeply in our minds. The revulsion is involuntary; it does not matter whether the swastika is used as a Nazi symbol or it is used in its much older form as a Native American symbol of power and the deity. This is just one example of the power of symbols.

Southerners who revere their flag as the symbol of truth and sacrifice must heed this example. The establishment of today misses no chance to vilify the Confederate battle flag. They want it to bring about the same response. In turn, we should never miss a chance to display our symbols in a positive manner. Patriotic display of the Confederate battle flag, the various Southern National flags, and the Great Seal of the Confederacy should again become commonplace. For years, the American Empire outlawed the display of Southern symbols. If we do not exercise our rights, we stand to lose them again.

Ribbons are popular symbols of innumerable causes today. The use of the gray ribbon is one that I have long promoted. The gray ribbon is the symbol of Confederate-American awareness and assertion. My personal gray ribbon sports a black band (added with a magic marker) in mourning for our long-dead U.S. Constitution and Bill of Rights. A gray ribbon is about as inexpensive as emblems can get, but it has the potential to be a powerful symbol. When explained, it is sure to provoke thought. Besides, free thought is what a true education is all about.

An effective preparatory phase program uses frequency and duration. For Southern reformers, this translates as saturation. Your message should be everywhere. For maximum effectiveness, your campaign should specifically target the individual when they are "alone in the crowd." By this, we mean when they are in the open public, but isolated from the support of other's attitudes and opinions. Examples of this would be at a sporting event, driving on a crowded expressway, or walking a sidewalk crowded with strangers. This is where a heavy scattering of images and messages meets with maximum reception. As mentioned earlier, the effectiveness of your preparatory education campaign determines the result of all future attempts at prompting the desired response.

The animating phase has only one goal and purpose—initiating a desired action in response to a stimulus that you provide. The principle is the same no matter whether you intend to initiate a vote for a certain candidate or the purchase of a product. You must offer a certain stimulus that will trigger human emotion to provoke a desired response. Emotions are not rational feelings. They cause humans to act in irrational ways. Where the emotions lead, the mind follows and justifies the action. It does not matter if the emotional action was in character for the individual or not. The mind will still rationalize and defend the emotional decision.

Here lies the key to all of this psychological double-talk. Once the individual has made a positive, emotion-based response to your program and his mind has rationalized and supported the response, his attitude changes. He is more prone to react positively to each additional influence. It is the natural law of inertia. Once the individual is moving in one direction, it is hard to stop and change direction. Sales trainers teach this principle. It has been around since ancient times. Ask a person a question you know they will answer, "Yes." Then ask another, and another. Each succeeding "Yes" response makes a "No" response less comfortable to the potential buyer. It is the "Yes set," a basic premise of human nature and a fundamental of salesmanship. What is education, if not the sale of ideas?[10]

It all blends together. Washington and Hollywood do the same thing daily. We must use our knowledge to convey thoughts and emotions to others. Once they are comfortable with those thoughts and emotions, they will be receptive to more. By arousing their basic human instincts and emotions, we can cause them to act. Once they act, they become more receptive to our message. The more they act, the more receptive they become, even to the point of ideas and actions that the Empire formerly made uncomfortable for them.

Recruit/Reinforce

In numbers, there is not only strength but also peace of mind. We should enlarge our team with dedicated members as the opportunity arises. Also, bear in mind that we can suffer casualties from burnout. Saving our people from oppression is a big job. To do it, we must keep the Concerted Action Team at its full strength and vigor. Occasionally, this requires a recruit or two.

However, the main goal of our recruiting at this point is to develop a "Database for Change." This list is a roll of people that our efforts have reached. These people have responded favorably to our message and are waiting for more. These individuals will form the basis of public opinion supporting Southern nationhood. How do we know who these people are? We have taken great pains to keep our privacy. One way is through telephone polls that you conduct. Keep up with those people who answer the Southron way all the time. Most phone books do still list the street or mailing address between the name and telephone number. This is a quick start. Generally, these people are reliable, but not as reliable as those who come to you on their own.

There are several ways to draw people to your movement. One is to go public immediately and start an active recruiting campaign. This may tip your hand too soon, though. If you have been very effective as a community influence, there may be those waiting for you to surface. Then, they can pounce on you. Why throw away all the safety and intrigue of privacy prematurely?

Perhaps a better way is to become accessible while remaining anonymous. One member of the team could get an extra, unlisted telephone line and couple an answering machine to it. Another could get an extra post office box. Print up cards, flyers, and brochures advertising a concerned citizens' group that is now organizing and desires to make a change. You could also put an ad in the paper or on the radio. Make an appeal over the state of affairs, politics, morality, illegal immigration, and so forth. Take a moderate stance and tell people to call or write if they feel as you do, and are fed up and looking for an alternative.

Naturally, when they call, you should give them a professional-sounding message encouraging them to leave their name, telephone number, and address. Call them back later in the evening and thank them for responding. Build them up and make them feel important. Let them know that you and some others are forming a citizens' group in the area. You are happy with the great response you have received, and would appreciate their participation. Let them know that the group should not require a lot of time. It should mainly consist of some good people getting together, sharing ideas, and trying to carry out some positive changes. Remember that everything said should be positive. Again, before you go, tell them how much you appreciate their important help. People crave a feeling of importance. It draws them to efforts that fulfill this basic human need. The same principle applies to answering letters. Remember that honey attracts more flies than vinegar.

Now that you are assembling your database for change, you should not sit idle. Instead, reinforce the decision of your respondents. A quick letter or postcard will assure that they feel appreciated and let them know the latest news of the area. Don't be afraid to encourage them to write a letter to the local editor or legislator. Certainly, request that they get their friends involved. Place their names on the mailing list for your newsletter.

Recruiting is the lifeblood of any movement. Without growth, there is only stagnation and decay. With this in mind, you should set goals on the amount of people you hope to reach. Develop a plan and stick with it. Remember the "rule of the tens." For every person who rallies to your cause, ten more will support you, but will not come forward now. For each person who supports the cause, but does not come forward, there is another ten. They will agree with you, but will never be active. For each of those ten, there are another ten. They will sympathize with your view if your campaign reaches and influences them. It adds up to a sizeable base of support. For every CAT team member there are 1000 sympathizers.[11]

As in all political movements and revolutions, the heart of your efforts should be playing the numbers game. The great advantage of the numbers game is that it is a winnable game if you use the right strategy. If by chance, your strategy fails, you can still win through grit, determination, and hard work. Otherwise, change your strategy. Do not let yourself be discouraged. Remember that one thousand people that there are for each active CAT member. Does the importance of small team efforts now become clear? In most counties, one thousand votes would make a decisive impact on any election. That is why politicians are so receptive to pressure groups. Politicians depend on votes for their job security. They know that for every complaint that they receive, there are possibly one thousand they do not receive. The complaints that they do not receive are the ones that frighten them. Each of those complaints could mean more than one thousand lost votes.

Judge from the population of your county. If your database for change equals 1 percent or more of your county's population, you could have the beginnings of sufficient strength and support. It is on this strength and support that we will rebuild our Southern Nation. The team concept is the closely guarded secret of our oppressors. The secret worked well for those meddling groups that work to deprive us of our values, our traditions, and our wages. The team concept is also the secret of all those nations who achieved their freedom in the modern era. The American Empire has deprived us of our destiny too long. With dedication, we could work ourselves free in possibly as little as five years. It is a lofty goal, but with enough teams in place and operating, we could do it. One Concerted Action Team in each county or parish of the South could very well be the vehicle of Southern freedom in so short a time.[12] One team in each community would be even better, even stronger. Of course, how hard we work really determines the pace of our progress. Remember that just because we have a certain state flag or a certain monument in place does not mean that the war is over. Every day is a battle. The Empire constantly engages us on all sides, in all media, with man's most devious weapons.

The battle for a free Southland, or even our continued existence, is a battle of and for the Southern mind. It is a contest to capture and recapture the Southern heart. It is a struggle to preserve our own personal identity, which someone else wants to destroy. The Southerner battles to save his soul from a meaningless and destitute bondage of an existence under the American Empire. Ours is a fight for the future of our children.

THE CONCERTED ACTION CONCEPT

O-R-D-E-R.
O—ORGANIZE: Organize the Concerted Action Team.
R—REDUCE: Reduce our program to its simplest terms.
D—DELUDE: Delude the opponent.
E—EDUCATE: Educate team members and the public.
R—RECRUIT/REINFORCE: Recruit and reinforce education.

CHAPTER IX

Stand and Be Counted

> Those who make peaceful revolution impossible will make violent revolution inevitable. John F. Kennedy[1]

Over the years, the South has witnessed the birth of many noble organizations and movements. We even witnessed the rise of some that were not so noble. We saw them rise and fall. Some of them were infants with great promise, falling before crawling, never having the chance of their first perilous steps. We have all seen it. Some of us were even foolish enough to try it. Every cause must have its pioneers. Those envisioned few that blaze trails through the dark, bloody ground of ignorance and fear are the salt of any age. Whether pushing through the Cumberland Gap, tossing tea into a harbor, or symbolically blocking the door of a university, those pioneers earn the malice of their contemporaries, but the respect of succeeding generations. Pioneering is hard and dangerous work. Sometimes you never reap the rewards you deserve. It is devastating to stand by and see your sown fields plowed under by someone else.

Still, pioneers forge ahead. Farming a new field, they announce their purpose to anyone who will listen. Using creativity, the old standby of pioneers, they present an impressive platform and develop engaging literature. They advertise for members through what media is at their disposal, and eventually they gain a scattering across several states: not a landslide, but a start.

In some areas, the new entity takes wing. Its membership grows and develops the beginnings of power. Fertile fields bear fruit as the pioneers begin to achieve their objectives. This is what all pioneers hope to achieve. Their labor is richly rewarded as they begin to make a difference. I wish it always happened that way, but it doesn't.

In other areas, the crop comes up and stands for a while, but there are barely enough plants to make a stand, let alone supply seed for the coming seasons. No matter how hard the pioneer works his field, the grain fails to boot and the cotton sheds its bolls. Morale bottoms and the exodus begins. The pioneer couldn't hire field hands, let alone expect them to volunteer. Funds are in even shorter supply than labor. His crop withers long before harvest.

No one wants to be a dirt scratcher. It is no fun to hoe a field full of weeds in the shadow of some other man's plantation. I have been there. No one has ever truly lived until he has been there. It is an experience like no other. Some fellow shows up decked out in more ribbons than Audie Murphy. He delivers the same speech that nine out of ten other "Audies" use. Then, he hands you a charter and ends the ceremony with the same words that God spoke when Noah departed from the Ark: "Go forth and multiply."

Something somewhere in the back of your mind says, "I thought we had."

About that time, reality and a tired feeling come over you. By the time the first thought travels to the front of your mind, you conceive another, "What do we do next?"

All of this will sound familiar to some of you. Chances are that those of you who recognize this scenario are also addicted to antacid. You might also have painful memories of "Audie's" next visit. That is the one when he shows up aiming to retrieve the charter that he earlier delivered. You refused to mail the charter back because you refused to admit defeat.

Twenty-twenty hindsight is wonderful stuff. If you use it right, it is called experience. With each failure comes the seed of even greater success. These hard-won seeds refuse to rest. They cry out to the pioneer to be sown again, even if he has to find a new field. Having failed at the local, the state, and at the regional level, I can share plenty of seeds with you. You can use my seed. Just promise to plant a crop.

The best advise that anyone ever gave to a people desiring to regain their freedom or pioneering an independence movement is found in a little-known booklet. Much to its original distributor's embarrassment, many other people than its intended audience read this small manual. It presents practical advice on getting the message of a political or cultural movement across to its prospective audience. Coincidentally, it is advice that issued from the American

Empire. The Central Intelligence Agency printed this guide for the Nicaraguan Contras in the mid-nineteen-eighties.

> The desired result is a guerrilla who can persuasively justify his actions when he comes into contact with any member of the People of Nicaragua . . . he should be able to give 5 or 10 logical reasons why, for example, a peasant should give him cloth, needle and thread to mend his clothes. When the guerrilla behaves in this manner, enemy propaganda will never succeed in making him an enemy in the eyes of the people.[2]

That is good advice for anyone, whether they plead for food and shelter in the jungle or for the future of a monument in Mississippi. The CIA's collective wisdom applies equally to pleading the case of our Southern Nation. When you ask something of anyone, their natural mental reflex is to question why (or why not) they should give you what you request. Now you can give them ten reasons why our Southern Nation should be free.

> 1. Southrons have a God-given right of self-preservation. The American Empire censors and discourages both Southern culture and Southern heritage, threatening the historical right of the Southern people to exist as a distinct cultural group.
> 2. The empire's education establishment dictates the education of Southern children. This leaves Southrons with no realistic chance for local input.
> 3. In the 1860s, the American Empire destroyed and confiscated the property of the Southern people while Southerners were acting within their rights. The injury did not end there. Because of this continuing campaign, Southerners suffer constant meddling and social engineering at the hands of non-elected federal judges and bureaucrats.
> 4. Due to its moral depravity, continued association with the American Empire serves only to promote similar moral decay in our own people.
> 5. Continued economic oppression coupled with a repressive tax system that will never change ensures that the American Empire will never allow the South to advance beyond its status as a second-class colony of the Empire.
> 6. The American imperial system is rotten with corruption from its highest to its lowest levels. The system is a self-fulfilling prophecy with no hope of meaningful reform.
> 7. The empire purposefully ships the South's already low-wage jobs overseas via corporate greed and imperial trade agreements.

8. A free society can exist only as long as there is the free exchange of ideas and freedom of association. The American Empire silences any Southern dissent by propaganda, harassment, blacklisting, or further oppression. Therefore, imperial American society is no longer a free society.

9. It is plain that Southern participation in the grand American experiment is no longer welcome (except as cannon fodder), since no traditional Southron is allowed a seat on the Supreme Court or any of the empire's controlling bodies.

10. The American Empire has encouraged the secession and recognized the independence of states seceding from other empires while repeatedly using force to deny the Southern people that same right. According to the laws of nations and precedents set by past actions of the American Empire, the South has a natural, legal right to its freedom and independence.

That is my personal top ten list of reasons. I am sure you can think of even more. Some of your reasons are probably better than mine. So put your mind to it. The real worry of our existence under the control of the American Empire is not what our reasons for wanting to leave are. It is that we have reasons to leave. In this case, they happen to be very good reasons. In particular, our reasons are better than those that the Declaration of Independence mentioned for leaving the British Empire.

Think about it. Even Ivan the Terrible and Adolf Hitler were never able to demand an accounting of every penny their subjects earned. The American Emperor does. If Grant and Sherman were alive today, they would be some of the first in line to revolt against the same Empire they helped inflict on the Southern Nation. Regardless of what such Yankee idols would do, Southrons do not need an armed insurrection. Violence is the imperial style of pursuing change. Today there are many smarter and more successful ways to revolt. Twenty-first-century Southrons fight by using their heads.

Of course, it does no good to start a movement if your movement flounders before anyone knows it exists. When developing any movement or organization, we must first form a base of dedicated members. Then, from that solid beginning, we seek to enlarge our following into a real social power. Southern partisans must get the message of Southern nationhood out to other potential partisans. We use advertising and public relations to achieve this goal. The science of public relations aims to motivate a person to do what they would not normally do. By applying some rudimentary public relations techniques, we alert the public to the presence of our movement and help them conceive their first impression of Southern nationalism. The scope of our efforts will depend upon the audience we target. One good example of a sweeping broad-based campaign is the Sons of Confederate Veterans' "1-800 My South" billboard campaign. While your particular group may not have the resources available for this type of campaign, it is the same principle in practice.

Most of us perceive advertising and public relations as a big-money game played by lawyers and corporations. Contrary to this common impression, the little fellow can win the game, too. Effective public relations is more than just getting your name out. You must also implant a mental picture that will penetrate the public mind whenever your name is mentioned. Our goal is to ensure that the mental picture of Southern nationalism is a productive, unifying image that the target audience is sure to welcome. The Southern image must convey a positive, realistic view of the South's true nature. This is crucial because our image is the first message that the public gets.

Like any other step we take, we must design our message to achieve specific goals. Paramount among these objectives is the need to attract active, intelligent young people to the Southern nationalist movement. Naturally, this means that our message must appear where our desired audience will receive it. We also need to present our case in an economically efficient form. Southrons must recognize that the science of persuasion relies less on bombardments of reason and more on emotional solicitation. Since modern mass-man is rarely convinced by logic, the best persuaders take care to mix emotions with their facts. Remember that your message is most effective when it is simple and engages the basic human psychological drives and desires. Tailor your campaign to achieve your goals effectively in your area.

People are born either male or female. No doctor ever approached an expectant father in the waiting room and announced that he had a new baby public relations specialist. As with any science, the disciplines of persuasion are learned through study and practice. This science is indispensable to any fledgling political or cultural movement. There might already be someone in your group with hidden aptitude as a public relations specialist.

That person might not know a unifying metaphor if it hit them in the face, but with practice, they can admirably use metaphors, parallelisms, and plenty of other terms that they do not recognize. If you do not have a person who has this aptitude or is willing to develop it, recruit one.

Southerners also acquire many advantages due to the amazing era in which we live. No matter who puts the words on paper, modern technology makes it easier to fight the publicity battle. Home computers and copy machines enable any home to be an information bureau. All that is necessary is dedication, creativity, and a critical eye. Flyers and brochures will probably compose the backbone of your starting efforts. Thanks to copiers and PCs, their production is easier and less expensive than just a few years ago. You can get professional-quality results, whoever punches the keys.

Remember to keep your message simple and digestible. Flyers or brochures must be easy to read. Use a clear crisp font that is not too cramped, and make sure there is plenty of white space. Nothing turns a reader off quicker than a cramped, densely typed sheet with narrow margins filled with never-ending paragraphs. Collect flyers and brochures. Then, analyze their layout. If you feel that one carries considerable impact, imitate it. Don't be afraid to gain from the experience of others.

Today, we have many other inexpensive means of getting our message across. One of the most common is placing a classified ad in magazines that cater to a related field that interests the target audience. This is an effective and economical means of enlarging your original operational base. Classified ads are cheaper than display ads and they have an extra advantage— they work. People actually do read the classifieds. The same ads that can sell the most worthless junk will also sell an idea.

In our rush to promote the cause, we tend to forget many free sources we can use in marketing our cause. Fledgling movements almost universally neglect public service announcements. Such community bulletins on radio stations are free in most cases. You just have to follow the station's rules. At the same time, tailor your message to fit the forum. It is the same with public event notices in small town papers. Not only are they valuable sources of free publicity, but they have considerable readership, especially in rural areas. In the struggle for Southern nationhood, we are limited more by the extent of our creativity than by our budget.

Of similar effect and of little expense are letters to the editor of these same publications. Have your friends help and send several letters following the same general formula. Your letters should beam with promise for the future of our movement. Your letters should be powerful, full of dignity and positive image.

From the start, strive to bring people into the fold who are known to sympathize with the Southern cause. By scanning the same letter columns we write to, we can find those who hold similar views. We can easily recognize them by the letters they write. Usually their name and hometown are published with their letter. A peek at a phonebook will often furnish their address or at least their telephone number. Contact these people. Each probably has a circle of friends who hold similar viewpoints. Maybe you can recruit them. At the least, let them know you appreciate their efforts.

Getting positive publicity in these same media outlets is important, but in the post-modern age, positive publicity is hard to get. It seems that you never hear any good news today. There is a genuine reason for this: The news media is an entertainment industry devoted solely to the pursuit of legal tender. In today's newsroom, bad news is good news. Pleasant articles or charming stories about dogs and kids simply do not sell enough advertising. (On the other hand, if the dog is a pit bull that goes around gnawing on kids, the market is wide open.) Even if a media outlet reports good news, it is in a small space, buried deep in the back pages.[3] Your primary goal in public relations is to develop this back-page notice. Positive exposure in the back pages avoids negative exposure on the front page. Rest assured, if your group is in the public eye and attempts to accomplish anything, you will eventually be exposed in one place or the other.

In the real world, negative exposure is at the forefront of forming public opinion. The penalty for bad press is automatic, whether you earned it or not. This is why many media experts compare negative exposure to the Black Death. Their estimation is correct. Bad press spreads like a plague, usually infecting everyone it contacts. Compounding this tendency, your first negative publicity always acts as a trigger and unleashes more bad press. The best way to handle negative exposure is to avoid it. Unfortunately, that is easier in principle than it is in practice.

The key to controlling bad publicity is to control all publicity. Your team should allow only official communication between a designated representative and the press or any other public establishment. Your comrades may not like the sound of this policy, but there is a good reason behind it. On more than one occasion, the press has bent otherwise innocent information to destructive purposes. What really hurts is when this information is taken from off-the-cuff remarks made by an organization's members or leaders. Many times those remarks resulted from concocted pressure, applied in a manufactured, heated situation for the benefit of reporters or the group's opposition.

No matter how well you control information, you will eventually come upon something less like plague and more like a venereal infection. This is usually an unprovoked attack by some self-appointed guardian of the public virtue. Often, he knows even less about the Southern cause than he does quantum physics. Still, that does not curb his desire to save us from ourselves. These people tend to share a common trait. They have a terrible time reconciling their convictions with reality. Such misguided but well-meaning people never miss a chance to announce the evil of some cause they know little about. They are different than the average rabid activist. These people occasionally carry some influence and respect. The best way to handle them is to ignore their actions unless they become too disruptive. This gives them less attention than if you were to respond to their ranting, so it diminishes their effect.

Publicity control is crucial to the future of any organization in its early stages. Naturally, we want people to know of our cause, but we still want to make sure there is a positive slant on the information they get. By controlling our publicity, we not only control their first impression of our cause, we control the way the public perceives us as they get additional information. Likewise, we prevent our critics from gaining the weapons of our own design that they would love to turn against us.

By controlling who does the talking, and what they talk about, Southern groups also have the power to avoid spontaneous public debates. These non-planned debates usually turn sour when reason conflicts with emotional argument. As Southern-rights advocates found in more than one heritage defense battle, the deck is always stacked in favor of the opposition in such an ad lib showdown. If it is not in their best interest, the opposition avoids argument. They know that if there is no guarantee of a win, the confrontation could do them more damage than good.

Interviews are similar to spontaneous public debates. The deck is stacked in favor of the establishment's agenda, or the interview would not occur. In newspapers, magazines, and other print media the odds are often so uneven as to make the attempt foolhardy. It is often said that you can't do battle with someone who buys ink (or electrons) by the barrel. This is often the case. Controlling which person talks is a good way to avoid such slanted interviews. These interviews are normally edited to give a crackpot image to the proponent of any ideas unapproved by the liberal establishment.

An example of this tendency that comes readily to mind is an interview that I saw the National Rifle Association's James Baker give on ABC's *Nightline.* Baker is normally a dignified and intelligent person. *Nightline* made him look paranoid and foolish in an edited interview that appeared spontaneous.

Direct communications with the press, no matter how small, are best handled through press release or articles written for publication. Even then, you do not have complete editorial control, but some control is better than none. Southern organizations usually overlook press releases. Perhaps it is the impression that we are not big enough or important enough to warrant the use of press releases. Attitudes like these are self-defeat in action. Through press releases, you have the advantage of controlling the content and timing the release of your information. Timing is valuable in playing public sentiment. If you do not try for advantages in developing public sentiment, there is little use in contacting the press anyway.

Remember to use the press to your advantage or the press will use you. A 3-person group that uses every means at its disposal to resist the Empire is already bigger and more important than a 100- or 1,000-person group that does not. Press releases, articles, advertisements, and other public relations efforts are like bread. They must be cast upon the waters. Perhaps the media will pay no attention to your efforts. Then again, maybe they will. Before we can reap, we must sow.

Despite our best efforts, there always comes a time when things go wrong. You find that you cannot hide behind the skill and knowledge of your chosen representative, or maybe necessity forces you into that role. Maybe a news crew or an innocent bystander corners you and just wants to know what is happening. How do you react? What do you say? When the camera lights are staring you in the face and the microphone is positioned just beneath your chin, what do you do? You have one ticket to disaster, and two correct choices.

We have all seen it on the evening news. The news crew stops a public figure or maybe a defendant's lawyer and asks him for a few remarks about a new government policy or a trial verdict. The result is a suave, smooth reply that may or may not answer the question. Still, it satisfies the reporters. They have something to carry back to the newsroom. The reply is cool. It looks professional. Well it should. Public figures and lawyers are professionals. An important part of being a professional politician, lawyer, or a political activist is to know what you will say before someone jabs a microphone in your face. As a rule, professionals never make off-the-cuff remarks. They plan their remarks well ahead of time, even if their chosen reply is simply, "No comment."

Professionals plan ahead because they expect reporters to want an opinion. Then they can plead their case to the public, their real jury. They know their shoelaces had better be tied and their fly zipped, because there is no second chance before the court of public opinion. If you make unplanned, unrehearsed remarks you will either appear stupid or arm your opposition. Who knows? Appearing stupid may be the hot item of an otherwise slow news day. Do not make off-the-cuff remarks. You will find that the habit only causes abundant pain without any gain.

On the other hand, there are two correct choices. The first correct choice is the hardest thing in the world to do. Say nothing. If you are not your group's chosen representative, if you do not know what you plan to say, or you have not rehearsed it, this is your choice. There are no exceptions. The easiest thing to do when confronted by someone who asks your opinion is to give it. Everyone wants their fifteen minutes of fame. It is always tempting to shoot your mouth off. Don't give in to the urge. If you do, you will sound like the man on the evening news who gives his impression of what the tornado sounded like. He has an excuse. He is in shock. You know better. If you have to say something, try a simple "No comment," or , "We will issue a statement at a later time."

Your other choice is to say the right thing. It is easier than saying nothing, but it still requires discipline. Saying the right thing involves planning. It involves practice, but don't worry. If your mouth is busy saying the right thing, it will be too busy to say the wrong thing.

When you plan what to say, start with the image you wish to portray to the media and the public. Then, work backward from there. As always, your message must be short and simple. This way there is no confusion about the meaning of what you said. Whatever the situation, never forget who your real audience is. Your target audience is not the media or whatever group you might confront. Your true audience is the public.

Also, remember that you have a limited amount of time to deliver your message to the public. Newspapers only carry short quotes from newsmakers. Radio and television use only sound bites. In the 1950s, an average news-camera scene lasted 35-50 seconds. Today, it lasts only 5.[4] So, be able to condense your entire message into one simple sentence charged with fact and emotion. Think of it as the same message you would write on a banner or protest sign. Anything longer than one sentence is not a sign; it is an essay. Sound bites and quotations used by the media are seldom any longer. The more reason, combined with emotional impact, that your one sentence contains, the more successful you will be at saying the right thing.

Planning what to say is important for groups, too. When preparing a demonstration or mass protest, everyone involved must know the rules. Plan everything from what the signs and banners say to what the group will chant or sing. Even the clothes that the individual protesters wear carry a message. Dress codes are never popular, but they are necessary to ensure that you convey the right image. For some reason, news cameras only focus on the best and worst dressed people in a crowd. If a protester dresses like a slob, the public sees only an instantly discredited cause supported by slobs. Protesters must also know what to say if confronted by the press. A good rule to follow is that you say what the sign you carry says, nothing more.

Saying the right thing is hard enough without trying to persuade others, but that is the whole purpose of saying anything. Still, when you try to persuade others, do you use reason or emotion? Past events give us some clues how the masses in the American Empire respond. The European propagandists of the early twentieth century designed their petitions to the American public based on the European tradition of appealing to reason. Both the British and French desired America's help in World War I, while Germany hoped we would at least remain neutral. These European propagandists all complained that their efforts were failures with the American public. When the American Empire exploited the public's sense of outrage over the German sinking of the passenger liner *Lusitania,* Americans rushed to war against the Central Powers. German propagandists, such as Joseph Goebbels, quickly learned the error of the European method. The largest, most savage war in history followed because Adolf Hitler masterfully used emotional appeals to persuade Germans to act in the most unreasonable of ways.[5]

Appealing to reason requires a reasonable audience. Usually, reasonable audiences are also well-educated audiences. Very few people in the American Empire are able to truthfully claim this label anymore. The Empire has ensured it. Why do you think that the quality of American education has declined so far, so fast? Uneducated masses are slaves to emotional appeals. Ruling by emotion requires far less effort than ruling by reason. In the distant past, the original American republic expended the extra effort. America's founders were all well-educated men who believed only in reasoned argument. They considered emotional demagoguery evil. That is why the original colonies won their independence only after developing a literate middle class.

Emotional arguments are most persuasive with the lowest-class members of a society. It takes little education or reason to respond with fear, outrage, or envy. That is why our emperors so often appeal to vague notions like "fairness." Such emotion-based appeals extend to an unseen attitude of class-envy. Even more often, we hear sound bites featuring some authority figure on the evening news exploiting our fears by declaring what we must do to avoid some real or imagined tragedy that looms in our future. The middle- and upper-class Bolsheviks used these same techniques to topple the czar. They learned from motivating Russia's many failed uprisings of hungry peasants.

However, in today's world a movement must rise above mere rabble-rousing. To win, a group must appeal to both reason and emotion. This way, their message receives some acceptance across all classes, while achieving its greatest impact with the larger middle class. The typical middle-class American is educated enough to respond to reason, while repressed enough to respond to emotional appeal. Most Southerners still consider themselves to belong to the middle class, so a combination of emotion and reason is necessary to attract a larger foundation of support. Saying the right thing always combines reason and emotion.

Nevertheless, when confronted with an attack against our

Southern Nation, the average Southron frequently finds himself speechless. For this reason, Southern nationalism seldom gains the serious attention our cause deserves. It is natural to be nervous in front of others, especially when you suspect that they do not share or respect your opinion. The one activity many people fear most is speaking in front of other people. The key is to practice until you learn to tap your fear as a source of energy.

You will find that every attack or criticism of Southern nationhood's potential has its responses. Plan your responses before critics confront you. The key is not so much in knowing the answers, but knowing how to deliver the answers. There are many ways to respond to attacks, questions, and criticisms. You can give a short answer and then leave. You might answer with a question. Another strategy involves refuting the critic or attacking his criticism. You can also respond with a patterned rhetorical flurry that gives your opponent no chance to lever a word in edgewise. The attitude of the critic and his choice of criticism dictates the zeal of your responses. Here are some common attacks and criticisms of our Southern Nation along with examples of how you might respond.

Criticism: "Southern independence? We already tried that. It doesn't work. It failed. The idea was discredited. The war settled the question."

This is the usual indoctrinated response to any mention of Southern nationhood. It shows that the imperial ministry of propaganda has done its work well, stamping out competing ideas and the reality of constitutional law while we were still school children. After all, the non-binding Pledge of Allegiance says we are "One nation indivisible." Right? Many so-called responsible conservative leaders also fall easily into this typical thinking trap. They place the crumbling almighty union above the people it was designed to protect.

Response one: Give a short answer. "If at first you don't succeed (or secede) try, try again."

Response two: Dispute the first part of the comment with fact. "Southern independence worked fine for four years under the worst possible conditions. Had it been given the chance, Southern independence would still be working today. The South never scrapped the idea of independence. Instead, we were conquered by the superior numbers of a meddling invader."

Response three: Dispute the second part of the criticism. "What has been discredited is the imperial system. It has failed the very people it was supposed to protect. In the meantime, it is outgrowing its original boundaries to the point of being harmful to its citizens. Recent surveys show that 39 percent of all Americans consider the federal government to be the biggest threat to the liberty of its citizens."[6]

Response four: Attack the third part of the comment. "All the war settled was the question of whether an industrial nation of 23 million people could lay waste to an agrarian nation of 10 million. Even with Southern soldiers outnumbered four to one, it still took four years to supposedly settle the question."

Response five: Answer the criticism with a question, to force a deeper, more accurate dialogue on the subject. "Since when does violence and conquest settle any question? Aren't trial by combat and 'Might makes right' the outmoded, discredited ideas? Do you teach your children that it is best to resort to violence to settle their disputes?"

Criticism: "Southern independence is impractical. The South would never make it alone."

This criticism is another typical result of imperial indoctrination. The empire loves for us to think that the South could never be successful as an independent nation. The criticism itself is nothing more than a tired propaganda statement, a statement that flies in the face of all reality. This argument is easily proven false by applying facts and reason. Arm yourself ahead of time with information from chapter five and always be ready to counter this all-too-familiar argument.

Response one: Give a short answer that leads into a more detailed discussion of the facts. "I'm sorry, but your statement is not wholly correct. If you will allow me, I will show you why."

Response two: Challenge the criticism using facts about the South's industrial and agricultural productivity. "An independent South would be the fourth most prosperous nation on earth, ranking between Germany and France. We would be almost self-sufficient since we make and grow almost everything we need here. We could raise our standard of living by keeping our money at home, instead of sending it to Washington. We could also keep our jobs home instead of exporting them to foreign lands."[7]

Response three: Challenge the statements using facts about the South's population. "An independent South would rank twelfth in population among the world's nation's. With 81 million people, we would hardly be a puny stretch of backwoods. Additionally, we would still have plenty of room to grow. Remember that the Third

World countries have the world's largest populations. These are also the world's poorest countries. Nations with populations well balanced to their resources, such as the South would be, are among the world's most prosperous nations."[8]

Response four: Challenge the statements with facts about the South's land area."Unlike larger nations such as the Russian Federation or Red China, the South's 860,000 square miles is much higher-quality land. None of it is tundra or desert. Almost all of our land is usable, and it includes some of the world's richest farmland. We also have a practical world monopoly on some crops. Even the South's mountains and wilderness areas are a vast storehouse of natural resources, which promises to keep our nation prosperous for centuries to come."[9]

Response five: Answer the criticism with questions that will force the critic to destroy his own argument if he dares answer. "What makes Southern independence impractical? Why would we not make it alone? Do we not grow or make the same products as the rest of the Empire? Can you name one factor or vital resource we lack that would doom an independent Southern Nation to failure?"

Criticism: "You are a bunch of racists/radicals. You are intolerant. You are in with the militias/K.K.K./religious right."

Whenever these kinds of remarks are used, you can bet there will be an audience around, even if it is no more than an unseen video camera. These kinds of statements are not valid criticisms. They are hostile attacks using the propaganda technique of name-calling. This kind of attack is also an open invitation to a confrontation that you are sure to lose. Do not bother arguing with the person who uses this kind of attack. His mind and possibly the minds of his audience are already made up. Under the best circumstances, your hope is to keep your composure and impress whatever non-committed onlookers are around.

Response one: Give a short answer, then disengage. "I am not." Leave the area if you feel that your safety or the safety of others is threatened.

Response two: Answer with a question, then disengage. "And what group are you associated with?" Again, leave the area. Chances are the person's only desire is to create a spectacle resulting in negative exposure to the Southern cause. He will probably never answer the question you asked. If he did, it would more than likely reverse the name-calling tactic, to his own embarrassment.

Response three: Challenge the attack with poise and dignity for the benefit of the audience. Issue your challenge in a rapid-fire manner without allowing your opponent to utter a coherent word. "I take it you don't agree with my cause. From the tone of your remarks, I also assume you think there is something wrong with anyone who doesn't agree with you. Apparently, you think that the whole Empire is full of supposed racists, bigots, and extremists who make it their daily mission just to get under your skin. "Quickly disengage and walk away before your attacker has time to formulate a response. Always be careful when responding to these kinds of attacks. Remember that you do not want to give your attacker further ammunition to use against the South. You will also do your family and friends little good as an additional martyr to the Southern cause.

Criticism: "You Southerners are just out to destroy America."

Though milder than the previous attack, this criticism is still an attack designed to provoke a negative emotional response from any onlookers that they will associate with the Southern cause. As with most emotion-based attacks, the deck will probably be stacked against you, and there will probably be an audience. Again, the key to winning in this situation is to keep your composure and impress any non-committed bystanders.

Response one: Give a short answer, then disengage. "No, we are not." Then, turn and walk away without providing your adversary any tools to use against you.

Response two: Answer with a question similar to the attack, then disengage. "And socialist, big-government types like you are not?" As earlier, turn and walk away.

Response three: Challenge the attack with composure and dignity, using rapidly asked questions for the benefit of any non-committed bystanders. "Did the thirteen original colonies destroy England by seceding from the British Empire? Did Ireland destroy England by seceding? Did India? Does Poland belong back behind the Iron Curtain?" Turn and quickly walk away before your critic has time to respond. Notice that these questions were all questions that would provoke an immediate negative answer. Even if the critic declines to answer any of them, the audience answers them in their minds, as they are asked, "No. No. No. No." These consecutive negative responses transfer their mental impact back to the original attack. This reverses the Socratic "yes-set" sales technique as you attempt to "un-sell" any spectators on the critic's original attack.

Criticism: "Leave the past buried. What are you trying to do, restart the war? You are living in the past. You are out of touch."

As with most criticisms featuring the word "You," this one is propagandistic. It carries a hidden message of "It's not worth it." In an even subtler manner, the critic implies that you are not worth it. He is out for a quick kill. He is either underestimating you, he is not prepared for discussion on the subject, or he is parroting something that he heard someone else say. Your responses should convey the attitude that Southern nationhood is worth bothering about.

Response one: Give a short answer designed to reroute the direction of the discussion. "Why would anyone want to restart the war? Would you?"

Response two: Respond to the criticism by attacking the critic. "Actually, people such as you live in the past. It is your ideas that are outdated. The time has long passed when a citizen could stick his head in the sand and entrust others to manage his future. Today, everyone must be ready to stand up for himself and his nation."

Response three: If the critic's behavior warrants it, respond by shaming him. "You seem to think that our Southern homeland and our people are not worth bothering about. I feel sorry for people like you. As for many other people, as well as myself, we feel that our future and our children's future is worthy of our concern."

Response four: Answer with a series of rhetorical questions designed to put the critic on the defensive while swaying any bystanders by emotional appeal. How can we learn from history if we bury the past? Which is more important, a government or the citizens that government was installed to protect? Are freedom and liberty outdated ideals? What is out of touch about caring?"

Criticism: "Your version of history is a myth. It is a past that never existed."

This criticism surfaces often these days. It is the kind of statement typically used by revisionist historians, but more often you hear it parroted by so-called community activists who desire to appear learned and superior. This kind of rhetoric is another propaganda technique patterned after the style that Joseph Goebbels used to confuse Germans. If it is repeated often enough, the public eventually accepts any false statement as fact. It is amazing how often the Empire and its supporters copy Nazi tactics. Study your Southern history and be well armed with the facts to combat this kind of attack.

Response: Give a short answer and prepare to follow up with the facts. "Prove it."

Don't worry. He can't. Be prepared to combat an insult veiled within a statement. Such as a response beginning with, "Everyone knows that . . ." or "Even you should know that . . ."

The secret of responding to these kinds of insults and winning is to study rhetoric. Rhetoric was a common subject in the schools our grandparents attended. Now, rhetoric is a lost art and even the word has taken negative meaning. With another of the useful arts and sciences taken out of the education system, the Empire has less to fear from its citizens. Few average people know how to talk back in a manner that will be taken seriously. To take steps toward learning the forgotten craft of oral combat, read Suzette Haden Elgin's *The Gentle Art of Verbal Self-Defense*.[10]

Criticism: "We should be thankful that we lost the war."

This cliché has to be the oldest Yankee propaganda statement there is. Our detractors often use this ploy, another Goebbels-style device. If you manage to stay awake and remember your studies, it is also the easiest attack on the South to disprove. There is only one reasonable response to this criticism.

Response: Reply with a short question. Be prepared to follow with the facts. "Why?"

Have mercy. Try not to overkill your critic if he actually thinks of a reason. I do not know why people still use this criticism. Perhaps they just cannot think of anything else to say. Your opponent has only two real options available. He can give reasons that you are sure to refute, or he can switch the burden of proof to your side by saying, "Why not?" In any case, never go into battle unless you are well armed with the facts.

Criticism: "Things are good. The economy is booming. Why rock the boat?"

Unlike attacks or propaganda statements, this is a fair question. As such, it deserves a fair and informative answer. Nevertheless, remember that reason alone seldom convinces anyone of anything. To persuade, we must fuse emotion into our explanation of the facts.

Response one: Give a short, thought-provoking answer. "Unless there was a family crisis your grandmother did not work outside of the home, did she? Things only look good on TV and in the business section of the newspaper. In the real world, it takes two people working. Then, they barely make enough of a living to scrape by."

Response two: Give a longer, more emotion-charged answer. "Things are good in Washington. That is where you send more than one-third of your earnings. Things are good with your creditors. That's where the rest of your money goes. Are we better off than our parents were? Their parents? Does your job satisfy you? Do both you and your spouse have to work to make ends meet? If you can, enjoy it. A lot of other people's jobs are taking the fast boat to Red China?"

Response three: Answer with the facts while presenting an alternative.

"There is a good reason to rock the boat. Our so-called economic boom is a boom on paper only. The economy is actually shrinking. The Empire creates just enough low-paying jobs to offset the high-paying jobs we lose to foreign countries. This sham just barely keeps the market moving. The real value of your labor decreases while the price of bread increases. Why not rock the boat? If we don't rock the boat, who will keep our rulers honest?"

Response four: Answer with a quick series of rhetorical questions. "If things are so good why do we make less money for the same work than people in other parts of the country? Food at the grocery store costs the same here as it does in New York or California. Why do our wages buy less each week? If things are so good, then why are you so far in debt? Why do our taxes continue to rise? Why are we the ones who must sacrifice so a privileged few do not have to work? If things are so good, why are our jobs moving overseas?"

Criticism: "What makes you think you can change things?"

This remark shows the sarcasm typical of the cynical age we live in. Cynicism is a common characteristic of life under a repressive regime. The critic is not necessarily trying to be a smart aleck. He is simply trying to convince himself one way or the other that our situation is either hopeful or hopeless using his natural defense mechanisms. Unconsciously, he could be reaching out to you for help.

Response: Answer with a short question designed to create further dialogue on the subject. "Why not?"

We hope that the critic will begin to give reasons to support his original criticism. Explain them away with statements of fact or ask further questions that he will have to answer for himself. Your goal is to guide the critic as he forms a new opinion. If his mind is open and you handle the situation right, his new opinion will be one that realizes the hope and promise of the Southern future.

Criticism: "What gives you the right to impose your views/morals on me?"

This one question has caused more people to cut and run than possibly any other collection of words in the English language. When any unwanted form of vice has decided to move in, this question has been responsible for destroying whole towns. It has wrecked countless lives and homes because it is one of the most frequently called moves in the liberal, left-wing playbook. The attack is a favorite tactic of homosexual activists and pornographers. They love it because it works. This tactic works because people fail to rebut the criticism out of an instinctive fear of imposing on other people. The statement uses erroneous logic shrouded in reasonable sounding terms. Your critic uses this tactic to appoint himself a victim and confuse the issue of just who is imposing what on whom.

Response: Stand your ground. Keep your composure. Counterattack the critic swiftly and forcibly, rephrasing his criticism at the end of your rebuttal. Here is a sample reply, printed as I once heard it voiced by a gutsy little old lady who knew how to stand up for her rights.

"We're not imposing anything on anyone. Our standards have been the same for one hundred and fifty years. We have never allowed strip clubs on Main Street and we are not going to start now just because you say so. This is our town. We were here long before you. How dare *you* come in and try to impose *your* morals on *us*."

This kind of counterattack usually catches the critic unprepared. His original approach was thwarted. Now, he must shift to another tactic. His wise choice would be reasoned debate. Instead, he usually ends up delivering a shrill name-calling attack. Stay cool. Continue your forceful counterattack with poise and dignity. Otherwise, just walk away. Leave him babbling and screaming in half-witted splendor. Do not feel sorry for him. He wouldn't shed a tear for you. Besides, if the media is watching, they will more than likely edit out his mistakes. Just remember that the media can never edit the impression you made on a live group of spectators. Neither can the media erase the fact that you cared enough to stand up for your nation.

Of course, these examples are not a script. They are illustrations designed to make you think. There is no way to include all the possible criticisms or attacks you might face. Likewise, I do not pretend to know all the answers, let alone know all of the questions. Every situation is different. The important thing is that you know there are possible responses to every question or criticism about Southern nationalism. Have no fear. Eventually, someone who despises the Southern cause is going to confront you. Study, practice, and prepare yourself. Southrons do not have to roll over and play dead just because our masters say so. Do your homework. Dare to challenge their assumptions. Don't be afraid to speak our truth to their power.

Remember that 20 percent of Southerners already support the idea of Southern independence. As the empire's activities grow even more oppressive, that percentage will grow on its own. Additionally, as each Concerted Action Team persuades more people to adopt the Southern nationalist philosophy, the support in that team's operational area swells even more. Many active teams equal many new believers. Twenty percent will rise to 30 percent, then 40, possibly even 50 percent. Contrast our progress with the fact that few of the successful revolutions and independence movements of history ever managed 20 percent of their public's support. Until the recent ballot in Quebec, I doubt that one has actually achieved so lofty a ratio of support as 50 percent. In the 1960's, the question of independence for Quebec barely managed 4 percent of the public's support. If the Quebecois can muster that kind support, just imagine what we can do, given the head start we have.[11]

Don't worry. Southern nationhood will happen. With knowledge and planning, we have nothing to fear. When people stand up and assert themselves, they never fail. Success is always theirs. Prepare yourself. That way you can be the greatest success possible.

THORNTON'S TOP TEN REASONS FOR SOUTHERN NATIONHOOD

1. Southrons have a God-given right of self-preservation. The American Empire censors and discourages both Southern culture and Southern heritage, threatening the historical right of the Southern people to exist as a distinct cultural group.

2. The empire's education establishment dictates the education of Southern children. This leaves Southrons with no realistic chance for local input.

3. In the 1860's, the American Empire destroyed and confiscated the property of the Southern people while Southerners were acting within their rights. The injury did not end there. Because of this continuing campaign, Southerners suffer constant meddling and

social engineering at the hands of non-elected federal judges and bureaucrats.

4. Due to its moral depravity, continued association with the American Empire serves only to promote similar moral decay in our own people.

5. Continued economic oppression, coupled with a repressive tax system that will never change, ensures that the American Empire will never allow the South to advance beyond its status as a second-class colony of the Empire.

6. The American imperial system is rotten with corruption from its highest to its lowest levels. The system is a self-fulfilling prophecy with no hope of meaningful reform.

7. The Empire purposefully ships the South's already low-wage jobs overseas via corporate greed and imperial trade agreements.

8. A free society can exist only as long as there is a free exchange of ideas and freedom of association. The American Empire silences any Southern dissent by propaganda, harassment, blacklisting, or further oppression. Therefore, imperial American society is no longer a free society.

9. It is plain that Southern participation in the grand American experiment is no longer welcome, since no traditional Southron is allowed a seat on the Supreme Court or any of the empire's controlling bodies.

10. The American Empire has encouraged the secession and recognized the independence of states seceding from other empires while repeatedly using force to deny the Southern people that same right. According to the laws of nations and precedents set by past actions of the American Empire, the South has a natural, legal right to its freedom and independence.

CHAPTER X

The Cause and the Cure

Nothing can seem foul to those that win.

William Shakespeare[1]

As Southrons, we know that our main purpose must be to vindicate the cause of our ancestors. The first Confederates and their
leaders wrote appeals to tell the world's future generations the true
nature of their fight. They knew that the benevolent Squareheads
would take advantage of their victory to distort the truth and
rewrite history. In a like manner, those same conquerors distorted
and rewrote our constitution. Confederate veterans knew that the
Yankees would reeducate their Southern descendants to the point
of denying their nationality. They also knew that eventually someone would turn around and listen to the Southern side of the story.

When someone tries to vindicate a cause of the past, they immediately run into a moral problem. You can never vindicate a cause
that you yourself would be unwilling to undertake. Above all, you
cannot vindicate the actions of your ancestors when you will not
even vindicate your own. The imperial establishment programs us
to believe that we better ourselves by not getting involved in any
cause, let alone Southern nationhood. That same establishment
also ensures that most of us have little free time. Most people do
not get involved until someone else or some intolerable incident
gets them started. Then they have no idea what to do. Still, deep
inside, Southrons have something much stronger than the establishment's imposed idea of not getting involved. It is our Southern
nature to resist and to be part of something bigger than we are. For
a Southerner, taking your stand is a highly personal endeavor. We
each do it, in one way or another, as we see fit and when we can see
an effect, or maybe when we have had all we are able to stomach.

The main objective is to get involved. Also, remember to have fun being involved.

Our acts of defiance are an integral part of the Southern psyche. It is our nature. What other conquered nation erects memorials to its heroes, always with the statue turning its back upon the victors? Yes, New England Brahmins would say that resistance is inbred in us. Many of our defiant acts do not take much effort. Neither do they have to be visible. The key is to be creative with all we do. We must encourage ourselves to act daily. Then, as we resist the Empire daily, we must look to our future while developing tools and ideas that will further aid our quest for Southern nationhood.

We must develop new ideas, attitudes, and tools in our quest for freedom. We are already acquainted with some of these ideas. Obviously, it wastes time to reinvent techniques that already exist. Instead, we must adapt these ideas and ideas from other captive nations' movements to our situation. This will speed our work. The idea is to start locally and rebuild our Southern Nation. Each rural Southern community has the potential to become a center of Southern nationalism. From these solid beginnings of Southern resistance, we can reach out to our neighbors and try our case in the court of world opinion.

DEVELOP THE ATTITUDE
OF SOUTHERN DEFIANCE

Southrons must first develop and hone their natural attitude of defiance to Yankee domination. It is already there inside us. We just have to learn to let it out. First, we express our contempt as individuals, then as groups and organizations, and at last as a nation. We must explore the vast reservoir of Southern defiance. Filled to overflowing, it is as much a part of our heritage as the Confederate battle flag or "Dixie." It is a blessing, not a curse, as the Empire would like us to believe. Used with diligence and dedication, our natural attitude of defiance is one of the tools that will help set us free of the Empire.

There is a tale about the early days of the so-called "Civil Rights Movement" that illustrates the kind of attitude we want to develop. At the peak of the movement, to be a member of one organization, you had to swear to do something every day to aggravate a white man. It did not matter if the act was large or small; they aggravated daily. They may not still swear this oath, but it appears some still carry on this practice. The same policy is proper for Confederate-Americans to adopt. Unlike most liberal strategies, it works. We could easily refine this practice to adapt to our non-racial needs. It could be part of a new code of Southern conduct to do something every day to aggravate the Empire. Nothing aggravates the Empire more than Southrons who refuse to be good indoctrinated imperial citizens. The imperials cannot stand a Southerner with an attitude of defiance. It shows the imperials that they are losing control.

Read a good pro-Southern book like *The South Was Right*, by the Kennedy brothers, or *Southern by the Grace of God*, by Michael Andrew Grissom. Another thought-provoking choice is *I'll Take My Stand*, by the Fugitives. For moral guidance and direction, the Bible should always be tops on your reading list. Join a pro-South organization such as the League of the South, the Sons of Confederate Veterans, the United Daughters of the Confederacy, or the Confederate Society of America, to name just a few examples. Register to vote, and always vote, doing so from a conservative, Confederate-American stance. While you are at the polls or anywhere else wear "badges of Southern nationhood," like a pro-South T-shirt or a gray ribbon. When your great-grandfather meets you on the other side, how will he greet you? He wore a uniform for his cause, and you will not even wear a simple T-shirt for yours?

Get a piece of gray satin or grosgrain ribbon from your local dry goods or department store. Loop it, put a pin through it, and wear it. You might want to add a black stripe or two with a marker. The stripes show our mourning for the Constitution and Bill of Rights. If you are dedicated to the cause, you will buy your own spool of ribbon and give ribbons out to your friends and relatives. Sure, everybody is wearing ribbons for this, that, or the other reason. Why not call attention to our cause? Besides, gray is a color none of the liberal activist groups has taken, yet.

If you do not already do so, then no reason exists why you should not fly a Confederate battle flag or one of the three patterns of Confederate national flag outside your home or business. You could also apply a bumper sticker to your vehicle. There are many available with Southern nationalist slogans like "The South Was Right!" or "Free Dixie." Show your true colors. Speak up. The friction you do not get will surprise you. One of the great advantages of living down South is that down here most people still respect your rights.

Many Southrons are taking their personal rebellion against the Empire one step further. They refer to the U.S. flag as the "Banner of Yankee Occupation," and refuse to pledge allegiance to it. They also refer to zip codes and area codes as "Yankee Occupation Codes." Your Social Security Number is now being more correctly termed as your "Imperial Identification Number." Just try leaving your Imperial ID Number off a check nowadays. Some Southrons are even returning to the practice of denoting that their letters are mailed from an occupied zone. This habit is said to have started as a protest in Little Rock during the Central High crisis of 1957. Those who started the practice got the idea from the way they addressed their mail while serving as occupation troops in Germany and Japan after World War II. Additionally, a growing number of Southrons now refuse to use the Yankee Occupation Code or the two-letter abbreviation for their state. They write, "Occupied Jackson, Mississippi" or "Occupied Charleston, South Carolina C.S.A." This small, painless act of linguistic defiance might cause someone to think, if only for a minute, of what we lost. As the fine Southrons of Crown Rights Book Company state in their ordering instructions:

> Such abbreviation and code designate a military district of the corporate UNITED STATES rather than a *dejure* state. Use of the "zip code" is voluntary (*Domestic Mail Services Regulations,* Section 122.32) and the United States Postal Service cannot discriminate against the non-use of the code (*Postal Reorganization Act,* Section 403, Public Law 91-375). Mail sent to us in disregard of this request may be subject to refusal.[2]

Every year, most of us fill out at least one Federal or state form. The odds are that you will come to a part of the form that should not be there at all. This is the section where they ask your racial/ethnic group. Put a check mark in the box that says other. In the blank space provided, write "Confederate-American." The government can do nothing about your answer. The instructions on the form say that this section is for statistical or affirmative action purposes only. We all long for the day when the United States Postal Service has to hire a certain percentage of Confederate-Americans. This practice is also good for the next United States Census. We should all stand up as a legitimate ethnic group so that we can receive "equal protection under the law." Part of that protection is that Southerners are free to practice lawful resistance to the Empire as much as we please. The attitude of defiance is the main ingredient in practicing that resistance.

SPEAK AND WRITE THE SOUTHRON LANGUAGE

Our native tongue is another tool that we can use to defy the Empire. The Southern language is one of the chief signs of our nationhood. It makes us unique from our conquerors. Our dialect is another trait that the Empire simply cannot stand about Southerners. Conquerors always try to stamp out the native tongue of their captive nations. This practice is an ancient tool of empires; it is a form of cultural genocide. That is why many *lost* languages had to be found once their nations broke the chains of empire. The English once outlawed the speaking of Gaelic in Scotland and Ireland. Now Gaelic is again the language of the Irish and is making a comeback in Scotland, as that nation moves closer to independence. For decades, Danish was the official language of occupied Norway. The Norwegian language was thought to have vanished. That is, until the early 1800s, when two young men with no formal training inherited the task of. reconstructing their native tongue. They did this by researching the speech of elderly Norwegians living in rural areas.[3] Likewise, Hebrew left the domain of dead languages with the rebirth of Israel in 1948.Now it is time for Southerners to show their defiance of the Empire by renewing their Southern language.

As in any other imperial domain, the American Empire moved early in its plans to stamp out its regional tongues. The ink from the First Amendment was still wet when Noah Webster took over as the self-appointed agent of the speech police. He sanitized the English language and reconciled it with New England's patterns of grammar and pronunciation to form an approved, sterile American language. This Yankeefied tongue was once foreign to Southrons.

The native Southern tongue is Southern English, not Yankee American. For years Southern schools used Oxford's dictionary and kept Webster's as only a reference book. When I was a freshman at the University of Arkansas almost twenty years ago, students who took freshman composition were told that no other school would honor their course credits. Why? We were told that the home of the Razorbacks was the last major school to use William Faulkner's English composition book, *Writing Good Prose*. Faulkner used the

British orthography and grammar native to the South. He refused to use Yankee Newspeak. For an example of the native Southern and English version of English, read older editions of Charles Dickens' *David Copperfield*, Sir Walter Scott's *Ivanhoe*, or one of Faulkner's novels, such as *Absalom, Absalom*. You will notice that some of the words are spelled in unfamiliar yet attractive ways, and that sentences are parsed and punctuated somewhat differently. Be forewarned Stick with the older editions, since some of the newer printings are actually translations. They have been sanitized to avoid offending the Empire's grammar police.

This is British (Southern) orthography. It is how we used to write. In our Southron language, the words "labor," "honor," and "color" are "labour," "honour," and "colour." In addition, proper Southern English uses more "S"'s than "Z"'s. The Southern equivalents of "specialize," "aggrandize," and "organize" are "specialise," "aggrandise," and "organise." Mr. Webster also made unnecessary apostrophes popular. Before Yankeefication, "won't," "don't," and "can't" were "wont," "dont," and "cant." In their rush to apostatize the English language, the Yankees even changed the way we write dates. If you have ever been in the American military, you probably noticed its unusual way of writing dates. "July 4, 1776" is the Yankee way of denoting Independence Day. To Southrons and soldiers, Independence Day is "12 April 1861," sans the comma. The military is resistant to change and still uses the old English method to avoid confusion. It is an army tradition. Remember that the U.S. Army got its start as British militia.[4]

Our native Southern language uses particular words in ways that the imperials do not. The three Southern meals of the day were breakfast, dinner, and supper. Later, the Empire's public school system forced us to eat lunch. Avoid using the word "lunch," since it is of a foreign tongue. Southrons eat dinner around noon. Strange people do lunch out in California. Furthermore, Southerners carry nothing in lunch buckets. We use dinner pails or dinner buckets.[5]

Undoubtedly, you have noticed that I have used the unfamiliar word "Southron" many times so far in this book. Once, this word was common throughout the South. Southron is an old Scots-Irish term that is interchangeable with the more common term Southerner. Get familiar with the word and use it to further your personal rebellion against Mr. Webster and his imperial jargon.

Of course, no discussion of the Southron language would be complete without mentioning our Southern accent. Our accent is under the same derisive imperial attack that any other symbol of Southern nationhood suffers. The imperial speech police have made it their duty to eliminate all our twangs and drawls. As well, they try to turn us all into auctioneers. They use the typical fat sheriff stereotype to propagate the myth that if you talk slow, you think even slower. In academia and business, most Southrons are told to lose their accent if they plan to advance. The Empire claims our twangs and drawls are the red badge of ignorance. If this campaign were inflicted on any other ethnic group, it would be vilified as discrimination and a violation of civil rights. The war against the Southron accent is perhaps the most effective of all the Empire's cultural eradication campaigns. It is so successful because of television sets, which blare a constant stream of Midwestern Newspeak in Southern homes, twenty-four hours a day.[6] Defy the Empire and your business associates by boldly and purposefully reclaiming your Southron accent.

VISIT OR ORGANIZE
SOUTHERN HERITAGE FESTIVALS

Around the turn of the century, many fortunate Southerners witnessed the United Confederate Veterans reunions. These were Southern cultural extravaganzas held annually around the South. They featured bands, parades, food, speeches, and a veritable celebration of Southern symbols to honor the remaining Confederate veterans. Each year a different city would host these reunions. Southern cities used all their resources to impress the visiting veterans and their families. These festivals did much to revive the dormant feeling of Southern nationhood in a lost generation.

Today the Southern cultural extravaganza is making a comeback. Throughout the South, such special events are again reviving the hidden spirit of Southern nationhood in a new generation. In a way, battle festivals and living histories started this trend. They quickly turned into reminders of what Southerners once had. Unlike the real battles, these events always had an automatic handicap. There was always a shortage of Yankees. It seems that just as when we played as children, no one wants to be the bad guy. Everyone wants to be a Confederate hero, even when we lose. Many of these special events grew into local festivals celebrating Southern culture and history. Eventually, they overshadowed the twenty or thirty souls shooting blanks at each other on the outskirts of town.

Now, annual Southern culture festivals are springing up all across the South. Despite the objections of the politically correct crowd, these festivals are growing rapidly. At some point during the year, there is usually one within driving distance of most Southern families. Unlike the Empire's bread-and-circuses-type events, Southern cultural festivals are designed for the whole family to enjoy. They are not just a means to separate you from your hard-earned cash. Southern heritage festivals are places to learn what we lost and what we can have again. They are places to feel at home with other Southrons while we learn about ourselves.

Of course, there is no reason to limit the number of existing festivals throughout the South. Each county or parish can have its own. You can also bring a Southern nationalist flavor to any already existing festival. Just add Southern events and booths. Likewise, you can remove the politically correct nature and add Southern nationalism to your county fair.

For the last several years, the Sons of Confederate Veterans and local reenactors have marched in Monroe, Louisiana's annual Mardi Gras parade. This Southern show of force started with just a few dedicated Southrons. Now it involves hundreds. There is nothing but cheers for multiple Confederate battle flags as they flutter in the chill night air on their way down Louisville Avenue. Likewise, Southern nationalists are free to participate in almost any public parade. Federal courts still say that you cannot be excluded.[7] Just remember to include music. Always include Southern music. The strains of "Dixie" always mixed well with cheers.

DEVELOP SOUTHRON ORGANIZATIONS
AND COALITIONS

As we drive forward into our future, Southrons must get organized and remain active. This is one of our weak points. It has enabled the Empire and the left wing to run over us for decades now. We cannot fight and defeat opponents who are more prepared to fight than we are. We have a strong base, but until we organize on a large scale, we will remain second-best. As with any fight, in the battle for Southern nationhood second place is reserved for the loser.

A good beginning would be to start local chapters of pro-Southern organizations. You might shy away from this idea because you think it is difficult or that you do not have the time. Looking below the surface, you will find that the national organization will be happy to help by lending its expertise and support. Start by forming a chapter to cover a four- to five-county area. Then, work and grow the organization until you have several members from each county. When that is accomplished, split the group into county chapters. As you grow, maybe you can further divide into community chapters.

While you grow, look for recruits and allies in other organizations devoted to similar causes, such as tax reform, the Second Amendment, or one of the third parties. Finding allies is especially important because it allows us to form coalitions to fight for Southern nationalist issues. This is another thing that Southerners have long ignored, much to our detriment. As we build broadbased coalitions and teams of organizations, we gain more strength and more political influence.

A good step forward was the first Confederate Summit, held at New Albany, Mississippi. There, representatives from almost every pro-South and Southern nationalist organization met and came to a consensus called the "New Albany Declaration." (See Appendix B) Another bold step forward is the tentative formation of a Confederate Alliance, as a league consisting of most pro-South organizations.

In addition, Southrons must learn to network with other independence movements around the world. In the U.S., that means the Alaskan and Hawaiian independence movements. In the outside world, we can learn much from the Quebecois and the Scottish nationalists. We have much besides good will to share with these movements. We can share information, strategies, and techniques. We can delight in their successes as they delight in ours.

A good example of one of those successes was the Hawaiian apology resolution that Emperor Clinton recently signed into law.[8] While this gave a boost to the Hawaiian Nation, it also made the road for Southern nationalists that much easier. If we organize more and work harder, we will see that we are that much closer to our freedom when Washington finally offers us an apology. It is coming. Just wait and see. One of the Empire' s great hypocrisies is that they think an apology makes everything right and erases the wrong forever. Southrons will show them the error of their ways.

USE THE CONVENTIONAL MEDIA

When we see Southern nationalism in the news, we know things are happening. Southern nationalists must learn to be heard and seen. We have already had some successes. Most major newspapers have run a story relating to Southern nationalism in the last four years. We have had some bad press, to be sure, but public response is usually positive. Exposure in the news brought many new recruits to the cause. Especially effective were the stories and articles that ran in the *Washington Post* and the *Wall Street Journal.*

Getting in the news is more art than science. It is public relations. Because of the left-leaning slant of most news stories, we know that the left is good at public relations work. They have been for years. Now, traditional Southerners are beginning to learn the art. Pro-Southern organizations have been blessed. We have some talented individuals who have done well as amateur public relations specialists. The rebirth of the SCV and the wide exposure given to the League of the South are prime examples of our ability to learn from adversity.

Sometimes getting coverage is as easy as writing a press release. This is something that few people know how to do. The rarity of these skills is why a few people seem to hold a monopoly on what we see and hear daily. Writing a press release is a skill that should be basic training for every Southern nationalist. Likewise, local chapters of pro-Southern organizations need to learn just who the media are in their area. It is a surprise to find how few people know just how many news outlets their area has. Most small local newspapers are happy to print stories on special events. Likewise, most television and radio stations announce public events as a portion of their community service requirement. These announcements are free publicity on the local level, but always reach for more. Learn the fine art of being heard and seen.

As the cause grows, our exposure will need to grow also. Eventually, a Southern nationalist organization or a coalition of organizations will have to look at hiring a professional public relations team. An important responsibility for them is to recognize that this new expenditure is an investment, not a cost. More exposure means more recruits, more strength, and more money. That is the goal of public relations for any organization. To reach that goal, we may need to hire a helper who has mastered of the art of being heard and seen. Professionals know that if you don't like the news, you can go out and make it yourself. In our case, we are not just making news. We are making history.

DEVELOP ALTERNATIVE SOUTHRON MEDIA

Because we get such a bad rap from conventional media, Southerners need to develop an alternative to conventional media.

Some prominent Southerners belittle alternate media development as a waste of time, with little return for the effort or the expense. However, alternative media actually makes our other efforts more cost-effective. Why withhold a dollar to save a nickel in the short term, especially if the return on your investment is much higher than the original dollar? As with public relations, we must recognize alternative media as an investment in our future. We can begin its development now, or be forced to do it later, when the cost is much higher.

The information superhighway was one of the first alternative media to be exploited by Southern nationalists. The League of the South pioneered this effort through the hard work of George Kalas, one of its early members. In early 1996, there was only one Southern nationalist site on the Internet. Now there are too many to track. Unlike most of the fluff that crowds the net, most Southern Internet sites are well designed, informative, and entertaining. Like the original pioneers that built the South, a brave few Southerners are pioneering the electronic world.

Another electronic frontier that Southrons are blazing a trail through is radio. Over the past few years, there have been several Southern nationalist radio pirates. Now the South is riding high on the legal airwaves. A few years ago, conservative and constitutionalist talk shows staked our initial claim on A.M. radio. Now there is a genuine Southern nationalist radio program, *Dixie Rising*. It also broadcasts over the Internet.

An even greater stride forward would be for a pro-South organization to set up a Southern radio network, using repeaters and satellite transmission, like the American Family Association did with American Family Radio. In less than a decade, AFR has grown to serve thirty-four states and Canada.[9] It is a very cost-effective operation, since it is listener-supported and self-financed. Beginning with the college towns and larger cities of the South, our "Radio Free Confederacy" could grow a similar revival of Southern nationhood. Our network could play country music until midnight and Southern rock from there until morning. Additionally, the network could take advantage of advertising from traditional Southron-owned businesses. AFR was the dream of just one man, until he shared his dream with others. Radio Free Confederacy could start as the work of a team.

As with radio, Southern nationalism first caught the attention of smaller publishers. It even spawned a few publishing houses dedicated to the Southern cause. Now larger international publishing

houses such as Pelican are taking notice. Why? Southern nationalism is a sure sale. An entire nation wants to see its name in print.
Likewise, the Southern cause has its modern periodicals. The Sons
of Confederate Veterans resurrected the old *Confederate Veteran*
magazine of the UCV in the 1980s. That was a solid beginning. Now
we have several excellent magazines such as *Southern Heritage* and
the more literary *Southern Partisan*. Several far-sighted Southerners
have also begun the first Southern nationalist newspaper, the
Edgefield Journal, in Edgefield, South Carolina.

The road of alternative media is open to the message of
Southern nationalism. We are already accelerating down that road,
regardless of the Empire's posted speed limit. As technology brings
new forms of entertainment and information transfer, the Southern
Nation will blaze those trails also. Our message will get out. Like
old black axle grease, Southern nationhood is a message that sticks
to all that get next to it.

DEVELOP FUNDING FOR SOUTHRON CAUSES

Often the limit of any effort' s success is the limit of its funding.
This is a sad but true secret. It is impossible to buy advertising space
without the bucks. Southern nationalist and pro-South organizations are masters of making the most out of every dime. We have
had surprising success with our low-budget campaigns. Each of
these successes also increased our exposure in both conventional
and alternative media, in turn bringing in more funds. Still, we
have more to learn. Sadly, often we find that the final line drawn in
the sand is the bottom line.

As means of gaining more funds, we can use the same media that
we use to spread the message of Southern nationhood. We can post
appeals on the Internet. Organizations can place advertisements in
newspapers and pro-South magazines. As we develop Southern
national radio, we can take to the airwaves in search of funds. In
addition, we must look to the possibility of corporate sponsorship.

Read the book *Patterns of Corporate Philanthropy*. There you will
get an idea of some of the outlandish causes that large corporations
give large sums of money to. You will agree that a real cause like
Southern nationhood needs some of their funds also. For this reason, it is in our best interest to organize aggressive campaigns to
solicit donations from major corporations, especially those that
bleed our Southern Nation of its natural wealth.

We can also cross our borders when asking for money. Most major secession movements use funds from both internal and external sources. Mainly Irishmen living in America funded the Irish independence movement. Why? They were the only Irishmen with any money. They gave it freely from 1840 to 1920, in an effort to free their captive homeland.[10] Likewise, Afghanistan's resistance to Soviet aggression was mostly funded by the outside world. Most of the donations came from citizens of Middle Eastern nations, but many Americans gave freely through the Afghan Freedom Fighters Fund. Many people of Europe admire the Southern cause. They would be happy to donate to a Southern Freedom Fighters Fund. So would the descendants of our exiled brethren in Brazil, the Confederados. Just like the Irish, they still have a natural hereditary affection for their ancestral Southern cause. As long as foreign money is not used for politics, there is no restriction on foreign donations.

These funds can be used to support the cause of Southern nationhood in many ways. We could develop subsidies for Southern art and literature. The same funds could also establish and grow alternate Southern educational institutions. Such a nest egg could keep those institutions independent of federal money and therefore independent of federal control. Further, we could give grants to Southern small business. This would keep Southern inventors and entrepreneurs out of hock to the Empire's Small Business Administration. It would free Southern genius to work miracles and develop Southern wealth while the money stays home. The new wealth might bring an infusion of hope to the war zones that we call cities. Developing these sources of funds is yet another way of breaking the chains of dependence that bind Southrons to the Empire.

FORM SOUTHERN AID SOCIETIES

Southrons know that charity begins at home. We have never been shy about giving to a worthy cause. Sometimes we gave money. Other times we gave blood, as in 1861-1875. The South is well known as the most charitable portion of the Empire. In many cases, this knowledge is used to bilk Southerners out of their hard-won cash. Many official and respected charities use very little of the money they collect for its intended purpose. This outrageous but true form of fraud is all the excuse we need to form alternate Southern charities and aid societies. These would be charitable institutions with an honorable Southern tradition of fiscal responsibility.

Since charity begins at home, Southern aid should also begin locally. We have always had a proud tradition of helping those less fortunate. We started long before Washington got into the charity business. We should continue to do so. There is no reason for a Southern nationalist or pro-Southern organization not to hold a holiday food drive for the needy members of their community. One local Confederate group in southern Arkansas even cut firewood for their elderly neighbors when its members learned of the money that some extortionists asked per cord. They dumped their loads of wood in the middle of the night at the elderly person's home, along with a note announcing that the firewood was a gift from fellow Southrons who cared. This should remind us that charity is good public relations, even when news of your kindness spreads only by word-of-mouth. In this case, the message is that the South can take care of its own, without the artificial help of the Empire.

There are many forms of charitable pursuits to be handled on the local level. Aid to the needy, sick, or elderly is just a small example. Using the power of the Southern mind, we can invoke the warmth of the Southern heart to carry the positive message of Southern nationhood. Try visiting the sick or those confined to the human warehouses that the establishment terms "nursing homes." These residents can always use a fruit basket to brighten their holidays. Local pro-South organizations can always pay a deserving student's college tuition for a small sacrifice of fund-raising time. Don't think that student won't remember who helped when he needed it most.

In addition, we need to incorporate large-scale Southern charitable institutions of our own. There are many various fields open to our charitable pursuits. Already mentioned are scholarship funds and aid to the needy. There are children's hospitals throughout the South that need our support. Medical research into typically Southern problems needs to be done. There are also starving children in our own states who need help just as much as the children of Africa. While the Empire propagandizes sending our dollars overseas, we can help our own instead. Remember, charity begins at home.

PARTICIPATE IN SOUTHERN
PROTESTS AND DISPLAYS

Turn on the network news almost any evening and you will usually find that someone, somewhere, is protesting something. The politics of protest are an integral part of the American scene. Those who stage these protests over what might seem to be silly causes know that if they plan, do their homework, and contact the right people, they stand a good chance of seeing their message plastered across the evening news.

Many Southerners are not comfortable with the idea of protesting. They think of unlawful, violent demonstrations, such as the Vietnam War protests of the 1960s and 1970s. Those memories create a distasteful image in many minds. However, the South needs peaceful demonstrations, not riots. Unlike the liberal yahoos we always see on the news, most Southerners are also too busy making a living to fly off to Neverland in defense of endangered snails. We can achieve greater participation from our own citizens by coordinating times and locations of protests, through the leadership of our pro-South organizations.

There should be at least two major protests per year for the cause of Southern nationhood. A good example of a current special event for the purpose of exposure and protest is the annual "Martyrs' Day" parade and rally, held in Kentucky. Set annual events are good, but in other cases, the element of surprise is desirable for maximum effectiveness. What might happen if an average-looking boatload of tourists in Charleston, South Carolina was to disembark and suddenly sit down in the middle of Fort Sumter? They might refuse to leave for some specified length of time, in protest of Northern aggression and continued meddling. Of course, this would only be a surprise to the National Park Service, since the media would have been informed about the protest just in time to cover the event.

There are certain rules to keep in mind about protests. Always dress in a respectable manner. Likewise, conduct yourself in a respectable manner. Always have a plan. Then stick with that plan. Start with the message or sound bite you want to get across, then plan your protest backward from there. Learn from the Left. They have been conducting successful protests for years. Many groups, especially the environmental watchdog groups, post instructions for carrying out successful protests on the Internet. Usually these manuals are complete with checklists of things to do and how to handle the media to achieve maximum coverage.[11] All of this is new to most Southrons. To get our message heard and get the maximum benefit from our efforts, traditional Southerners must learn to do what other nationalities have already learned to do well.

ESTABLISH A SOUTHERN
NATIONALIST POLITICAL PARTY

Once the South's solid support for the Democratic Party earned us the nickname "The Solid South." This is amazing, considering that the Democratic National Party abandoned us for the flavor of black votes in 1948. Then later, after Southerners begged their way back in, they gave us the boot in 1968, as Southern conservatives were ejected in favor of Yankee liberals.[12] Recently the Solid South has been a Solid Republican South, especially during the GOP revolution of 1994. Unfortunately, the Republican National Party has rejected the principles that Southrons revere. Since the Republicans have abandoned us, the Solid South is again in search of a political home.

This leads many Southerners to believe that the time has come to establish a Southern nationalist political party. We must face many challenges for a Southern party to merely exist. For such a party to succeed, it must first develop a wide base of support. It would, of course, need to be representative of a conservative, pro-family, and states' rights constituency. A Southern nationalist party would actually have to deliver on the promises that the GOP has reneged on since 1994. Likewise, for our party to succeed it would need to appeal to the same white Southern support base that the Republicans abandoned in November 1998. This means addressing issues such as immigration, gun control, an unfair tax system, and rampant Big Brother-type government. With attention to the real issues, hard work, and dedication, we might possibly gain a balance of power in some local and state elections.[13]

There have been two or three attempts at forming such a Southern political party. While some attempts were serious, others were not. In one spurious instance, the members even refused to sign their names to their own writings. Maybe this will change. The new Southern Party made its debut in August 1999. As it grows and develops, its shows promise of being a viable political outlet for traditional Southern voters. One possible way the Southern Party could initially gain impact would be to merge the existing membership of the other, less-effective Southern nationalist parties. Then we could try to place a candidate on the presidential ballot as a protest vote. This is the same strategy used by several small parties, such as the Green Party. Such a Southern protest might amass more than one million Southern votes.[14] That is a sizeable protest, but it is a technique that some complain would withhold votes from what might be an important candidate.

Another option would be to work through the structure of an existing third party, such as the Reform Party, the Libertarian Party, or the U.S. Taxpayers Party. While the electoral system is rigged in favor of the two main political parties, the Reform Party has sometimes managed to overcome the odds and knock a dent in the two-party cartel. One recent example was the election of retired professional wrestler Jesse Ventura as governor of Minnesota. Still, such upsets are exceptions to the rule. The more practical hope for a third party would be to gain several seats in Congress. There, they could wage a campaign of obstruction like Irishman Charles Stewart Parnell once did. Parnell almost owned the British Parliament at the turn of the century.[15] In any event, it is certain that Southrons must find a political home that will not betray our trust. Until we do, politics will be one field that we desperately need to redevelop. It is a field we cannot afford to neglect, since it is a key to our release from the Empire.

––––

As you read over these tools to further our future, notice that some are already under development. Many Southerners already have the attitude of defiance. This attitude spreads rapidly through our people with each new imperial atrocity. This same attitude of defiance is fueling the rebirth of our Southern language and its accompanying accent. Southern heritage festivals are springing up across the South at an increasing rate. Southern nationalist and pro-South organizations are developing their base and uniting through conferences like the Confederate Summit and the newly formed Confederate Alliance.

Southerners are learning to be heard and seen using conventional media. As shown by Southern national radio, the new Southern nationalist newspaper, and our use of the information superhighway, we are also making great strides forward in developing our alternative media. This will be a Southron media, free from imperial censorship. In the area of fundraising, several pro-South organizations now receive percentages from credit card companies and long distance services. Southern aid societies are also off to a start. The protests to keep the Confederate battle flag on the

Georgia state flag and atop the statehouse dome in Columbia, South Carolina, as well as Kentucky's annual "Martyrs' Day" event, show that at least part of the Southern population is learning new ways to stand up for our Southern Nation. As time progresses, Southerners will also find an eventual home in the form of a Southern political party.

The further development of these tools will be our guide to the future progress of the Confederate movement. In fact, we will be able to tell how close the Southern Nation is to its final goal of freedom from imperial domination by the development of these tools. When they are in place, we will be upon the threshold of the dream of our great-grandparents. Our Southern people will be that much closer to winning the Southern dream. We can only build the future, if we dare to dream the future.

TEN SOUTHERN THINGS TO DO

1. Develop the attitude of Southern defiance.
2. Speak and write the Southron language.
3. Visit or organize Southern heritage festivals.
4. Develop Southron organizations and coalitions.
5. Use the conventional media.
6. Develop alternative Southern media.
7. Develop funding for Southern causes.
8. Form Southron aid societies.
9. Participate in Southron protests and displays.
10. Establish a Southern nationalist political party.

CHAPTER XI

The Greatest Conquest

No sceptre or throne, nor structure of the ages, nor broad empire, can compare with the wonders and grandeurs of a single thought.   Albert Pike[1]

It is an often-neglected law of nature: What we think determines who we are. It determines what we do and whether what we do is good or bad. Our minds often even predetermine whether we win or lose. You can blame whomever you want to for your shortcomings, but like it or not, sometimes we are the ones who are the most to blame for our failures. You are what you are because of the thoughts that dominate your mind. You can accept it or not. That is just the way the mind and the world work.

Many times, we can tell the outcome of any contest before it begins. Just observe the attitudes of the participants. The end result of a spelling bee, a ball game, or even a war often depends not on the will to win, but the belief that a person, team, or cause can win. History demonstrates this tendency many times. A disappointment in any kind of struggle is often the result of an avoidable loss of faith. It is the same in the South as anywhere else. That is why July 1863 was the month we lost our freedom.

For most of May and all of June 1863, General John Pemberton's small Confederate Army of 30,000 men faced what he suspected was 100,000 federal troops across the trenches of Vicksburg, Mississippi. His men valiantly fought off every attempt the invader made at storming their works, but the losses were heavy on both sides. Pemberton and his men did not have to be in this situation. Twice Pemberton disobeyed orders to hurl Grant's invaders back across the Mississippi River before they got a solid foothold. When he finally did act, Pemberton left half his troops in Vicksburg, while his junior officers lead doomed defenses at Port Gibson and Baker's Creek. In the latter battle, an entire Confederate division found itself cut off from the retreat route back to Vicksburg. Through the skillful leadership of its commander, the division escaped northward, ending its part in the campaign. Due to his lack of resolve, Pemberton suckered himself into a siege before the Yankees were even in front of his trenches. Now, he and his men faced a more dangerous situation. Hemmed in by Grant's well-reinforced army, the risk was much greater than the active defense he was ordered to lead in the first place.

Because of Pemberton's lack of faith and strategy, the citizens, as well as the garrison of Vicksburg, suffered. The constant pounding of the Yankees' heavy guns sapped the strength of Confederate soldier and civilian alike. Further, the Yankee gunners were indiscriminate about their targets. They fired on groups of women and children leaving church just as quickly as they did gray-clad soldiers. Food supplies ran short, but the men wearing the gray still had plenty of fight left in them.[2]

Mentally, John Pemberton succumbed long before the troops under his command. Hoping to receive better terms from Grant, he chose to surrender on the fourth of July. The troops cursed their general for giving in so easily. As the soldiers saw it, Pemberton betrayed the sacrifice of their many dead and wounded comrades. The civilian population of Vicksburg was equally upset. Many remembered that Pemberton was born up North and speculated that his curious surrender on the fourth was an act of treason. In all fairness to Pemberton, his problem was probably the same curse that haunted him throughout his military career—he consistently lacked faith in himself and his troops.

Outside Jackson, Mississippi, General Joseph Johnston readied a large Confederate force to relieve Vicksburg. News of Pemberton's surrender reached him just as the columns readied to move. Johnston was livid. The relief of Vicksburg would surely have been an epic feat of military history. Trapping Grant between two armies deep inside Confederate Mississippi would leave the Federals little choice but to abandon their siege, along with most of their heavy guns. Grant's only escape route led deeper into hostile country. Any of the options open to Grant would have disastrous results to at least part of his command. Had Pemberton held Vicksburg one week longer, the war in the west might have ended with a decisive Confederate victory. History does not record what General Johnston's exact words were when he was informed of Vicksburg's fall, but most likely those words were not suitable for delicate ears.[3]

Further down river, at Port Hudson, Louisiana, General Franklin Gardner and his Confederate force faced even more lopsided odds than Pemberton. Since, May 21, his 6,500-man army had resisted valiantly against 35,000 Federals under General Nathaniel Banks. Unlike his Vicksburg counterpart, Gardner obeyed his orders. Overwhelmed, his men were driven back to Port Hudson and trapped against the Mississippi. His men foiled every attempt the Yankees made to storm the Port Hudson defenses. As the Federals crept close, taking cover in galleries made of cotton bales, the Confederates used their creativity. They burned out their attackers, firing flaming arrows from hastily constructed bows. When rifle ammunition ran short, they picked up spent Yankee bullets, melted them down, and molded more. When artillery ammunition ran short, the defenders gathered the Yankee shot and unexploded shells that littered the ground inside their works. They distributed the missiles to their guns according to the proper size and promptly returned them to their original owners.[4]

Though the battle at Port Hudson was the longest siege ever to take place on American soil, the defenders still had plenty of fight left. Nevertheless, when word of Vicksburg's fall reached Gardner on July 8, all hope was lost. Soon even more Federals would arrive to push his Confederates into the river. Unlike Pemberton's choice, Gardner's decision to surrender was the humane thing to do for his men.

At the same time that Pemberton was contemplating surrender, General Robert E. Lee's Army of Northern Virginia was in a fight for its life at Gettysburg, Pennsylvania. Neither side had wanted a fight at this particular place, but they got all the fight they could ever want anyway. Lee fought blind. The early troop movements cut off the Confederate cavalry under J. E. B. Stuart from the main force. This isolated Lee from any knowledge of his opponent's movements. Even worse, this was the army's first major battle without General Thomas "Stonewall" Jackson. His accidental death at Chancellorsville drained much of the spirit from the Confederate force. The largest land battle ever fought in North America raged for three days, with staggering losses to both sides. In the end, Lee's troops withdrew. They were beat up, but they were still an army.

These defeats in the field were major setbacks to the Southern cause, but they were not the end. By themselves, these losses were not even the turning point. The real disaster was not the stacking of arms along the Mississippi. The disaster was not the blood trail that Lee's men left as they trudged back to Virginia. The real disaster came about a week later, as type was set and presses rolled. That was the real turning point. The newspapers spread hope in the North and despair in the South.

It was not Robert E. Lee's fault. The Army of Northern Virginia recuperated and proved it could still win battles. Similarly, the armies from Port Hudson and Vicksburg reorganized and merged into the Army of Tennessee and the Trans-Mississippi Department. They worked wonders under competent leadership. While Braxton Bragg's lack of faith transformed the triumph of Chickamauga into the debacle at Chattanooga, the survivors of the same army performed miracles when led by Joseph Johnston. Military science teaches us that the attitude displayed by the commander usually determines the attitude of his troops. However, the future of the whole hinges upon the attitude of the nation.

While it is true that the setbacks of July 1863 were tragic, they were not final. Until the newspapers reached their readers, the Southern attitude was one of victory through perseverance. Then, in one week the Southern outlook decayed. The news of July poisoned the soul of the Confederate States of America. Southerners began to lose their faith that we would ultimately win. They deprived themselves of their edge. July 1863 was the month we lost, but it was in the second week, not the first. That was the week we lost the war.

The decisive difference was the change in public attitude. These losses caused the Southern home front to seriously entertain the possibility of losing for the first time. Likewise, the same events gave the North their first vision of hope. As negative reports spread and fed the fear, a cloud of despair settled over the South. The gloom stifled and choked the life out of the Confederacy. As the cloud shut out the light of hope, the new lack of faith sowed the seeds of defeat. The change in attitude was more effective than Lincoln's blockade at beating the South. No one is defeated until he accepts defeat as reality. The loss of the War for Southern Independence was a defeat of the Southern mind.

Defeats of the mind are just as potent and often even more powerful than defeats in the field. This is because the human mind is the most powerful weapon available to man. Like any sword, the mind has two cutting edges. The mind can generate victory out of defeat, but it can also transform triumph into disaster. Beginning with the debacles of July 1863, the North took the Southron's most powerful weapon, his mind, and turned it against him. For nearly a century and a half, it has been a very effective strategy. We are totally blown away by our own thoughts.

The mind is a most effective weapon. Our thoughts are its ammunition. As with any weapon, the mind does not discriminate how it is used. Absent a strong conscience, our weapon willingly serves evil as quickly as good. Probably the low point in the history of human mental capacity was the German Nazi regime of the 1930s and 1940s.

On the other hand, the human mind has had its high points too, with some prime examples being the emergence of Greek democracy and the beginnings of the original Roman Republic. However, even in the same era as great mental strides, the fallibility of the mind without strong moral guidance is clear. The European Renaissance saw great leaps forward in art and science, as well as the beginnings of the Protestant Reformation. At the same time, humanity sank to typical lows with the corrupt antics of Pope Alexander VI and the rest of the Borgia family.

Like any carelessly wielded weapon, an irresponsibly used mind is easy to turn against its bearer. This flip-flop is a classical tactic used by conquerors. Through propaganda and force, they turn the minds of their captive nations into weapons of pacification. This keeps the peasants docile and easy to rule. The American Empire is especially efficient at subverting the native mind. The imperials waste no effort to keep Southrons in their place. They offer unjust social engineering in the guise of jurisprudence, force under the camouflage of statesmanship, and propaganda through an illusion of education. According to the imperials, the South is a bastard stepchild in need of enlightenment. Our people are ignorant, barefoot racists. Our native culture is backward. The Empire further declares our heritage and philosophy of life evil, our religion fanatical and extreme. Using their proven, winning strategy, they take the Southerner's most powerful weapon and club him with its blunt end.

Today, increasing numbers of Southrons realize that the Empire's criticisms are all a passel of lies. We know that the sound bites just aren't so. This knowledge is what our captors fear most.

They know that once we commoners know the truth, their days are numbered. When Southerners refuse to believe their lies anymore, it is the end of the Yankee Empire. Truth is nourishment for the mind. Southrons are tired of junk food. Our minds crave a more balanced diet.

Remember what the Kennedy brothers wrote, "You are not free because you do not believe you can be free."[5] The mind is the most precious resource of a captive people, but to be of value the mind must be strong. Like any other organ or muscle, our minds need food and exercise. Just like lifting weights to develop our biceps, we must develop our minds to perform at their full potential, lifting heavier concepts, pulling deeper thoughts, and throwing larger ideas. When your mind operates at full potential, you think at maximum power, using magnum creativity.

René Descartes, a great thinker of the European enlightenment, declared, "I think. Therefore, I am."[6] Descartes understood thought. He knew that thought is a form of energy, just as heat or electricity. Recognizing that applied energy is force, Descartes reasoned the same laws that rule the other forces of the universe govern the application of thought. Descartes knew that thought, correctly applied as any other force, yields power, and with it the ability to do work.

Descartes also used his logic and reason to prove the existence of God. Beginning with the logic of Descartes, we can apply our own Southern brand of reasoning and prove the existence of our Southern Nation.

> I think. Therefore, I am.
> We think. Therefore, we are.
> We think we are a nation. Therefore, we are a nation.
> We think our nation can be free. Therefore, our nation can be free.
> We think our nation will be free. Therefore, our nation will be free . . .

This little play on words is the other side of the imperial broken record. A healthy chain of thought like this is the kind of attitude our oppressors fear. When we dare to think contrary to the Empire's imposed line of thought, we break the mental chains that hold us captive. We unleash our dormant power. Our rulers know that where the mind goes the body follows. That is why they stress the supposed impracticality and foolhardiness of Southern nationhood. They fear the release of our natural Southern genius.

Southern genius? Yes, there is such a thing, and our people have it in abundance. Genius is simply the use of the mind at above-average levels. Most Southrons already do this as a by-product of our culture. It is a necessity while simply trying to survive in the world of the Empire. Most scientists agree that few humans ever use more than 10 percent of the potential of their minds. They also agree that the great geniuses of history had brains with little if any difference from that of the average human. The brain of Albert Einstein has been studied by every means possible. While scientists have found some differences between his brain and the average brain, Einstein's brain still worked much the same way yours does.[7]

Thought is a glorious capacity. Thinking elevates the soul. Our higher thought capabilities give only men, among all other animals, the ability to commune with God. This ability is the key that unlocks the treasures of the universe. The energy directed by a single thought sometimes produces greater results than a revolution. The sermons of Martin Luther yielded greater conquests than the armies of Alexander or Julius Caesar. Peter the Hermit never held a political office, but he almost single-handedly united all of Europe and launched the Crusades. On the other hand, James II was driven from his throne by little more than a silly drinking song. A thoughtful mind is truly a dangerous implement.

The difference between you and the great thinkers of history is a simple, almost absurd truism: Since the great minds had no more mental capacity than the average man did, they used more of what they had. They took advantage of more of their minds' potential. They did not settle for a mere 10 percent. From the invention of the wheel to the discovery of DNA, people who refused to impose limits on their capacity for thought accomplished the great achievements of mankind. Civilization advanced because a select few people refused to accept the standards of ignorance embraced by science and so-called learned society in their day. As Galileo found, even if his body was in chains, his mind could still be free.

Boundaries to thought are boundaries to achievement. A man can be no more than his mind says he will be. This is an accepted fact, even in the least mental of activities. Whether you, your peers, or imperial society set your boundaries matters little to your mind.

Those boundaries are still mental chains that imprison the potential of a man's thoughts. They are the limit of all he will ever be.

All limits and mental chains are frustrating. It is dangerous to curtail man's potential for thought. Like a baby shark in a ten-gallon aquarium, the confinement suppresses man's growth. Frustrate man's growth and the result is "bonsai man," his whole existence contorted to serve the wires and pruning of his gardeners. Thus limited, our bonsai man turns to destructive pastimes as a substitute for achievement. Instead of applause, he seeks drugs alcohol, and gangs.

Visit any prison. You will find that the career-criminal convict population has an average IQ of 92. That figure is ten points below the average for law-abiding people.[8] Still, a portion of the convict population is of above average in intelligence. They could have been doctors. They could have been teachers. Maybe some could have been bankers or brokers who would have handled far more money by honest means than they ever could by stealing. Instead of a productive life, the inmate chose a life of crime. Some were told by a parent or other respected authority figure that was all that they would ever be, that they would never amount to anything. Some lacked a good example or shunned moral guidance. Others believed they were too smart to get caught. Ironically, their destructive behavior robbed them of their intelligence. A policeman of average intelligence found it easy to catch many of them. What separates these wasted lives from productive citizens is a tall concrete wall, razor wire, and the misuse they made of their potential. Knowledge and reason is corrupt without faith and a moral conscience. The convicts' real imprisonment began when they accepted negative influences in their lives.

Repeated exposure to negative influences is poison to the mind and the soul. Today's constant bombardment of filth and despair imbeds itself deep within your subconscious mind. When least expected and least needed, it pops back to the top in the conscious mind and, if allowed, will steer our course through life. This is why television is so devastating to children. It ruins adults, also. In the modern empire, Jerry Springer is our guru. Howard Stern is our spiritual advisor. Both preach sermons of debauchery and destruction, with occasional breaks to advertise the latest psychic hotline. Instead of uplifting us, media brings us down to the level of the least, commonest denominator of imperial society. We were warned to resist this onslaught by the Bible. The false prophets of materialism, perverts, and psychics we willingly expose ourselves to will be our undoing. We would do well to remember God's warning.

> There shall not be found among you any one that maketh his son or his daughter to pass through the fire, or that useth divination, or an observer of times, or an enchanter, or a witch,
>
> Or a charmer, or a consulter with familiar spirits, or a wizard, or a necromancer.
>
> For all that do these things are an abomination unto the Lord: and because of these abominations the Lord thy God doth drive them out from before thee.[9]

To get out of a negative rut we must purge the negative from our lives. Just as DDT, negative influences are hard to remove once stored in the body's tissues. They imbed themselves easily into our subconscious minds. The only way to remove negatives is to replace them with positive influences. Unlike negatives, positive influences are hard to install. The brain craves negative influences much as it craves carbon monoxide. Both are equally poisonous. The only way to replace either is by saturation with the life-saving alternative. For carbon monoxide, that means breathing pure oxygen. Likewise, negative influences can only be replaced by a bombardment of positive influences. Read your Bible. Read pro-South literature. Daydream about what a free Southern homeland would be like. Keep that mental image in your mind and think of it when you feel down.

One of the quickest ways that the Yankee establishment casts Southerners into a mental rut is by destroying the Southern self-image. This is another classic tactic of empires, akin to censoring a people's native culture. It is simply another, more covert, form of cultural genocide. Think about it; if the Empire really had our best interest at heart, wouldn't our oppressors avoid this unnecessary drain on Southern humanity? Our true best interests are nowhere in the Empire's concerns or plans. Because people who are down on themselves rarely get up, the destruction of the Southern self-image is a focal point of the Empire's mental war on the South. However, the effects of this type of attack are not permanent unless you want them to be. Developing a positive Southern self-image easily reverses the damage.

Building a positive Southern self-image is the same as building anything else. You must first identify the material you have at hand and what kind of foundation you have to build on. So start by taking inventory. Take a piece of paper and list your assets. Start with your positive qualities. Are you dependable? Are you a hard worker? Do you pay your bills? Do you think ahead? If you do, then write it down. While you are at it, write down all the things that you have accomplished in life. It does not matter how small or trivial you think your accomplishments are. Write them down. Don't just sit down for an hour and zip out your list. Reflect deeply and work on your inventory for several days. Chances are that you will find that you are not as far in the hole as you thought. As the old saying goes, "The Lord didn't make no junk."

Now that you see that you are not a total basket case, you need to reinforce that fact. Start by reading inspirational writings. The stories of people who overcome the odds or succeed in spite of their handicaps are fuel for achievement. Take the counsel of men who build the human spirit, like Dale Carnegie, Zig Ziglar, or Dr. Norman Vincent Peale. There are many from which to choose, so you will never get bored. Also, learn from people who could best be described as successful failures. Babe Ruth struck out more than any other player in Major League Baseball, yet he is still considered a success. Likewise, Mark McGwire and Sammy Sosa also have hefty strikeout percentages. Their lesson is an important one. They failed a lot because they tried a lot. They know that in life as in baseball the only way to avoid failure is to not try. Your success rate is directly proportional to your failure rate. Therefore, to increase your success rate, you actually increase your failure rate. It sounds weird, but you naturally raise both your failure and success rates by trying more. Build your confidence by tackling small tasks first. Then, try for greater challenges.

Another way to improve your Southern self-image is to improve your appearance and your relationship with others. It is no secret that what you see on a person's outside reflects what you will find on his inside. At least, that is the way other people perceive you. So, if you want to be positive and have a healthy Southern self-image, then do your best to look the part. You do not have to overdress. Just be neat and well groomed. Always maintain eye contact with the people you meet and converse with. Don't be afraid to smile. Smiling warms the water more than anything else. In addition, it never hurts to share a judicious compliment with others from time to time. By making others feel better about themselves, you naturally improve your own self-image.

While you are at it, you can make yourself feel even better by devoting some time to the service of others in need. When you help a person who is down, you lift two people up. In today's negative-tainted world, we can always use an extra boost.

As always, there are also things we must be on our guard against. We must avoid harmful, destructive influences. Do not ruin all your hard work on your Southern self-image by accident or through neglect. Because of this, we must be careful with whom we associate. We have all heard of guilt by association. Make sure that you do not entrap yourself. Stay away from those people who always cast a shadow of gloom over everyone around them. You know the type. They have a little dark cloud perpetually hanging around above their heads. Have enough sense to come in out of the rain. Don't let them choke out your sun. Also, avoid those people who constantly demean the value of other people. To make up for their own inadequacies, these twisted individuals try to make sure that no one else rises above their level. If you hang around them long enough, their campaign of sabotage against the human spirit usually succeeds.

Furthermore, avoid anyone who indulges in harmful behavior such as drinking, gambling, drugs, and pornography. There is a reason that such people always invite others to participate. It is because that they know what they are doing is wrong. Naturally, they love a crowd, so they can use the standard excuse that everybody does it. They want you to justify their actions by proving everybody does do it.

Pornography is especially dangerous, because it is a *stealth* vice. It is a simulated experience. Research shows that simulations like pornography cause just as much harm to you as the real thing does. Actually, these simulations are more harmful, since their damage sneaks up on you. Studies show that three simulated experiences carry the same impact as one physical experience.[10] This means that watching the average hardcore porn film is the same as participating in several degenerate sex acts. Similarly, watching the typical Hollywood slasher picture causes your mind and your self-image to experience the trauma of actually witnessing two or three horrible deaths. Unknowingly, you self-inflicted these wounds by doing no more than clicking a remote, buying a ticket, or opening a magazine. Be careful what you feed your mind. You are what you eat.

Climbing out of the imperial mental rut sounds like a lot of work. In fact, it is not. Like any mired vehicle, you expend much more effort by remaining in a rut and spinning your wheels while desperately hoping to get out. Instead, you get nowhere, except into a deeper rut. Anyone finding themselves hopelessly stuck in the mud knows that they will not get going again until their wheels

are out of the ruts and back on solid ground. There is rarely relief
such as that you experience when you finally get traction and start
moving again. After you're moving, just keep it between the ditches
and remember that no one on earth can make you feel inferior to
them without your permission. Never give the imperials that permission. The Southern Nation is a positive place.

While renewing our own Southern self-image is the brick to
build our future, we must go further to ensure the rebirth of our
Southern Nation. We must help our neighbors see the light of a
better tomorrow. We are appointed to the task by our knowing better. We are the ones assigned the responsibility of finally jerking the
stool of everlasting repentance out from under the seat of our
nation. This is not a particularly easy job. Southerners have been
sitting on the stool so long that we have worn it to a comfortable
and familiar shape. Southrons must learn to be more effective at
countering the official imperial propaganda. We must inspire our
people to a new Southern mindset.

The best way to defeat the stigma of Yankee domination is
through leadership. To produce a positive Southern self-image in
our neighbors, we must show them the Southron way. The key to
leadership is a lesson that the sergeants who run the army's Non-
commissioned Officers Schools constantly hammer into their students. They know that the best way to lead is to lead by example. To
lead our fellow Southerners by example, we must show our positive
Southern lives and avoid negative influences. They must see that living the Southern life is living the good life. Become involved in
your community to provide a positive Southern influence. Be active
in your church. Start or help with existing youth organizations such
as the Boy Scouts. Influence and provide sound Southern leadership to the civic groups you attend. Your leadership goes a long way
toward restoring the healthy self-image of the Southern people.

Your example positively affects those who encounter you on a daily
basis, but how do we effect the lives of those that we have little influence over? Sure, our example is important to our peers, but we must
reach more people. How do we show the advantages of Southern
nationhood to the many that we need to reach? This work is designed
for the Concerted Action Team. We know that the battle for Southern
nationhood is a battle for the Southern mind. Our ammunition is
thought. Unlike a soldier's time on the firing range, we do not have to
try for a mental direct hit. Instead, we desire a ricochet that will create

a chain reaction of thought in our desired targets' minds. Because ours is a mental war, the battles are not won by your typical fighting. Our battles are won through hard work. The smarter we work, the less energy we waste and the more battles we win.

The human animal has a herd instinct, like most other mammals. If we lead, someone will follow. Just don't expect them to all try to bust down your door at once. Despite our initial unrealized results, we must continue our work, building positive Southern self-images in those around us. They will in turn spread their new Southern self-images to others. Speaking from experience, this starts out as a lonely job, but so does any other type of reform. However, if you hang in there you will eventually see results far exceeding your expectations. Like the mythical baseball diamond in the middle of the cornfield (or cotton patch in our case), if you build it, they will come.

Sure, we have plenty to overcome in our quest to restore a healthy self-image to the Southern people. It is a lot of work. The Empire purposefully portrays the South as evil. Its media ministry of propaganda assigns our accent to only its most evil or ignorant characters. They miss no trick to show us as barefoot, inbred hicks. The imperial model of a Southerner is that of a hookworm-infested bigot who has carnal knowledge of at least a hundred head of livestock. Through the empire's efforts, Ned Beatty lost much more than his manhood on the Chattooga River.

In chapters seven and eight, we became acquainted with the New Nazarite and the Concerted Action Team. The goal of these developmental programs was to build repeated positive pro-Southern influences in your life and the lives of others. The program in chapter seven clears away the briar patch that repeated exposures to negative influences allowed to grow in your mind. We plant a cash crop instead. The positive influences we purposely provide fertilize that crop so that it outgrows the weeds. As long as we avoid adding any more negatives, we will have a bumper crop at harvest time.

The Concerted Action Team program in chapter eight lets us expand the farm and puts us into the land-clearing business. Positive farming practices are still only part of the solution. While we can rid the soil of its weeds, we still are not using our most fertile soil at its full potential. Thought and a positive Southern self-image are only fuel for our mental tractor. It takes more than fuel to win a tractor pull. We need water, oil, and other lubricants, too.

In the same way, positive thought must be combined with positive emotion to yield the most horsepower.

Thought, when teamed with emotion, gives us an extra boost of power; but not just any emotion will do the job. Positive emotions such as love and faith are the only ones that unleash this power. Negative emotions such as fear and hate sap our strength. A high jumper that fears he will not clear the bar usually doesn't. A child who hates broccoli usually becomes an adult who hates broccoli. It takes positive emotion to get a positive result. Although you may not realize it, you are probably acquainted with this fact already. Its most common example is prayer. Effective prayer is not simply thought pointed at God. Prayer requires thought plus emotion to bridge the gap between the natural and supernatural spheres. Thought combined with a positive emotion such as love is prayer with strength. This is how we come to experience the power of prayer.

> If ye have faith as a mustard seed, ye shall say unto this mountain, Remove hence to yonder place; and it shall remove; and nothing shall be impossible unto you.[11]

Faith is the head chemist of your mind. The same faith unleashes your potential and breaks your chains. No man has to accept artificial limitations. Beethoven was deaf. John Milton went blind. Robert Burns was a drunkard. Still, they unleashed their potential using faith. The whole world is richer due to their triumphs.

When the mind combines positive thought and positive emotion, it operates at a higher potential. We think on a higher level than otherwise possible. Ideas seep into our mind, seemingly from nowhere. This is what is meant by creative thought. The more practice the mind gets at creative thinking, the stronger it becomes, wielding more quality and quantity with each new thought.

Inducing this state of mind is the secret of the great inventors, scientists, and philosophers of history. It really shouldn't be a secret at all. This frame of mind is easy to induce. First, we must find a place and an atmosphere where we can relax and think freely. For many people this is a quiet, dimly lit room. For others, it is a center of activity. Personal comfort and personal preference are really the determining factors. In any event, have a pencil and a piece of paper ready for note-taking.

Second, try clearing the mind of all thought. For a few moments, just blank out everything. This frees up space in the mind for the coming rush of ideas. Third, think warm positive thoughts about a subject or object that induces positive emotion. I know your teacher told you not to daydream, but that is essentially what you want to do in this step. Daydream about something you really love or some goal you long to achieve. This combines thought with emotion and triggers the creative thinking process. Before long, you find yourself thinking vivid, colorful thoughts about your subject. Carefully insert the subject you want to study or the problem you want to solve into the picture and you will find that your thoughts easily switch to that task. Now your thoughts are in high gear. You are using your brain at a greater potential than you would otherwise. With practice, you will find this creative state easier to achieve. You can even change the conditions that trigger the creative state. You will see that it is easy to think creatively. However, there is a way to enhance your mind's potential even further.[12]

Have you ever noticed that you can detect that someone else is having a bad day before you even ask him? That is because your mind senses a limited amount of the activity of other minds. Whether you call it intuition, vibes, or a sixth sense, it happens. It is not as powerful as magicians and mentalists claim, but it is part of human nature, a portion of the grand design of creation. When people work together as a team, this phenomenon is one of the advantages they gain. When team members have a positive mental outlook, that positive mental energy flows and exchanges between the team members' minds. Often people describe it as an electricity in the air. The team feels better and easily accomplishes more. They find that they can do things that they thought were impossible.[13]

Science does not have a ready explanation for this natural synergistic effect. Some scientists deny it even exists. On the other hand, successful business organizations know the laws of physics and use them to their advantage. Many corporations promote brainstorming sessions as a problem-solving tool. Since thought is energy, the collective thought of many minds yields even more energy. As problem-solving groups focus the positive energy of their collective minds on a question, their minds think in unison. They tap a higher creative capacity as they work. Ideas and solutions flow naturally, freely, gaining force and momentum from this habitual inclination of man. Dr. Norman Vincent Peale also noticed this tendency. He found it particularly important in prayer, especially when seeking divine intervention.[14] It is a Biblical truth as well.

> Again I say unto you, That if two of you shall agree on earth
> as touching any thing that they shall ask, it shall be done for
> them of my Father which is in heaven.
> For where two or three are gathered together in my name,
> there am I in the midst of them.[15]

It is no secret that teamwork enhances labor. Likewise, prayer groups find more answers to their requests. The effect works to the same advantage with creative thought. Often we face a dilemma that we just can't reason out as individuals. We know there has to be an answer, but we just can't grasp it. When this happens, do not despair. Just apply the power of creative thought as a team. The team thought process is much the same as it is for an individual desiring greater creative potential.

Just as in the corporate world, brainstorming is our ticket to creative team thought. Start by gathering your team in a quiet calm place. Make sure at least one or two people have a pencil and paper handy to record the ideas. A good start would be to open with a prayer. Strive to induce a positive tone from the start by reminding the participants that every problem is an opportunity in disguise. Then the team members sit and reflect calmly for a while without talking. Identify your problem, separating its different parts and symptoms. Then, just start tossing out ideas and writing them down. Do not discuss the ideas yet. Don't criticize them. Just throw out ideas and write them down.

As more and more ideas flow, the positive mental energy created by the group further stimulates the members' minds. This induces an even higher state of thought as the participants' minds change gears. This natural effect enhances the creative power of the group, as ideas flow faster and more freely. Your alliance of brains taps the divinely provided universal storehouse of knowledge and mental power. When these problem-solving juices start to flow, the dam soon bursts. It floods the room with potential solutions. You will come to feel that there is no problem too big to solve if you use this method.

Before long, you will generate a sizeable list of ideas. Then, slow down and select those ideas that have the most potential for success. Discuss the options and plan in a positive manner. Take possible solutions apart and reassemble them in different ways. See what fits your situation best. From your pool of ideas, develop a plan and a backup plan. If you still do not come up with a workable solution, then break the problem down into smaller components and brainstorm them separately.[16]

Creative thinking, whether done alone or as a team, supercharges man's mental power. The more we use our minds the easier it gets. As we flex our mental muscle, our minds grow proportionately. Usually, modern man is so busy that he neglects to exercise his most powerful muscle. He jogs around all over town while his head turns to flab. This is how we get stuck in a mental rut. It is a shame. The ladder is right there within reach. We just need practice at climbing. Once we learn to climb, we will see how easy it is to soar.

While we plan, we must remember that our main fight is a struggle to eradicate the hollow promises of the Empire's materialist non-culture. In its place, we must restore Southern values, Southern culture. This requires Southerners to make some uncomfortable changes in attitude in the face of imperial opposition. Our struggle is a mastery of what the Eempire claims to be outdated values. Our poor belittled ideals outshine propaganda. These ideals are love, dignity, respect, honor, courage, and truth. The battle of minds is the new field of honor, a humane battlefield absent of bloodshed.

As Southern leaders, we must be the role model for our fellow captives. As said earlier, we must lead by example, but this time lead by group example. Remember that what you show on the outside reflects what you hold inside. Be positive. Radiate hope and confidence. You know we will win; show this knowledge. To a captive people, all problems are opportunities in rude form. You are a salesman selling Southern opportunities. You are selling ideas to a people who do not know that they really want them. Your product is not plastic junk. You are selling ideas that they really do need.

A great way to start your sales pitch is by promoting the display of Southern cultural emblems. The rest of the Empire is deprived. They have nothing to steer by except what Hollywood provides them. We have so much more. No other region of the Empire, except maybe the former Hawaiian kingdom, has its own flag. We have several styles to choose from. At one time, the display of the Confederate battle flag, as well as the first, second, and third pattern Confederate national flags, was illegal. There are no more beautiful flags than those of our Southern Nation. Our Southern Saint Andrew's cross flags are some of the few among the nations of the world that dare to display Christian symbols. Naturally, we should do more to show them off. If we do not, we stand to lose our precious right to display them again.

Our Southern songs are under similar attack. Once, almost every

Southern radio and television station played "Dixie" at sign-on and sign-off. If your local stations do not, call them. Tell them to start again. Don't be afraid to express your feelings. That is what the rebel yell is for. Write letters to the editorial pages of newspapers by the bushel, or even guest columns if you are so inclined. Hold up Southern heroes for the world to see. Men like Davis, Jackson, Forrest, and Lee are role models for the entire world to follow. If you can't stand all those "X" shirts you see being worn about, wear your own, an "L" shirt.

Furthermore, never miss a chance to support your fellow Southron who is doing his part for the cause. Those who stand up for their nation may be tough, they might be rugged individualists, but they are still vulnerable. They need to know they have our appreciation. Many of those radio and television stations that used to play "Dixie" at sign-on and sign-off quit doing so because they got several complaints and not a single "Thank you." It takes much less effort to preserve a tradition than it does to reestablish a tradition. Likewise, it is much more effective to be pro-active than it is to be reactive. Show your support for those brave few who stick their necks out, before complaints lead them to the chopping block.

Especially support political displays of Southern pride. When presidential contender Pat Buchanan laid a wreath at the grave of his Confederate veteran grandfather, the news media immediately trashed him. Liberal spin doctors had a field day.[17] The outcry of support for Buchanan never made the news like the condemnation did. Still, Buchanan saw that he was not alone. His detractors saw this, too. Showing our support for other Southrons encourages others who would never act alone. When you see someone stand up for the South, tell them how much you like it. Their next stand will be even more solid when they are secure in the knowledge that friends stand behind them.

Of course, they have friends. The South is a friendly place—except maybe downtown Atlanta after dark. Regardless of our inner-city jungles, people here still speak and show courtesy to total strangers. This is important. We can show that you get more with the South than other regions. It is easy to see. When was the last time you went to Iowa for your vacation? Nobody does. Instead, people vacation down here. There is nothing up North that anyone wants to see. When you go South, you get family, security, peace of mind, and a promise for the future, as well as a more hospitable climate.

When we gain an independent Southern Nation, we will get those same benefits times ten. Sell this image. It is the real South, not the Northern stereotype.

With the South you get family. Moreover, in the South it is hard to draw the line where family ends and community begins, even in the suburbs of our large cities. In the South, family is the only thing that matters. Tell your children what it was like to have grandparents. Carry them to the old home place on weekends. There, you learned from the old folks about real life in the real old days. Usually, it was around a table heaped with honest-to-goodness Southern food. Help others smell Granny's lovingly baked ham.

With the South, there is security. Even our politics show it. Our legislators have no fear of their constituents. That is, unless that particular politician is up to no good. Our statesmen do not try to grab our guns, because they know we need them. They know that none of us are safe unless we have them. In addition, they know that the South, unlike the rest of the Empire, is ruled by moral consciousness. No Southern politician's career can hope to survive the contempt of his electorate. It was a lesson Bill Clinton pretended to learn in his second term as governor of Arkansas.

Of course, like any other place on earth, we have problems. Unlike other places, most of our problems are either directly caused by or aggravated by the Empire. If we do away with the cause of the problem, most of the symptoms will also disappear. As was the Northern outlook at the founding of the United States, the Yankee Empire's philosophy is still "might makes right." Theirs is a pagan philosophy that Southrons reject. Southerners need fear no one but God.

With the South, there is peace of mind. Our life is a slower pace. We know that things will always happen that are beyond our control, but we can always overcome. The land and the Southern people will still be here after the smoke clears. We may have to repair a little bit after hurricane season, but the rest will grow back with time. Southerners do not need to rush. We just need the basics. If a Southerner does not get the latest mass-produced plastic trinket for Christmas, he knows it is no big deal. There is no need to shoot up the workplace. Our Southern philosophy is that God will provide as long as we do our part. There is no need for worry. Life is to enjoy.

With the South, there is great promise for the future. We are a blessed people. We have everything we need, right here. Few nations can boast of self-sufficiency. We can. Through our self-sufficiency, we can have peace, prosperity, and strength. Long after the rest of the Empire deteriorates into a Northern version of a banana republic, we will be living the Southern dream.

When you have the South, you have it all. That is no exaggeration. You can see all the evidence that plainly lies around you. It is the fabric of dreams. In our case, it is the Southern dream. What we must do now is help others see this bold Southern vision. We must get the word out. Our families, our friends, and all our other Southern neighbors must see the magnificent future that awaits them.

Still, we will never convince some. Do not think that you must convert everyone. Instead, bypass those who refuse to believe. Others hunger for what we offer. Spend your energy reaching those Southerners. You will be surprised how the doubters rise and try to take all the credit later. Strange, but history shows that it always happens that way.

Maybe you could show some of your more reluctant Southern peers what they stand to lose without Southern nationhood. Help them see the future of life in the Empire. Show them a once great empire that must now borrow from its neighbors for its very existence. Show them a superpower that will not allow its armies to win wars. Let them see the big kid in school that all the other kids bow to, then laugh as soon as his back is turned. Remember, that is just the way you used to do the schoolyard bully. In this cased it is not a crudely lettered sign, but a bold, permanent tattoo on his backside that says, "Kick me."

Show them how the third world ducks for cover every time the emperor gets caught with his pants down. The world knows the cruise missiles will fly to divert his subjects' attention. The other nations of the world ridicule the same Empire that ridicules the Southern Nation. They know as Thomas Paine did that oppression only feeds the mental strength of the oppressed. They laugh at the gurgling noises made by Leviathan in his death agonies. The world knows no empire that swallows and holds nations captive against their will has ever survived more than a couple of centuries. Most of them do not last near as long. Our Empire is no different. Why go down with a sinking ship?

The battle for Southern nationhood is foremost a battle for the Southern mind. It is a struggle that the Empire's ministry of propaganda has bet everything to win. They will use every weapon at their disposal to ensure our continued compliance with the imperial regime, because without us there is no more Empire. Then who would pay their salaries? The propagandists' arsenal is a frightening array of weapons, as barbaric and fearsome as anything the North or its politicians could ever come up with. The Empire and its allies control all means of communication, production, and distribution, as well as an education establishment dedicated to furthering the goals of its ruling class. Still, we have the edge. The imperials are paid mercenaries. Ours is an all-volunteer force fighting a battle for freedom against a heretical view of reality.

Southerners know what reality is. We are up to our necks in it. Our reality is low pay and poor working conditions. The current Southern reality is being thankful for substandard housing while we pay for the welfare class and illegal aliens to get their housing built up to code for free. In our reality, someone else determines what our hard-earned dollar buys. The ruling class determines how many Southern sons go to fight, how many don't come back, and even where they are buried afterward. As my community just found out, the Empire even controls who our new neighbors are. Likewise, other Southerners have little control of who their new neighbor is. This is our current reality. Enough is enough. Even Grant and Sherman would lead a rebellion against this regime. It is time for the men and women of the South to stand together and forge a new reality.

Instead, the Yankee establishment wants us to adopt their version of reality. They force us to pay homage to their skewed view everywhere from the home to the school to the marketplace. Their plan hopes to corrupt us into abandoning the Southern view of reality. In their eyes, the emperor is above law. He can lie and creatively parse grammar. Even then, it is not lying, let alone perjury. Their version of reality is a globalist, universalist heresy. Southrons should already recognize it as a physical and spiritual poison. Their ideology hinges on a global political game of Russian roulette. The Southern reality instead is rooted in the Bible and common sense. We find it foolish to throw away what God created and man fought to keep whole. The Southern reality will not yield willingly to concocted multicultural fallacies and fairy tales of a universal world brotherhood.

The Southerner knows that God defines reality. Reality, like truth, is not relative. There is truth and there are lies. Only truth can be reality. Reality is always there in black and white, no matter what the Philosophy Department at Harvard says about gray areas. Reality is harsh, but it is truth. In nature, there are no lies. The real lion king is not fuzzy and warm, nor is he necessarily noble. He is a ruthless predator who feeds off only the weak and helpless. That is his purpose. God made him that way. He reflects reality.

Words also reflect reality. That is why the imperial establishment loves to deface the meaning of words. When they tamper with the meanings of words, they tamper with the commoner's view of reality. That is why the Empire enjoys so-called politically correct speech. Its weak excuses for words distort man's view of reality. Therefore, in imperial jargon, abortion mills become "family planning centers." Those who glorify the murder of unborn babies are "pro-choice." On the other side, those of us who believe only in the Bible-based relationship between man and woman are suddenly intolerant homophobes. This is how the Empire forces its view on its subjects. It is a word game designed to change our view of reality.

There can only be one reality. Still, reality is not a fixed system, except where God's revealed truths are concerned. His moral truths can never be changed. All else—man's political, social, and economic reality—can be changed. This is man's sphere of influence. Man can change his reality for good or bad. A people can change their political systems on a whim. They can wisely or foolishly throw away old customs and institute new ones. Their economic reality can shift with the mood of the nearest banker, but only God can change His reality. Changing the reality of man's sphere is little more than mental warfare. When you win a people's minds, you win the war without shedding blood. As one noble Southron wrote, "The mastery of mind over mind is the only conquest worth having."[18]

THE LOGICAL SOUTHRON WAY OF THINKING

I think. Therefore, I am.

We think. Therefore, we are.

We think we are a nation. Therefore, we are a nation.

We think our nation can be free. Therefore, our nation can be free.

We think our nation will be free. Therefore, our nation will be free . . .

Believe it! Achieve it!

CHAPTER XII

Conclusion:
Deo Vindice Resurgam

> Secession filled me with hope, not as the destruction but as the redemption of Democracy. I deemed that you were fighting the battles of our liberty, our progress, and our civilization; and I mourn for the stake which was lost at Richmond more deeply than I rejoice over that which was saved at Waterloo.
>
> Lord Acton[1]

Even in his last days as one of the South's greatest public servants, Jefferson Davis never lost an attitude of hope for the Southern future. He knew that eventually the Southern cause would prevail. That same attitude of hope is the outlook that Southerners desperately need today. I aimed to fulfill that need from the time I start working on this book. I promised myself that I would do my best to give you hope for the Southern future. While the rest of the American Empire looks back on its best days, we can look forward to ours.

In 1861, the Confederate founding fathers had the same hope for the future that the original American founding fathers had in 1776. Both groups tried their best to transmit that attitude of hope to the nations that they founded. The original founding colonists' plans went astray as greedy men stole the old republic and substituted the American Empire. Likewise, the Confederate founders saw their dream crushed under foot, only to rise again in a new generation. Still, all of them had the same kind of hope that a father has as he sees his new child enter the world. As new fathers fret over what name their children will wear through life, the Confederate fathers concerned themselves with what message of hope they could adopt to inspire their people.

The Confederate founding fathers were especially optimistic with their message of hope. They adopted the motto, *Deo Vindice,* Latin for "God will vindicate." Clearly, the Confederate founders did not expect to lose. They had every reason to look forward to a bright future. Unfortunately, we lost. Tragically for Southerners, our conquest left us stuck with a motto not wholly suitable for a captive nation. *Deo Vindice* is passive. The motto encourages Southerners to set around waiting for a lightning bolt from above to suddenly vindicate our cause and set us free.

It is time for Southerners to shake the cobwebs out of their collective heads. There is no need to sit idle waiting for God to vindicate the Southern cause. He already has. Just look around at all the decay so evident in the American Empire. It seethes with daily corruption from its top to its bottom. Crime is rampant as gangs rule city streets. Even in small towns, drugs and drive-by shootings gradually become normal. The Empire's moral and social stagnation gives off a stench that overrides all the public filth lying beneath the surface. It will only get worse as more of the Empire's corporations ship our jobs overseas. Then our masters will wonder in amazement why we do not have money to buy their products. Turn your nose to the air. Do you smell it? It is the stench of death, the death of the American Empire. The imperial version of an industrial system is failing just as the Fugitives warned in *I'll Take My Stand.*

Southerners, the age of empire is over. God has vindicated your ancestors, your cause, and you. If I have not presented enough evidence to convince you, I'm sorry. Read additional pro-Southern books. Eventually you will be convinced. You will come to the same conclusion as many other Southerners. We are the Southern Nation and we are being dragged to our death as the remains of the American imperial system drowns in its own bodily wastes. A proud and self-reliant people deserve a better fate. That fate is now in your hands. The road to the Southern future is open. Now, what are you going to do about it?

Do you feel like you have been hit with a brick weighted with heavy moral responsibility? You have. I took the same hit on the chin at Smackover, Arkansas in 1992. I faced the same dilemma. I had to decide what to do about the future of my Southern Nation. *How could I help save my people?* Like me, you have five different options. All five hold either promise or consequences. Be sure that you choose wisely.

First, you could do nothing. It doesn't matter whether you dismiss my argument or you just don't care. If you do nothing, or choose not to choose, you have made your choice. The Empire will run its predestined course. Before you commit to option number one, I suggest that you read Thomas Chittum's *Civil War II*. Chittum knows from experience what happens when multi-ethnic empires collapse. Having served in Vietnam with the American army in the 1960s, the Rhodesian Territorials in the 1970s, and the Croatian Army in the 1990s, he is well qualified to tell the tale. It is not pretty. It is usually tragic and bloody. As a rule, all multi-ethnic empires collapse in chaos and misery. From the Babylonian Empire right down to the Soviet Union and the American Empire, it always happens.[2]

Second, you could sit around and wait for further vindication while pursuing change through the Empire's existing two-party system. I hope you don't hold your breath while waiting. Both of the establishment's main political parties have demonstrated many times that they love the imperial system much more than they love you. In any event, it does not matter how hard you try for reform using the existing system; the wheel will roll back around to option number one. If there is any up side to this option, it is this. The results will further prove that the South was right to begin with.

Third, you could immigrate, but where would you go? Switzerland is an option. It is a free county. They understand liberty and limited government, but it is terribly cold there. There is also no promise that the Swiss would welcome immigrants who will not bother to fight to improve conditions in their home country. Why should they? We do not. Immigration is still an option though. If you know of a land of freedom and liberty with more beauty and promise than the South, go for it. Just remember that someday in your Promised Land you will probably wind up fighting the heirs of the American imperial collapse (under options one and two) as they search for greener pastures to pillage.

Fourth, you could resist the Empire using violence. This is always the least promising avenue of resistance. For openers, violence always produces more violence. Usually, innocent people get hurt the worst. Also, remember that violence is bad public relations. When you fight against the system, you need all the support you can muster. Besides, when you adopt the tactics of the Empire, the odds are automatically stacked in the Empire's favor. Expect to be squashed before you get started. Given the Empire's recent brutality toward anyone that espouses politically incorrect beliefs, the use of violence is a poor prospect. I doubt that the victims of Waco would line up to be re-incinerated just to make some weak political statement that no one would ever be allowed to hear.

Your final option is probably the most appealing choice. You can resist the Empire, but resist using your head instead of using bombs. You will find the program for pursuing this option already outlined for you in the preceding pages of this book. Use it to rebuild our Southern Nation the only sure way. This is the same way other captive peoples have rebuilt their nationality; one person at a time, one family at a time, one community at a time. This is the only successful route to peaceful revolution. It is the proven road, pioneered by other captive nations of the twentieth century.

Those are your five choices. They are the very same choices that every other captive nation has faced. Some made their choice wisely, while others did not. Even if Southerners try to avoid making our choice, we will be forced down one of these five roads. Of course, it would be best to choose the least painful route to ourselves now, without coercion later. I have tried to map out that route for you. The initiative is yours now. Choose wisely.

By close attention to the route we choose, we will rebuild our nation not on hatred of the Yankee race, but upon love for our own people. We will seat our bastion of Western Judeo-Christian civilization on the firm soil of our love for our fellow Southrons. That is the only way to really build, because building is a labor of love. This is only fitting, because Southerners are a loving people. From birth, our families teach us to love our neighbor. Our rich culture and heritage naturally endow us with a strong, deep-seated love for our Southern Nation and its traditions. We love our beautiful countryside and are most at home when we are close contact with God and nature. Our adoration extends even to the sweetness of the Southern air we breathe. Because of all this, we revere and love our Creator even more. He chose to bless us with this bountiful land and its people. As Dr. Michael Hill, president of the League of the South, said, " Our dream will be made real only when we love each other enough to die for each other."[3]

Part of finding that love are our efforts at rebuilding our Southern nationality. It also involves rekindling that familiar Southern fire that lives in all of us. So, when the Empire or one of its privileged groups demand that we remove a Confederate battle flag or a monument to our fallen heroes, there is a simple solution. Take the advice of one of the few honorable men who have ruled over the Empire and just say, "No." When the Empire orders that we give up a Southern tradition, the answer should be another automatic, "No." When they tell us to change our Southern way of life to better fit in with their plans, "No." If the empire suggests that we disarm for our own good, "No." When they order us to change the Southern way of thinking, "No!"

What can the Empire do about it? Will they oppress us? Will they slander or libel us? Could they occupy us with troops? Could the Empire's judges subject us to social engineering? Would they bomb us? Kill us? The Empire already does all these things, and will continue to do so whether we resist or not. So, why worry?

For openers, we can amend our attitude by amending our motto. Remember that earlier I said *Deo Vindice* is passive. Let's adopt a more positive, active attitude by adopting a more positive, active motto. Of course, we will keep the *Deo Vindice* part. There is nothing really wrong with that. However, we can add a phrase that is forever identified with the South. I propose we amend our motto to read, *"Deo Vindice. Resurgam."* In English, *resurgam* translates as, "I shall rise again." That reflects the proper outlook of a captive people who long to be free. God will vindicate. I shall rise again. It is hard to get more positive or active than that.

Next, to demonstrate our positive nature, we must learn to use the power that we already have to build a political base. This is best done one step at a time. Start by electing a Southern nationalist to the local school board. Then, elect another, and another, until we have the balance of power on that board. Next, do the same for the town council. Then take the fight to the county or parish level. These small, basic decision- and policy-making bodies are where the real power begins. From there, we then work our way into the statehouses by electing Southern nationalists to our state legislatures. That is how Hawaiian nationalists are succeeding. Just like them, we can elect governors, congressmen, and senators who support the Southern cause. Starting at the bottom, where it really counts, is the way to successfully build a solid nationalist political movement. That way the whole structure of the system works toward the cause of Southern nationhood.[4]

Before we can accomplish our freedom, Southerners must once again believe in ourselves and the cause of our Southern Nation. We must help our people regain their Southern pride. The average Southron needs to develop enough faith in his homeland to ask an average Northerner just what is it that gives him and his Empire the authority to sit in judgement over a better and more honorable people than their own. You, like Moses, must have enough faith to walk up to Pharaoh and demand, "Let my people go."

Developing that faith is getting easier for Southrons. It is easier because we are winning. Every new attack on our Southern heritage brings us more support. Every hate crime directed against a Southerner, every flag that falls, every new outrage, jolts more Southrons awake. Likewise, each new wave of third-world immigration that wades ashore is another nail in the coffin of the Empire. The attention that each new attack on the South brings serves only to further spread the cause of Southern nationhood. In reality, each new attack is a win for the Southern people. The fact that mere Southrons and their cause draw the attention of these attacks is another sign that the imperials fear us above all other threats to the Empire's continued existence.

A few years ago, Arkansas wore the mantle as the most reconstructed Southern state. This was a drastic break from our past and the result of many years of a scalawag governor named Clinton's influence. However, you can drive down any major highway in Arkansas today and chances are that you will see a Confederate flag floating proudly above at least one home. Usually, this home belongs to one more family that the Empire has alienated to the point of throwing them at the Southern cause.

The Southern people want no more than what is due them. Southerners have a right to a government that has their consent. The American Empire has lacked our consent for more than 135 years. We have a right to the rule of law based on a strong constitution without meddling and social engineering from non-elected judges and bureaucrats. We deserve fair wages paid in sound money, coupled with low taxes that ensure that we and not empires receive the fruit of our labor. Southrons deserve a just government with moral as well as fiscal accountability. Our dream is a nation where right and wrong bind the president as much as they bind the average citizen. We deserve liberty, political equality, and a return to secure property rights. The South deserves its independence. We will get it, too. With God's help, we will win it all. Southerners instinctively know that the way to stand tall is to begin on our knees in prayer. The Lord helps those who help themselves.

Deo Vindice. Resurgam.

APPENDIX A

Declaration of Constitutional Principles

March 12, 1956

The unwarranted decision of the Supreme Court in the public school cases is now bearing the fruit always produced when men substitute naked power for established law.

The Founding Fathers gave us a Constitution of checks and balances because they realized the capable lesson of history that no man or group of men can be safely entrusted with unlimited power. They framed this Constitution with its provisions for change by amendment in order to secure the fundamentals of government against the dangers of temporary popular passion or the personal predilections of public officeholders.

We regard the decision of the Supreme Court in the school cases as a clear abuse of judicial power. It climaxes a trend in the Federal Judiciary undertaking to legislate, in derogation of the authority of Congress, and to encroach upon the reserved rights of the States and the people.

The original Constitution does not mention education. Neither does the 14th amendment nor any other amendment. The debates preceding the submission of the 14th amendment clearly show that there was no intent that it should affect the system of education maintained by the States.

The very Congress which proposed the amendment subsequently provided for segregated schools in the District of Columbia.

When the amendment was adopted in 1868, there were 37 States of the Union. Every one of the 26 States that had any substantial racial differences among its people, either approved the operation of segregated schools already in existence or subsequently established such schools by action of the law-making body which considered the 14th amendment.

As admitted by the Supreme Court in the public school case *(Brown v. Board of Education)*, the doctrine of separate but equal schools "apparently originated in *Roberts v. City of Boston* (1849), upholding school segregation against attack as being violative of a State constitutional guarantee of equality." This constitutional doctrine began in the North, not in the South, and it was followed not only in Massachusetts, but in Connecticut, New York, Illinois, Indiana, Michigan, Minnesota, New Jersey, Ohio, Pennsylvania and other northern States until they, exercising their rights as States through the constitutional processes of local self-government, changed their school systems.

In the case of *Plessy v. Ferguson* in 1896 the Supreme Court expressly declared that under the 14th amendment no person was denied any of his rights if the States provided separate but equal public facilities. This decision has *been* followed in many other cases. It is notable that the Supreme Court, speaking through Chief Justice Taft, a former President of the United States, unanimously declared in 1927 in *Lum v. Rice* that the "separate but equal" principle is "within discretion of the State in regulating its public schools and does not conflict with the 14th amendment."

This interpretation, restated time and again, became a part of the life of the people of many of the States and confirmed their habits, customs, traditions, and way of life. It is founded on elemental humanity and common sense, for parents should not be deprived by Government of the right to direct the lives and education of their own children.

Though there has been no constitutional amendment or act of Congress changing this established legal principle almost a century old, the Supreme Court of the United States, with no legal basis for such action, undertook to exercise their naked judicial power and substituted their personal political and social ideas for the established law of the land.

This unwarranted exercise of power by the Court, contrary to the Constitution, is creating chaos and confusion in the States principally affected. It is destroying the amicable relations between the white and Negro races that have been created through 90 years of patient effort by the good people of both races. It has planted hatred and suspicion where there has been heretofore friendship and understanding.

Without regard to the consent of the governed, outside agitators are threatening immediate and revolutionary changes in our public-school systems. If done, this is certain to destroy the system of public education in some of the States.

With the gravest concern for the explosive and dangerous condition created by this decision and inflamed by outside meddlers:

We reaffirm our reliance on the Constitution as the fundamental law of the land.

We decry the Supreme Court's encroachments on rights reserved to the States and to the people, contrary to established law, and to the Constitution.

We commend the motives of these States which have declared the intention to resist forced integration by any lawful means.

We appeal to the States and people who are not directly affected by these decisions to consider the constitutional principles involved against the time when they too, on issues vital to them, may be the victims of judicial encroachment.

Even though we constitute a minority in the present Congress, we have full faith that a majority of the American people believe in the dual system of government which has enabled us to achieve our greatness, and will in time demand that the reserved rights of the States and of the people be made secure against judicial usurpation

We pledge ourselves to use all lawful means to bring about a reversal of this decision which is contrary to the Constitution and to prevent the use of force in its implementation.

In this trying period, as we all seek to right this wrong, we appeal to our people not to be provoked by the agitators and troublemakers invading our States and to scrupulously refrain from disorder and lawless acts.

Signed by:
Members of the United States Senate

Walter F. George, Richard B. Russell, John Stennis, Sam J. Ervin, Jr., Strom Thurmond, Harry F. Byrd, A. Willis Robertson, John L. McClellan, Allen J. Ellender, Russell B. Long, Lister Hill, James O. Eastland, W. Kerr Scott, John Sparkman, Olin D. Johnston, Price Daniel, J. W. Fulbright, George A. Smathers, Spessard L. Holland.

Members of the United States House of Representatives

Alabama: Frank W. Boykin, George M. Grant, George W Andrews, Kenneth A. Roberts, Albert Rains, Armistead L Selden, Jr., Carl Elliott, Robert E. Jones, George Huddleston, Jr.

Arkansas: E. C. Gathings, Wilbur D Mills, James W. Trimble, Oren Harris, Brooks Hays, W. F. Norrell.

Florida: Charles E. Bennett, Robert L. F. Sikes, A. S. Herlong, Jr., Paul G. Rogers, James A. Haley, D. R. Matthews, William Cramer.

Georgia: Prince H. Preston, John L. Pilcher, E. L. Forrester, John James Flynt, Jr., James C. Davis, Carl Vinson, Henderson Lanham, Iris F. Blitch, Phil M. Landrum, Paul Brown.

Louisiana: F. Edward Herbert, Hale Boggs, Edwin E Willis, Overton Brooks, Otto R. Passman, James H. Morrison, T. Ashton Thompson, George S. Long.

Mississippi: Thomas G. Abernathy, Jamie L Whitten, Frank E. Smith, John Bell Williams, Arthur Winstead, William M. Colmer.

North Carolina: Herbert C. Bonner, L. H. Fountain, Graham A. Barden, Carl T. Durham, F. Eric Carlyle, Hugh Q. Alexander, Woodrow W. Jones, George A. Shuford, Charles R. Jonas.

South Carolina: L. Mendel Rivers, John J. Riley, W. J. Bryan Dorn, Robert T. Ashmore, James P. Richards, John L. McMillan.

Tennessee: James B. Frazier, Jr., Tom Murray, Jere Cooper, Clifford Davis, Ross Bass.

Texas: Wright Patman, John Dowdy, Walter Rogers, O. C. Fisher, Martin Dies.

Virginia: Edward J. Robeson, Jr., Porter Hardy, Jr., J. Vaughan Gary, Watkins M. Abbitt, William M. Tuck, Richard H. Poff, Burr P. Harrison, Howard W. Smith, W. Pat Jennings, Joel T. Broyhill.

APPENDIX B

Adopted in summit at New Albany, Mississippi, October 12, 1996, by members of all major Southern heritage groups; undertaken in the spirit of the Albany Congress of 1754.

THE NEW ALBANY DECLARATION

All the natural world is based on loyalty to hearth and kin. Yet, in the West, historical regard for the integrity of distinct peoples and cultures is being submerged in a multicultural "melting pot." It will, if carried to its logical conclusion, overwhelm peoples of European descent. By subverting natural affinities, those in power commit the crime of genocide against Western peoples. It is the natural right of all peoples to seek their own survival and safety. Given the pace at which changes are unfolding, it has become necessary to seek political solutions that would have hitherto been unthinkable, that is, the irrevocable separation of threatened peoples from governing bodies that no longer further their safety and well-being.

No distinct people is more threatened than the European-derived peoples who constitute the American South. In 1861, the United States government waged a war of destruction and annihilation against the Southern people, a war provoked in part by abolitionists, who agitated ceaselessly for destruction of Southern whites by military force and servile insurrection. This call for their own murder met the only response any sane people could possibly make. The Southern people fought back, surrendering only when the weight of the invader became more than life itself could bear. While the factors influencing the political climate have changed in the intervening century, nevertheless it is self-evident that Abraham Lincoln's war of aggression against people of his own blood, and for the benefit of those of another descent, is now being re-enacted throughout the West.

By such means are a proud and brave people brought to ruin. Indeed, the situation today is far worse because it afflicts all the West. Nowhere in the civilized world is there sanctuary from the dissolutive multicultural tendencies inflicted in 1865 only on the South. If we are to survive, this spiritual malignancy cannot stand. We, the Southern people, are resolved that, whatever the risks to ourselves, we must take those steps necessary to secure the existence of our people and a future for our children. Therefore, and to that end—

———

In the 131st year of our physical and spiritual occupation by the United States Government, we the unreconstructed Southern people, do proclaim the following:

I. NATURAL RIGHTS OF A FREE PEOPLE

1. That we are a Christian people of Northwest European descent, with predominately Anglo-Celtic institutions, traditions, culture, and heritage; wherever we may abide, we are bound by blood, loyalty, and sentiment to the American South, comprising: Alabama, Arkansas, Florida, Georgia, Kentucky, Louisiana, Maryland, Mississippi, Missouri, North Carolina, Oklahoma, South Carolina, Tennessee, Texas, and Virginia.

2. That our historical and cultural identity was forged over a 400-year period of exploration, settlement, and endeavor that created our distinct character, dialects, folkways, values, and civilization. The War for Southern Independence was the crucible that transformed us into a people with a single purpose and destiny.

3. That we have an unalienable right to self-determination and to continued existence as a distinct people. These unalienable rights were bought with the courage, tenacity, and sacrifice of ancestors who fought and died in the War for Southern Independence, the American Revolution, and every American conflict where duty's call beckoned.

4. That the ideals of liberty and sovereignty undergirding were in large measure given voice by the genius and resolve of Southern statesmen; the transcendent principles they embraced, codified in the Virginia Declaration of Rights, the Declaration of Independence, and the Bill of Rights, have served as an enduring inspiration to all people who aspire to self-government.

5. That no power on earth is morally justified in depriving our people or our posterity of safety, independence, or substance; to this end, separation and independent nationhood are morally just measures for securing the safety of a free people.

II. THE DISPOSSESSION
OF THE SOUTHERN PEOPLE

6. That the hallowed battlefields and cemeteries of 1861-1865 bear silent witness to the destruction wrought by the United States government in league with Northern financial interests and social radicals for the purpose of subjugating and obliterating the Southern people, to wit: abolition, aggression, conquest, disenfranchisement, reconstruction, and amalgamation.

7. That during the military occupation known as Reconstruction, the South endured destructive physical, economic, and social depredations by carpetbaggers, scalawags, and freedmen; Reconstruction ended not because of benevolence, but by the indomitable resistance of the Southern people, despite which the federal government continued its policy of economic exploitation until World War II, keeping much of the South in unrelieved poverty.

8. That we, as well as all Americans of European descent, are suffering a second, more terrible reconstruction, one that began in the late 1940's with the schism in the Democratic Party over the "Civil Rights" plank, that escalated with the Brown school desegregation decision of 1954, and that achieved dominance with the "Civil Rights" Act of 1964 and the Voting Rights act of 1965.

9. That the moral and societal dissolution engendered by this Second Reconstruction was thrust on us through propaganda, deceit, and force of arms by adherents of the Marxist, universalist ideology known as liberalism, an ideology alien to the Southern people, contrary to God's laws, and destructive of all who are deceived by it.

10. That the tidal wave of Third World immigration unleashed during this Second Reconstruction imperils not only our right of self-government but our continued biological existence, as indeed it imperils all Western peoples.

11. That in furtherance of the illusion of a multicultural "Tower of Babel," an unholy alliance of government, media, and, regrettably, Christian churches in error are directing a relentless campaign of slander and abasement against our institutions, traditions, symbols, and

history through destructive laws, biased reporting, and teaching of false universalist doctrines.

12. That the assertion of equality among races, sexes, and moral belief systems is contradicted by every shred of natural evidence; as a people, we condemn inter-racial unions which are destroying our society and our peoples' very existence. [Author's note: This is not to be misconstrued to condemn the well-established principle of equality of opportunity or to imply that only white people can be Southerners.]

13. That much of the subjugation of the Southern people has been fostered by weak or inept Southern leaders who, due to venality, cowardice, or lack of vision, refuse to confront the hard choices needed to preserve our heritage and our children's future.

III. THE SOUTHERN CREED

14. That as Southerners, we affirm our faith and devotion to God, Family, and Country, and to the traditions that have sustained our people for uncounted generations; Southern ideals of honor, chivalry, courage, and discipline are timeless virtues, unchanged by the decadence of the modern age. While respecting freedom of conscience we are a Christian people, with Christian institutions.

15. That we believe that equality is the sworn enemy of liberty, and we recognize a natural, hierarchical social order and adhere to a political system where the best members of society are enabled to rise to positions of leadership and civic duty.

16. That the agrarian origin of the Southern people confess a deep affection for nature and for the land; responsible stewardship over nature's bounty has ever been the duty of all Southerners.

17. That we respect traditional social norms defining the role of the family, the relationships between men and women, and the ideals of Southern Manhood and Southern Womanhood.

18. That we have a long and distinguished martial tradition that precludes soldierly participation by women and other races.

19. That kindred folk who marry into Southern families and adopt Southern ideal and traditions may become naturalized Southerners. We welcome kindred folk who, without the benefit of family ties, adopt the Southern way of life; conversely, Southern nativity alone does not confer Southern nationality.

20. That while maintaining the integrity of Southerners as a distinct people and culture, we seek renewed fraternal ties with kindred peoples and friendly relations with all people of goodwill.

IV. RESOLVE FOR SELF-DETERMINATION

21. That we shall never accept the defeat of the Confederacy, the subjugation of our people, nor the eradication of our symbols as the final judgment of history, nor shall we accept the alien domination of Southern churches, schools, media, commerce, industry, government, or, through these institutions, alien control of Southern life.

22. That defense and preservation of Southern symbols, monuments, relics, and history are sacred charges to every Southerner; in defense of this heritage no honorable retreat or compromise is possible.

23. That the Confederate Battle Flag is the banner of the Southern people and stands preeminent as the most powerful symbol of liberty and Southern nationhood in a constellation of venerable Southern symbols. "Dixie" is the anthem of that nation. That we will stand when it is played and sing it with boldness and pride.

24. That those who love the South are committed to the health and prosperity of its people, the rejuvenation of its culture, the unbiased recording of its history, and the lifting of occupation and control of the South by non-Southerners.

25. That we pledge "our lives, our fortunes, and our sacred honor" to the creation of a secure homeland for our people and a future for our children, and we shall use all moral means, consistent with the right of self-preservation, to achieve that end.

That true Southerners, like our reconstructed Confederate ancestors, have an abiding faith in providence and the rightness of the Southern Cause, and that we do affirm that faith by adherence to the principles of this declaration.

Signed this 12th day of October 1996, at New Albany, Mississippi.

APPENDIX C

Suggested Reading for Southrons

BOOKS

1. *The Holy Bible*. The Bible is the most important book on this list for Southrons to read, study, and draw faith from.

2. *I'll Take My Stand*, Twelve Southerners, Louisiana State University Press, Baton Rouge, Louisiana, 1977 Reprint. Originally published in 1930, in this historic work the "Fugitive Agrarians" warn Southerners about abandoning their culture for the false messiah of industrialism. It is uncanny how accurate their predictions were.

3. *Southern by the Grace of God*, Michael Andrew Grissom, Pelican Publishing Co., Gretna, Louisiana, 1988. This is the book that many consider to have started the Southern heritage revival.

4. *The Last Rebel Yell*, Michael Andrew Grissom, Rebel Press, Wynnewood, Oklahoma, 1991. This is the second book of Grissom's Confederate heritage series.

5. *The South Was Right!*, James R. and Walter D. Kennedy, Pelican Publishing Co., Gretna, Louisiana, 2nd edition 1994. Many leading Southern nationalists refer to this book as the "Bible" of Southern nationalism.

6. *Why Not Freedom*, James R. and Walter D. Kennedy, Pelican Publishing Co., Gretna, Louisiana, 1995. The Kennedy brothers expand their study to include government misdeeds across the American Empire.

7. *Was Jefferson Davis Right?*, James R. and Walter D. Kennedy, Pelican Publishing Co., Gretna, Louisiana, 1998. Davis finally gets what he requested—his day in court. The Kennedy brothers establish an unassailable legal defense of the one Confederate the American Empire feared to put on trial.

8. *Facts Historians Leave Out: A Confederate Primer,* John S. Tilley, Bill Coats Ltd., 1406 Grandview Dr., Nashville, Tennessee, 1951. The fact that this small book finished its twenty-fourth printing as of November 1993, speaks for itself.

9. *The Coming of the Glory,* John S. Tilley, Bill Coats Ltd., 1406 Grandview Dr., Nashville, Tennessee, 1995. Originally published in 1951, this book gives the real facts about slavery, secession, and reconstruction.

10. *A Confederate Catechism,* Lyon Gardiner Tyler, Crown Rights Book Company, Wiggins, Mississippi, 1997. This reprint of Tyler's 1935 edition furnishes a good background for those who are unfamiliar with the Southern cause.

11. *America's Caesar: Abraham Lincoln and the Birth of a Modern Empire,* Greg Loren Durand, Crown Rights Book Company, Wiggins, Mississippi, 1999. This new book exposes the Lincoln myth for the passel of lies it really is.

12. *War for What?,* Francis L. Springer, Bill Coats Ltd., 1406 Grandview Dr., Nashville, Tennessee, 1990. Springer presents an excellent case on the North's true reason for waging the war, the total economic and cultural destruction of the South.

13. *The Uncivil War: Union Army and Navy Excesses in the Official Records,* Thomas Bland Keys, Beauvoir Press, Biloxi, Mississippi, 1991. This study indicts the Northern invaders of war crimes, using their own published reports and correspondence.

14. *Time on the Cross: The Economics of American Negro Slavery,* Robert W. Fogel and Stanley L. Engleman, Little, Brown and Co., Boston, Massachusetts, 1989. Dr. Fogel won the 1993 Nobel Prize for his work that lead up to this eye-opening economic study of how the slavery system actually worked. Of course, liberals and black groups universally denounced his work.

15. *Cracker Culture: Celtic Ways in the Old South,* Grady McWhiney, University of Alabama Press, Tuscaloosa, Alabama, 1988. McWhiney explains the cultural differences between North and South and why the two sections will probably never get along.

16. *A Defense of Virginia and Through Her the South,* Dr. Robert L. Dabney, D.D., Sprinkle Publications, Harrisonburg, Virginia, 1977 reprint. Dr. Dabney served in the war as Stonewall Jackson's chief of staff before writing this eloquent defense of the Southern Cause based on theology and law.

17. *Southern Tradition at Bay,* Richard Weaver, Regnery Gateway, Inc., Washington, D.C. A student of the Fugitives gives his spirited defense of Southern culture and policy.

18. *Southerner Take Your Stand,* John Vinson, South Press, HC-3 Box 52, Monterey, Virginia, 1993. Vinson's booklet defends the true South and suggests a plan for Southern Renewal.

19. *The Gray Book,* The Gray Book Committee, Arthur Jennings, Chairman, Sons of Confederate Veterans, Hattiesburg, Mississippi, 1918. Reissued several times, this is the Southern response of truth against the U.S. government's W.W.I propaganda campaign comparing the South with Germany.

20. *So Good a Cause: A Decade of Southern Partisan,* Ed. Oran P. Smith, Foundation for American Education, Columbia, South Carolina, 1993. This collection is ten years of the best articles and interviews from *Southern Partisan* magazine.

21. *Guns, Crime, and Freedom,* Wayne LaPierre, Regnery Publishing, Inc., Washington, D.C., 1994. This is one of the best books ever written on the topic of gun control and the gun-grabbers' true purpose, people control.

22. *Civil War II: The Coming Breakup of America,* Thomas W. Chittum, American Eagle Publications, Show Low, Arizona, 1996. Chittum paints a frightening picture of what he has witnessed first-hand—the tendency of multi-ethnic empires to disintegrate in a flurry of violence.

PERIODICALS

Southern Partisan (quarterly magazine)
P.O. Box 11708
Columbia, South Carolina 29211
(800) 264-2559

Southern Heritage (bi-monthly magazine)
P.O. Box 3181
Merrifield, Virginia 22116
(703) 591-3960

The Edgefield Journal (monthly, soon to be weekly, newspaper)
P.O. Box 628
Edgefield, South Carolina 29824
(803) 637-3789

Chronicles: A Magazine of American Culture
(Though not an exclusively Southern journal, *Chronicles* takes a scholarly and impartial look at American culture. It particularly supports the traditional Southern opinion in the so-called "culture war.")
P.O. Box 800
Mount Morris, Illinois 61054-8082
(800) 877-5459

APPENDIX D

Some Southern Resources

SOUTHERN RIGHTS ORGANIZATIONS:

The League of the South
P.O. Box 40910
Tuscaloosa, Alabama 35404-0910
(800) 888-3163

The Confederate Society of America
P.O. Box 1103
Warrensburg, Missouri U.S. Occupation Zone 64093
(660) 492-3632

Southern Defense Initiative
2000 Nathan Bedford Forrest Complex
Post Office Box 6280
Jackson, Mississippi 39288-6280
(601) 664-0200

The Council of Conservative Citizens
(Though not strictly a Southern organization, the CC of C is on the
    front lines of the battle for Southern rights.)
The Council of Conservative Citizens
P.O. Box 9683
St. Louis, Missouri 63122

SOUTHERN HERITAGE ORGANIZATIONS:

The Sons of Confederate Veterans
P.O. Box 59
Columbia, Tennessee 38402-0059
(800) MYDIXIE

The United Daughters of the Confederacy
328 North Boulevard
Richmond, Virginia 23220-40057
(804) 355-1636

The Heritage Preservation Association, Inc.
P.O. Box 98209
Atlanta, Georgia 30359-1909
(800) 863-4943

SOUTHERN POLITICAL RESOURCES:

At the present, there is only one Southern nationalist political party that shows promise. That is the Southern Party, which just recently started and is already growing at an incredible rate.

The Southern Party
PO Box 2582
Chesterfield, Virginia 23832
E-mail: freevirginia@aol.com

SOUTHERN LEGAL RESOURCES:

The Cause Foundation
P.O. Box 1235
Black Mountain, North Carolina 28711
(828) 669-5189

The Southern Legal Resource Center
P.O. Box 1235
Black Mountain, North Carolina 28711
(828) 669-5189

SOUTHERN EDUCATIONAL RESOURCES:

One result of federal judges meddling with the traditions of The Citadel and Virginia Military Institute was that alumni from those schools banded together to found a private military academy with its curriculum and traditions based on Southern heritage and our historical Southern concept of Christianity. The new Southern Military Institute is a traditional engineering and science college. It is the only all-male, four-year military college remaining in the United States.

The Southern Military Institute
8000 Madison Boulevard
Suite D102-390
Madison, Alabama 35758
(800) 394-1699

SOUTHERN MEDIA:

Dixie Rising!
A weekly Southern nationalist radio program first broadcast out of WNAH-AM in Nashville, Tennessee. The show is now available over the Internet on RealAudio and is expanding into the cable television market. For more information try www.dixierising.com.

The Big Show
John Boy and Billy's Southern-flavored morning show broadcasts via satellite out of WRFX-FM in Charlotte, North Carolina. Melding their unique humor and classic rock music, they continue to expand their network, which now broadcasts all the way over in Japan. To find a local station, check them out at www.thebigshow.com.

INTERNET RESOURCES:

www.dixienet.org—The League of the South home page.

www.deovindice.org—The Confederate Society of America home page.

www.pointsouth.com—CSAnet, the E-Voice of the Old South and a good collection of Southern resources.

www.freedixie.net—Jim Langcuster's Southern Traditionalist home page.

www.dixiecaust.org—This page remembers the DixieCaust, along with the Empire's wartime atrocities and its continuing campaign of cultural genocide directed at the South.

www.confederate.net—The Confederate Network, the largest and most comprehensive directory of Confederate sites on the Internet.

www.hpa.org—The Heritage Preservation Association home page.

www.cheta.net/slrc/—The Southern Legal Resource Center home page.

USENET NEWSGROUPS:

alt.thought.southern—A newsgroup dedicated exclusively to Southern Nationalist ideas. It is chronically plagued by an intrusion of anti-South bigots.

alt.revolution.counter—A newsgroup that explores counterrevolutionary thought, including Southern nationalism.

NOTES

INTRODUCTION

1. Dr. Michael Hill, League of the South Conference, Mobile, AL, 21 June 1997.

CHAPTER I

1. Jefferson Davis, First Address to the Confederate Congress, Richmond, VA, 18 November 1861.
2. Michael Grissom, *The Last Rebel Yell* (Wynnewood, OK: The Rebel Press, 1991) iv.
3. That portion of the Berlin Wall, along with its accompanying sculpture, was at the time destined for the new George Bush Presidential Library in College Station, Texas.
4. Mr. Bill's war story is retold here with his permission.
5. Burke Davis, *The Civil War: Strange and Fascinating Facts* (New York, NY: The Fairfax Press, 1982) 223.

CHAPTER II

1. Patrick Henry, The Virginia Convention, Richmond, VA, March 1775.
2. Conversation with James L. Bays, Crossett, AR, 8 December 1995. The author does not accept or condone the use of the term "Civil War." The phrase is only used as quoted.
3. James Ronald Kennedy and Walter Donald Kennedy, *Why Not Freedom?* (Gretna, LA: Pelican Publishing, 1995) 245.
4. Thomas Jefferson, The Declaration of Independence, July 1776.
5. John J. Robinson, *Born in Blood* (New York: Evans and Co., 1989) 101-4.

6. James Ronald Kennedy, "A Strategy for Southern Freedom," *The Southern Patriot* January-February 1995, 5-6. Also, "Vote Gives Scotland Own Parliament," *Arkansas Democrat Gazette* 13 September 1997, 6a.

7. "The Quebec Secession Vote," *The Southern Review Newsletter* May 1996, 4.

8. Address delivered before Congress, 12 January 1848. As quoted in Greg Loren Durand, *America's Caesar: Abraham Lincoln and the Birth of a Modern Empire* (Wiggins, MS: Crown Rights Book Co., 1999) 51n-52n. Also, John Shipley Tilley, *The Coming of the Glory* (Nashville, TN: Bill Coats Ltd., 1949, 1995) 58, 87.

9. Joe Miller, "Native Southerners, Southland, U.S.A.," Bulletin of the Arkansas Council of Conservative Citizens, November 1995, 4.

10. Donald Kennedy and Ronald Kennedy, *The South Was Right!* (Gretna, LA: Pelican Publishing, 1994) 10. Used by permission of the publisher, Pelican Publishing Company, Inc.

11. Marion P. Hammer, "Fear of Government," *The American Rifleman* March 1997, 12.

12. "Survey Finds Tolerance for Confederate Flag," *The Washington Times* 4 July 1994.

13. Kennedy, "A Strategy for Southern Freedom," 6.

CHAPTER III

1. As quoted in Tanya K. Metaska, "Sliding Down the Slippery Slope," *The American Rifleman* June 1997, 30-31.

2. Noah Webster, "An Examination into the Leading Principles of the Federal Constitution Proposed by the Late Convention Held at Philadelphia," as quoted in Palmer Stacy, *The Right of the People to Keep and Bear Arms* (Raleigh, NC: We the People Institute, 1995) 2.

3. Ibid., 4.

4. Jefferson, The Declaration of Independence.

5. Kennedy and Kennedy, *Why Not Freedom?* (Gretna, LA: Pelican Publishing, 1995) 52, 225.

6. Michael Grissom, *The Last Rebel Yell* (Wynnewood, OK: The Rebel Press, 1991) 299-300.

7. Ibid., 300.

8. Georgie Patton, "Guts, Brains and 'Leadership,'" *Looky Here* Vol. 1, Issue 3, 25.

9. Lee as quoted in *The South Was Right!*, by Donald Kennedy and Ronald Kennedy, 42-43.

10. David Lawrence, "The Worst Scandal in Our History," *U.S. News and World Report* January 26, 1970, 95-96.

11. Ibid.

12. (18 USC 1385) as explained in FM 100-19 Domestic Support Operations (Washington, DC: Headquarters, Department of the Army, 1993), §3 p. 1-3.

13. Kennedy and Kennedy, *The South Was Right!*, 175-76.

14. Ibid., 21-22.

15. Ibid., 37.

16. John Hofhiemer, "Newton County Wildlife Association 20 years of single-minded tree hugging," *Earthkeepers' Journal* October 1995, 6-7.

17. "Public Land Policy," *Congressional Quarterly Researcher* 17 June 1994, 529-49.

18. Bruce McMath, "Land Swap Questions Unanswered," *Earthkeepers' Journal* October 1995, 5.

19. Ibid., 5.

20. Hofhiemer, 7.

21. Andrew Lytle, "The Hind Tit," *I'll Take My Stand* (Baton Rouge, LA: Louisiana State University Press, 1977) 205.

22. *Statistical Abstract of the United States* (Washington, DC: Department of Commerce, 1992) xvi, 369.

23. Jimmy Love, "General Motors Unpacks Carpetbags in Tennessee," *Confederate Underground* Winter 1994, 8-9.

24. Ibid., 8.

25. Ibid., 8.

26. *Statistical Abstract of the United States* 371.

27. John Shipley Tilley, *Facts the Historians Leave Out: A Confederate Primer* (Nashville, TN: Bill Coats, Ltd., 1951, 1993) 34.

28. Ibid., 34.

29. D. James Kennedy, *The Dumbing Down of America* (Ft. Lauderdale, FL: Coral Ridge Ministries, 1997) 2-3. Also, *Statistical Abstract of the United States* 830.

30. Jefferson, "Letter to George Wythe-13 August 1786," *Thomas Jefferson: Writings (New York, NY: American Literary Classics, 1984) 857-860. Also, Jefferson, "A Bill for the More General Diffusion of Knowledge-1779,"* Saul K. Padover, The Complete Jefferson (New York, NY: Duell, Sloan, and Pearce, 1943) 1048-54.

31. John C. Hagee, *Day of Deception* (Nashville, TN: Thomas Nelson, Inc., 1997) 73-74.

32. Friedrich Nietzsche, *Thus Spake Zarathustra* 1885.

33. Jefferson, "Letter to the Danbury Baptist Association-1 January 1802," *Thomas Jefferson: Writings* 510.

34. Timothy C. Morgan, "Racist No More? Black Leaders Ask," *Christianity Today* 14 August 1995, 53.

35. Francis W. Springer, *War for What?* (Nashville, TN: Bill Coats, Ltd., 1990) 20.

36. Wayne LaPierre, *Guns, Crime, and Freedom* (Washington, DC: Regnery Publishing, Inc., 1994) 192-93.

37. Tom Brokaw, NBC News Special Report, 19 April 1993.

38. "SWAT Team," *Southern Partisan* 2nd Quarter 1994, 15. This woman's name was given in the original article but is omitted here to spare her any further embarrassment.

39. Hagee, 54-55. Also, Jay Grelen, "Ten Commandments Judge Looking for a Federal Fight," *Christianity Today* 8 December 1997, 60.

40. "C.I.A. admits to operations at Mena," *Arkansas Democrat Gazette* November 9, 1996, 1a.

41. Joseph D. Shapiro, "America's Gambling Fever," *U.S. News and World Report* 15 January 1996, 53-61.

42. LaPierre, 206.

43. Robert Lichter and Stanley Rothman, as cited by Sen. Jesse Helms in Oran P. Smith, ed., *So Good a Cause: A Decade of Southern Partisan* (Columbia, SC: The Foundation for American Education, 1993) 303-4.

44. Ibid.

45. "Index of Leading Cultural Indicators," *Time* 29 March 1993, 18.

46. Dick Sutphen, "The Battle for Your Mind," Unpublished manuscript in the author's possession. Also, Ann Landi, "You Are Getting Very Sleepy . . . ," *Redbook* November 1994, 118-20.

47. Proverbs 29:18, KJV.

48. Ezekiel 3:20, KJV.

CHAPTER IV

1. Jefferson, "Letter to John Tayor-1 June 1798," Willson Whitman, *Jefferson's Letters* (Eau Claire, WI: E.M. Hale and Co.) 187-88.

2. This definition is based on Boyd C. Shafer, *Faces of Nationalism* (New York, NY: Harvest Books, 1972) 14-15.

3. J. Steven Wilkins, "The Theology of the South," *Southern Patriot* November-December 1994, 12.

4. The official title of the articles was "The Articles of Confederation and Perpetual Union." Paul Boyer, et al, *The Enduring Vision* (Lexington, MA: D.C. Heath and Co., 1996) iii-vii.

5. John Shipley Tilley, *The Coming of the Glory* (Nashville, TN: Bill Coats Ltd., 1949, 1995) 103-5.

6. Springer, 13-14, 27.

7. Tilley, *Facts Historians Leave Out* 34.

8. Tilley, *The Coming of the Glory* 74-80.

9. Tilley, *Facts Historians Leave Out* 34.

10. Dr. H. Van Holst, *John C. Calhoun* (Boston, MA: Houghton, Mifflin, and Co., 1899) 75.

11. Elmo Ingenthron, *Borderland Rebellion* (Branson, MO: Ozark Mountaineer, 1980) 9.

12. Van Holst, 349.

13. Allen E. Roberts, *Freemasonry in American History* (Richmond, VA: Macoy Publishing, 1985) 135-36.

14. Albert Pike, *Morals and Dogma* (Charleston, SC: Supreme Council for the Southern Jurisdiction of the Scottish Rite, 1871) 70.

15. Robert Selph Henry, *First with the Most: Forrest* (Wilmington, NC: Broadfoot Publishing Co., 1987) 440-42.

16. Ibid., 444.

17. Ibid., 446-47.

18. Frank Lawrence Owsley, "The Irrepressible Conflict," *I'll Take My Stand* 63.

19. Robert C. Wood, *The Confederate Handbook* (New Orleans, LA: 1900) 92.

20. Ibid., 108.

21. Gen. Stephen Dill Lee CSA, United Confederate Veterans Reunion, Richmond, Virginia, 1896.

22. Aaron Delwiche, *Wartime Propaganda* (Institute for Propaganda Analysis, 1995) 4-13.

23. Sons of Confederate Veterans, *The Gray Book* (Hattiesburg, MS: Sons of Confederate Veterans, 1918) 35-40, 51-53.

24. Virginia Rock, "Biographical Essays," *I'll Take My Stand*, 361-410.

25. John Gould Fletcher, "Education Past and Present," *I'll Take My Stand*, 117.

26. Smith, 195.

27. Ben F. Johnson III, *Fierce Solitude: A Life of John Gould Fletcher* (Fayettevillle, AR: University of Arkansas Press, 1994) 202-3.

28. Smith, 321-26.

29. Ibid., 321-22.

30. Kennedy and Kennedy, *Why Not Freedom?*, 272.

31. The campaign to cleanse the SCV of Southern nationalists is well documented by a spinoff organization called the "Loyal Order of White Trash" in their journal, *Looky Here.*

32. "Murder of a Patriot: Confederate Activist Assassinated," *Confederate Underground*, Winter 1994, 1-3.

33. *League of the South Grand Strategy* 1995 (Tuscaloosa, AL: The League of the South, 1995).

34. *The Confederate Society of America* (Plaquemine. LA: Confederate Society of America, 1995) 5.

35. Michael Masters, "Rebirth at New Albany," *Confederate Sentry*, April-May 1997, 6.

CHAPTER V

1. Ulysses S. Grant, *Memoirs and Selected Letters* (New York, NY: Literary Classics of the United States, 1990) 746.

2. William Lamar Cawthon, Jr., "The South As Its Own Nation," *The League of the South Papers* (Tuscaloosa, AL: The League of the South, 1995).

3. Ibid.

4. Ibid.

5. Ibid.

6. Ibid.

7. Ibid.

CHAPTER VI

1. Victor Hugo, *History of a Crime*, 1871.

2. Kennedy and Kennedy, *The South Was Right!* 42-43.

3. Robinson, 101-4.

4. Edgar O'balance, *Terror in Ireland* (Novato, CA: Presidio Press, 1981) 2-3, 12-13. Norman MacKenzie, ed., Secret Societies, (New York, NY: Crescent Books, 1967) pp. 178-94.

5. Thomas Edward Shaw (T.E. Lawrence), *The Seven Pillars of Wisdom* (Garden City, NY: Doubleday, 1926) 18-21, 24-27, 42, 74.

6. Calvin Kytle, *Gandhi, Soldier of Nonviolence* (New York, NY: Grosset and Dunlap, 1969) 37-39, 80-81, 155.

7. Carl Bernstein, "The Holy Alliance," *Time*, 24 February 1992, 28-36.

8. Priit J. Vesilind, "The Baltic Nations: Estonia, Latvia, and Lithuania Struggle Toward Independence," *National Geographic*, November 1990, 2-37.

9. Richard Shenkman, *Legends, Lies, and Cherished Myths of American History* (New York, NY: William Morrow and Co., 1988) 84.

10. I Timothy 5:8 KJV.

11. Donald W. Livingston, Ph.D., "Secession and the Modern State," *League of the South Papers* (Tuscaloosa, AL: The League of the South, 1996).

12. Ibid.

CHAPTER VII

1. Benjamin Franklin submitted this as his suggestion for the motto of the United States in July 1776.

2. Numbers 6: 1-21 KJV.

3. Acts 21: 20-31 KJV.

4. Dr. Michael Hill, "Presidents Message . . . ," *Southern Patriot*, November-December 1994, 9.

5. I Timothy 6: 3-5 KJV.

6. Edward Bernays, *Propaganda* (New York, NY: Horace Liveright, Inc., 1928) 28.

7. I John 8: 32 KJV.

8. Dr. James Dodson's books are widely available in bookstores. You can reach Focus on the Family at Focus on the Family, Colorado Springs, Colorado 80995; 1-(800) A Family; or www.Family.org.

9. Ultima Thule was the settlement at the end of the trail of Tears on the Arkansas-Oklahoma border. It was named for a phrase meaning the edge or end of the world.

10. John Vinson, *Southerner Take Your Stand* (Monterey, VA: South Press, 1993) 1, 14.

11. Annie G. Massey, "The Secession of Arkansas," *The Confederate Veteran* November 1931, 414-18.

12. Romans 8: 28 KJV.

13. Romans 8: 31 KJV.

CHAPTER VIII

1. Sun Tzu, *The Art of War* (London, UK: 1910).

2. MacKenzie, 206-9.

3. Jacques Ellul, *Propaganda* (New York, NY: Alfred A. Knopf, 1965) 12-14, 20, 122-23.

4. Henry, 156-57.

5. Shelby Foote, *The Civil War: A Narrative, Volume I* (New York, NY: Random House, 1958) 399-400.

6. Rob Howe, Sarah Skolnik, and Don Hamilton, "The Bootstrap Method," *People,* 2 February 1996, 55-57. Also, "Mfume Says NAACP Has Retired Debt," *Jet,* 4 November 1996, 4.

7. Ellul, 15.

8. Ibid., 15, 32.

9. Ibid., 6-9.

10. Ibid., 25, 27-30.

11. The "Rule of Tens" is based on a scaled-down version of the quality control model we use in the paper industry.

12. 1,301 counties and parishes in the South as defined by the Congressional Quarterly times 5 (the average CAT team size) = 6,505 Southrons working toward Southern independence. Apply the Rule of Tens and multiply this number by 1,000 and you have 6,505,000 new supporters of Southern nationhood just from the initial work of concerted action teams. Add Missouri to the mix and the total rises to 7,075,000.

CHAPTER IX

1. John F. Kennedy, from a speech given in 1962.
2. *Psychological Operations in Guerrilla Warfare* (Washington, DC: Central Intelligence Agency) 3.
3. Michael Medved, "Television News: Information or Infotainment?" *Imprimis*, July 1999, 5-8.
4. Ibid., 6.
5. Delwiche, 8.
6. Hammer, 12.
7. Cawthon.
8. Ibid.
9. *The Universal Almanac 1993* (Kansas City, MO: Andrews and McKeel, 1992) 132-56.
10. Suzette Haden Elgin, *The Gentle Art of Verbal Self-Defense* (Englewood Cliffs, NJ: Prentice Hall, 1980) 86-127.
11. "Quebec Secession Vote," 4.

CHAPTER X

1. William Shakespeare, *King Henry IV*.
2. Reprinted with the permission of Crown Rights Book Company, Wiggins, Mississippi CSA; *see also* Domestic Mail Manual, A010.1.2d.
3. James E. Kibler, Jr., "More Than Y'all: The New Southern Language," *Southern Patriot*, January-February 1996, 3.
4. Ibid., 4.
5. Ibid., 4-6
6. Grisom, 42-45, 51-53. Grissom devotes an entire chapter to the causes of the Southern accent's demise.
7. Federal and state judges have handed down several rulings stating that organizers of public events cannot bar Confederate heritage groups from parades or other public events. One recent ruling against the Atlanta Committee for the Olympic Games was detailed in "Court Forces ACOG to Accept Confederates," *Confederate Underground*, Summer 1996, 7.
8. "The Hawaiian Apology Resolution," United States Public Law 103-150, signed into effect 23 November 1993. Sen. Slade Gorton (R-Washington) was reported by the Senate Congressional Record, 27 October 1993, to have argued, "The

logical consequences of this resolution would be [Hawaiian] independence."

9. "American Family Radio: From Sea to Shining Sea," *American Family Association Journal*, July 1999, 22.

10. O'Ballance, 17-18, 22-23.

11. One of the best manuals obtainable on the Internet is *The Ruckus Society Media Manual*, available at www.ruckus.org. A manual of purely left-wing strategy is *How to Win: A Guide to Defeating the Radical Right in Your Community*, published by the National Jewish Democratic Council in Washington, D.C. (Warning: The rhetoric in this manual will probably offend most people.) There is even an anti-Confederate strategy manual circulating on the Internet.

12. Kennedy and Kennedy, *Why Not Freedom?*, 272.

13. Michael Hill, "A New Political Party?," *Southern Patriot*, November-December 1998, 1-2., "Is the GOP Brain-Dead?," *Citizens Informer*, Summer 1997, 1.

14. Even with the lowest percentage of voter turnout in sixty years, "third party" candidates actually determined both the 1992 and 1996 presidential elections. The third parties took 20 percent of the vote in 1992 and more than 10 percent in 1996. Even Ralph Nader's quickly organized Green Party mustered 651,000 votes in 1996. Given the amount of support Southern nationalism already has, a well-organized Southern party could easily do better.

15. Kennedy, *Strategy for Southern Freedom*, 5-6.

CHAPTER XI

1. Pike, 201

2. Gordon A. Cotton, *Yankee Bullets, Rebel Rations* (Vicksburg, MS: Office Supply Company, 1989) 69.

3. Edwin C. Bearss, *Decision in Mississippi* (Jackson, MS: Mississippi Council on the War Between the States, 1962) 424-30.

4. Edward Cunningham, *The Port Hudson Campaign* (Baton Rouge, LA: Louisiana State University Press, 1963) 103-6.

5. Donald Kennedy and Ronald Kennedy, *The South Was Right!* 10.

6. Renee Descartes, *A Discourse on Method IV*, 1637.

7. Sharon Begley, "The Puzzle of Genius," *Newsweek*, 28 June 1993, 51.

8. Bruce Bower, "Criminal Intelligence," *Science News*, 15 April 1997, 232-34.

9. Deuteronomy 18: 10-12 KJV.
10. Zig Ziglar, *See You at the Top* (Gretna, LA: Pelican Publishing Co., 1984) 85.
11. Matthew 17: 20 KJV.
12. Charles Clark, *Brainstorming* (Garden City, NY: Doubleday, 1958) 155-61.
13. Napoleon Hill, *Think and Grow Rich* (New York, NY: Fawcett Crest, 1960) 205-11.
14. Dr. Norman Vincent Peale, *The Power of Positive Thinking* (New York, NY: Fawcett Crest, 1952, 1996) 43-45.
15. Matthew 18: 19-20 KJV.
16. Clark, 69-78.
17. Vinson, 11.
18. Pike, 31.

CHAPTER XII

1. Acton to Lee, as cited in Livingston.
2. Thomas W. Chittum, *Civil War II* (Show Low, AZ: American Eagle Publications, 1996) 2.
3. Dr. Michael Hill, League of the South Conference, Mobile Alabama, 21 June 1997.
4. George Kalas, "Putting Secession Back into the American Political Debate," *The Southern Review Newsletter,* April 1994, 5.

APPENDIX A

The Congressional Record, 84th Congress, second session (March 12, 1956), 4459-64. In all, 19 of 22 Southern senators signed "The Southern Manifesto," along with 82 out of 96 Southern representatives.

APPENDIX B

Mr. William Rolen, delegate to the Confederate Summit of October 1996 and publisher of the *Confederate Underground* newspaper, furnished this text of the New Albany Declaration.

INDEX

Abjuring the realm, 127-28
Acton, Lord, 217
Adams, John, 77, 116
Adams, John Quincy, 76
Adams, Samuel, 79
Affirmative action, 57, 71, 180
Afrikaner Broederbond, 142
Agent Orange, 51
Agrarian, 87, 90
Agriculture, 49-51, 53, 74, 103
Aid societies, 189, 193
Alabama, 50, 88-89, 93, 96-97, 104
Alaskan and Hawaiian independence movements, 185
Alexander, Lamar, 52
Alien and Sedition Acts, 77
All the King's Men, 90
Alternative media, 187, 188, 193
American Crisis, The, 61
American Empire, 30, 39, 40, 46, 49, 55-57, 61-62, 65, 70, 73-74, 92-93, 95, 103, 105, 109, 112, 127, 143-44, 149, 153, 156-58, 165-66, 181, 199, 217-19, 222
American Family Association, 187
American Family Radio, 187
Animating stage, 147, 148, 150
Anti-Federalists, 75
Anti-slavery societies, 78
Appomattox, 47
Aquinas, Saint Thomas, 117
Arabs, 36, 112, 114
Area codes, 180
Arkansas, 44-45, 89, 137, 190, 213, 222
Articles of Confederation, 74
Atlanta, Georgia, 212
Atlanta Journal-Constitution, 37
Australia, 121

Babylonian Empire, 219
Baker, James, 163
Baltic republics, 33, 40
Bandwagon effect, 146, 147
Banks, Nathaniel, 197
Banner of Yankee Occupation, 145, 180
Baton Rouge, Louisiana, 93
Beauregard, P. G. T., 112
Berlin Wall, 24
Bernays, Edward, 130
Bible Belt, 63
Bill of Rights, 41, 75, 149, 179
Birth of a Nation, The, 86
Black (race), 45, 65, 76, 87, 92-93, 106, 192
Borgia family, 199
Brainstorming, 209-10

Braveheart, 86
Brazil, 109
British Empire, 43, 113, 121, 158, 170
British (Southern) orthography, 182
Buchanan, Pat, 212

Cabot, Arkansas, 44
Calhoun, John C., 77-78, 107
California, 173
Calvin, John, 137
Canada, 109, 121
Captive nations, 39, 40, 112, 116, 121, 142, 178, 181, 199, 218, 220
Carnegie, Dale, 204
Carpetbag rule, 81, 83
Carpetbaggers, 50, 82-84, 88, 148
Casinos, 67, 68
Census, 46, 52
Central government, 31, 35, 57, 59, 75, 77
Central Intelligence Agency, 67, 157
Charity, 189, 190
Charleston, South Carolina, 180
China, 109
Chittum, Thomas, 219
Christianity, 136, 137
Christians, 89, 98
Citizens Informer, 97
Civil rights, 92-93, 178, 183
Civil War II, 219
Clay, Henry, 78
Clinton, William Jefferson, 25, 33, 42, 93, 185, 213, 222
Code of Southern conduct, 179
Colonies, 37-38, 40, 60, 74, 76, 166, 170
Committee for Public Information, 86-87
Committees of Correspondence, 141
Common Sense, 61
Computers, 22, 60, 131, 144, 147, 160
Concerted Action Team, 143-46, 151, 153, 175, 206-7
Confederacy, 49, 56, 80, 108, 123, 145, 149, 198
Confederados, 189
Confederate Alliance, 98, 185, 193
Confederate-Americans, 149, 179, 180
Confederate battle flag, 25, 26, 37, 83, 85, 96, 149, 178, 179, 184, 193, 211, 220
Confederate Society of America, 97, 143
Confederate States Constitution, 41
Confederate States of America, 44, 108, 121, 198
Confederate Veteran, 84, 188
CONFORSOLS, 26
Connecticut, 63, 73, 76

252

Consent, 39, 49, 71, 107, 120, 222
Council of Conservative Citizens, 97
Creative thought, 208-10
Creativity, 149, 155, 160, 197, 200
Cultural emblems, 33, 211
Cultural genocide, 56, 181, 203
Culture, 25, 36, 38, 41, 53, 56, 73-74, 79, 94-
    96, 98, 106, 126-28, 133-36, 157, 183, 199,
    201, 203, 211, 220
Culture Wars, 23, 143-44
Czech Republic, 34

Davidson, Donald, 91
Davis, Jefferson, 21, 74, 83, 212
Declaration of Independence, 117-18, 120,
    158
Defiance, 23, 27, 115, 178, 180-81
Delaware, 109
Democratic Party, 192
Demonstrations, 165, 191
Deo Vindice. Resurgam., 221-22
Descartes, René, 200
District of Columbia, 109
"Dixie," 135, 178-79, 184, 212
Dixie Rising, 187
Dixiecrats, 92
Dobson, Dr. James, 132

Economic colony, 54, 55
Edgefield Journal, 188
Education, 129-35, 142, 147-50, 157, 166,
    172, 199, 215
Eisenhower, Dwight D., 92
Elgin, Suzette Haden, 172
Emotion, 166, 171, 172
England, 38, 40, 50, 74, 120, 170
Environmental Protection Agency, 43
Estonia, 27, 33, 115
Ex post facto laws, 48

Faith, 23-24, 55, 62, 118, 123-26, 136-38, 195-
    96, 198, 202, 208, 221-22
False gods, 62, 89, 118
False prophets, 24, 62, 202
Family, 36, 45, 51, 57, 89, 91, 106, 118, 120,
    126-27, 131-33, 137-38, 148, 172, 184,
    192, 212-13, 220, 222
Farmer's Home Administration, 43
Federalists, 75
Feral man, 123
Fifth Amendment, 43
First Amendment, 41-42, 181
Fletcher, John Gould, 89-91
Fleurs-de-lis, 27
Florida, 104
Focus on the Family, 132
Forrest Gump, 111
Forrest, Nathan Bedford, 81-83, 144-46, 212

Fort Sumter, 191
Four Principles of Southern Freedom, The,
    38
Fourteenth Amendment, 39, 47-49, 58
Fourth Amendment, 43
France, 63, 77, 90, 109, 168
Free men of color, 56, 76
Freedom of: association, 44, 119, 158; eco-
    nomic choice, 118; the press, 77, 103;
    religion, 41; speech, 42
Freedom riders, 93
Freemasonry, 79-80
Fugitive Agrarians, 51-52, 88, 90-91, 179, 218
Funding, 188

Gaelic, 32, 56, 94, 112-13, 181
Gandhi, Mohandas, 34, 114
Gardner, Franklin, 197
General Motors, 52-53
Genius, 189, 201
Gentle Art of Verbal Self-Defense, The, 172
Georgia, 52, 65-66, 84, 89, 93, 96, 111, 145
Georgia State Flag, 96, 194
Germany, 27, 29, 71, 86-87, 108-9, 121, 165,
    168, 180
Gettysburg, Pennsylvania, 197
Gordon, John B., 84
Gore, Albert, Jr., 25
Gore, Albert, Sr., 92-93
Grant, Ulysses S., 85, 101, 158, 195-96, 215
Gray Book, The, 87
Gray Jackets, 91
Gray ribbon, 145, 149, 179
Great Britain, 76
Great Depression, 50, 88, 91
Great Society, 94
Greek democracy, 199
Greenville, Mississippi, 67
Grissom, Michael Andrew, 24, 95, 179
Gross Domestic Product, 108
Gun control, 192
Guns, Crime, and Freedom, 68

Hancock, John, 79
Hartford, Connecticut, 76
Hate crimes, 222
Hawaiian apology resolution, 185
Hawaiian kingdom, 211
Hawaiian nationalists, 221
Heritage, 25, 34-35, 41, 56, 73, 89, 95, 98,
    106, 112-14, 123, 126-27, 133-34, 141,
    146, 157, 162, 178, 199, 220, 222
Heritage Preservation Association, 96
Hill, Michael, 220
Hitler, Adolf, 62, 158, 166
Hobbes, Thomas, 120
Homosexuals, 42, 57, 60, 68, 70, 71, 174
Hussein, Saddam, 30

"If the South Would Have Won," 101
I'll Take My Stand, 51, 90, 179, 218
Illegal immigration, 57-58, 151
Illinois, 35, 52
"I'm a Good Ole Rebel," 46-47
Imperial Identification Number, 180
Imperial Rome, 39
Imperialism, 127
India, 34, 114-15, 117, 121, 170
Industry, 29, 50, 52-54, 68, 74, 77, 104-5, 142, 161
Internal Revenue Service, 43-44, 95
Internet, 96, 131, 187-88, 191
Invisible Empire, 82
Iraq, 30
Ireland, 32, 71, 113-14, 116-17, 135, 141, 170, 181, 189
Israel, 78, 112, 123-25, 181
Italy, 96, 109

Jackson, Andrew, 76-77, 212
Jackson, Mississippi, 180, 196
Jackson, "Stonewall," 74, 137, 197
James, Fob, 97
James II, 201
Japan, 29, 40, 109, 180
Jefferson, Thomas, 31, 32, 42, 60-61, 63, 73, 77, 117, 118, 130
Johnston, Joseph, 196-98

Kalas, George, 187
Kennedy brothers, the, 22, 36, 96, 179, 200
Kennedy, John F., 45, 155
Kentucky, 77, 78, 89, 104, 108, 109, 191, 194
Kentucky and Virginia Resolutions, 77
KGB, 33
Klein, Henry Blue, 88
Korea, 25, 109
Ku Klux Klan, 81-82
Kuwait, 30, 40

Language, 36, 38, 74
Lanier, Lyle, 89
Latvia, 27, 33, 115
Lawful resistance, 181
Lawrence, T. E., 36, 47, 114
Leadership, 85, 95-96, 113, 191, 206
League of the South, 25, 96-97, 127, 143, 179, 186-87, 220
League of the South Papers, 97
Lee, Robert E., 47, 74, 112, 137, 197-98, 212
Lega Nord, 96
Legislating morality, 66
Liberal welfare voting block, 31
Liberals, 22, 23, 74, 77, 93, 174, 191-92, 212
Libertarian Party, 193
Lincoln, Abraham, 35, 46, 78, 198
Lithuania, 24, 27, 33, 115
Little Rock, Arkansas, 25, 45, 49, 89, 90, 92, 180
Locke, John, 117, 120

Long, Huey, 46
Louisiana, 21, 56, 67, 89, 104
Louisiana Purchase, 56, 76
Luther, Martin, 137, 201
Lytle, Andrew, 51, 89

McWherter, Ned, 52
Madison, James, 77
Magruder, "Prince John," 145
Martyrs' Day, 191, 194
Maryland, 109
Massachusetts, 56, 73, 76, 78, 81
Maxwell House Hotel, 82
Media, 30, 37, 55, 62-63, 65, 68-70, 126, 129, 138, 142, 148-49, 161, 163-65, 174, 186, 191, 193, 202, 207, 212
Mena, Arkansas, 67
Meredith, James, 93
Military, 40, 42, 45-48, 77, 79, 106, 116, 121, 141, 180, 182, 196, 198
Militia Act of 1792, 42
Miller, Zell, 25, 96
Minority set-asides, 57, 71
Mississippi, 26, 45, 50, 81, 88, 93, 97, 105, 157, 196-98
Mississippi Delta, 103
Mississippi River, 55, 67, 76, 195
Missouri, 89, 108
Monarchists, 77
Monroe, Louisiana, 97, 184
Moral decay, 105, 135, 157, 176
Moral persuasion, 34
Morals and Dogma, 80-81
Morton, John W., 82
Multiculturalism, 55, 56, 61, 97, 215
Multi-ethnic empires, 219
Mussolini, Benito, 62

Nashville, Tennessee, 81
Nation (defined), 73
National Association for the Advancement of Colored People, 146
National Education Association, 60
National forests, 50
National Rifle Association, 96, 163
Nationalism, 33, 86, 87, 91, 114, 185, 221
Native American(s), 47, 134, 135, 149
Natural law, 94, 119, 121, 150
Natural resources, 49, 87, 104, 169
Natural rights, 98, 117-19, 121
Nazarites, 124-29, 131-33, 135, 137, 139, 207
Nazis, 29, 40, 64, 79, 121, 129, 130, 149, 171, 199
Negative influences, 202-3, 206-7
Negative publicity, 161
"New Albany Declaration," 98, 185
New Deal, 91
New England, 56, 74-77, 105, 178, 181
New Hampshire, 75-76
New Jersey, 48-49, 52
New York, 75, 173

New York Times, 128
Nicaraguan Contras, 157
Nietzsche, Friedrich, 62
Nissan, 53
Nixon, Herman Clarence, 89
Nixon, Richard M., 94
North Carolina, 105
Northern Confederacy, 76
Norwegian language, 181
Nullification, 35, 77
Nuremberg trials, 121

Ohio, 48, 49, 58
Oklahoma, 52, 104, 108-9
Oklahoma City bombing, 37
Ole Miss (University of Mississippi), 45, 93
101st Airborne Division, 45, 92
Oregon, 48, 49
Original American republic, 39, 117, 166
Otis, James, 79
Ouachita National Forest, 50
Owsley, Frank Lawrence, 83, 88
Oxford, Mississippi, 45, 93
Oxford's dictionary, 181

Paine, Thomas, 60
Parliament, 32, 43, 71, 193
Parnell, Charles Stewart, 193
Parsons' Regiment, 137
Passive resistance, 34
Peale, Dr. Norman Vincent, 204, 209
Pemberton, John, 195
Pennsylvania, 58
Persian Gulf, 26, 30
Persuasion, 159
Peter the Hermit, 201
Pickering, Timothy, 76
Pike, Albert, 80-81, 89, 195
Pioneers, 87, 155-56, 187
Poland, 33, 40, 64, 115, 117, 121, 170
Politburo, 33
Politically correct, 25, 41-42, 64, 183-84, 216
Popular culture, 128, 148
Pornography, 129, 131, 205
Port Hudson, Louisiana, 197-98
Positive emotions, 208-9
Positive influences, 203, 207
Positive publicity, 161
Posse Commitatus Act, 48
Prayer, 42, 63, 107, 208-10, 222
Preparatory phase, 147, 148, 150
Press, 44, 82, 96, 147, 161-65
Press releases, 86, 163, 186
Prison, 58-59, 71, 202
Property rights, 44
Protected minority, 42
Protests, 165, 180, 190-93
Public relations, 95, 158-59, 161, 163, 186-87, 190, 219
Publicity, 131, 160-62, 186
Pulaski, Tennessee, 88

Quebec, 24, 27, 33, 98, 117, 121, 175

Racism, 57, 64, 65, 86, 92, 169, 170
Radical Republicans, 92
Radio Free Confederacy, 187
Randolph, Innes, 47
Ransom, John Crowe, 88
Reason, 159, 165-68, 172, 200, 202, 210
Reconstruction, 30, 49-50, 56, 67, 81-83, 92, 93, 109, 127
Reconstruction Acts, 48
Reform Party, 193
Religion, 42, 63-64, 70, 74, 79, 90, 125, 135-37, 199
Republicans, 47, 92, 94, 192
Resistance, 33, 78-81, 92-93, 178, 181, 189, 219
Resources, 23, 34-35, 50-51, 104, 141-44, 148, 169, 183, 200
Rhetoric, 30, 58, 136, 171-72
Rhode Island, 75-76
Richmond, Virginia, 49
Rights: due process, 118; free exercise of religion, 118; to fruit of own labor, 118; keeping and bearing arms, 42, 118; lawful self-defense, 119; life, 119; property, 118; the pursuit of happiness, 118; revolution, 120; speedy trial by a jury, 118; to be let alone, 118
Robert the Bruce, 32, 113
Role models, 112, 116-17, 122, 211-12
Roman Republic, 199
Roosevelt, Franklin Delano, 91
Rule of the tens, 152
Russian Federation, 109

Saint Andrew's Cross, 27, 211
Saint Andrew's Lodge, 79
Saint Augustine, 117
Saint Patrick, 32
Saturn, 52, 53
Scalawags, 22, 25, 82, 83, 97, 148, 222
Schoolchildren, 167
Schools, 59, 61-64, 67, 71, 77, 83, 85, 90, 93, 106-8, 136, 147-48, 172, 181-82, 214, 221
Scotland, 27, 32, 98, 112-13, 121, 135, 181
Scots-Irish, 74, 182
Scots National Party, 32
Scottish Rite of Freemasonry, 80
Secession, 24, 30, 33, 35, 56, 60, 75-76, 121, 158, 189, 217
Second Amendment, 42-43, 185
Security, 36, 44, 107, 115, 118, 122, 138, 153, 212-13
Self-defense, 98, 117-18
Self-determination, 35, 37-38, 44, 46, 111, 117
Separation of church and state, 42, 63
Slavery, 48, 64, 75, 80
Slogans, 149, 179
Slovakia, 34

Smackover, Arkansas, 21, 218
Smyrna, Tennessee, 53
"Social Contract," 120
Social engineering, 45, 54, 56-57, 157, 199, 221-22
Social Security Numbers, 180
Solid South, The, 192
Solidarity, 115
Sons of Confederate Veterans, 85, 87, 143, 159, 179, 184, 188
South Africa, 27, 141
South Carolina, 77, 188, 191
South Carolina Exposition, The, 77
South Was Right!, The, 21, 36, 179
Southern accent, 182
Southern Baptist Convention apology, 64
Southern by the Grace of God, 95, 179
Southern cultural extravaganzas, 183
Southern Freedom Fighters Fund, 189
Southern Heritage, 188
Southern heritage festivals, 184, 193
"Southern Holocaust," 67
Southern language, 181-82, 193
Southern Manifesto, The, 92
Southern nationalism, 24, 86, 91, 95-96, 98, 142, 143, 159, 167, 175, 178-79, 184-85, 187-88, 192, 193, 221
Southern nationalist political party, 98, 192
Southern Partisan, 93, 188
Southern Party, 98
Southern Renaissance, 94
Southern self-image, 203-7
Southron (defined), 182
Sovereignty, 35, 75, 120
Soviet Empire, 33, 115-17
Soviet Union, 71, 91, 219
Spain, 109
Spontaneous public debates, 162
Spring Hill, Tennessee, 52-53
Stalin, Joseph, 62, 120
States' rights, 35, 192
States' Rights Party, 92
Stephens, Alexander, 83
Stone Mountain, Georgia, 24
Stone of Scone, 32
Strategy, 98, 123, 135, 146, 152, 167, 192, 196, 199
Support, 146, 152, 153, 166, 175, 192, 212, 222
Sweatshops, 52
Symbols, 74, 79, 83-84, 96, 149, 183, 211

Tariffs, 50, 77
Tate, Alan, 89
Tax reform, 185
Taxes, 30, 50, 51-54, 56, 57, 95, 157, 173, 176, 222
Team concept, 141-42, 148, 153
Television, 41, 58, 68-70, 128, 132, 134, 145, 165, 183, 186, 202, 212
Ten Commandments, 67, 119

Tennessee, 81, 89, 90, 92, 104
Texas, 56, 65, 76, 104, 109, 116
Thirteen colonies, 116
Thirteenth Amendment, 48
Toxic wastes, 55
Tradition, 32, 105-7, 116, 134, 138, 153, 189-90, 220-21
Tucker, Jim Guy, 44
Tuscaloosa, Alabama, 93

Ultima Thule, 135
Unalienable rights, 36, 41, 111, 117
United Confederate Veterans, 84-85, 183, 188
United Daughters of the Confederacy, 85, 87, 143, 179
United Kingdom, 109, 113
United Nations, 66
United States Census, 180
United States Constitution, 41, 46, 48, 149
United States Forest Service, 50, 51
United States Postal Service, 180
United States Taxpayers Party, 193
University of Arkansas, 181
U.S. News and World Report, 47

Vanderbilt "Phalanx," 91
Vermont, 75, 76
Vicksburg, Mississippi, 67, 195-98
Viet Cong, 29-30
Vietnam War, 26, 29, 109, 191
Virginia, 64, 75, 77, 96, 198
Vision, 70, 198, 214
Voting Rights Act, 44

Waco, Texas, 64, 65, 219
Wade, John, 89
Wallace, George, 46, 94
Wallace, William, 32, 94, 113
War for Southern Independence, 53, 116, 198
Warren, Joseph, 79
Warren, Robert Penn, 89
Webster, Daniel, 78
Webster, Noah, 43, 181-82
Welfare, 41, 45, 54, 57-58, 70, 215
Wesley, John, 137
West Virginia, 109
Williams, Bill, 25
Williams, Hank, Jr., 101
Williams, Hank, Sr., 102
Writing dates, 182

Yankee domination, 79, 81, 85, 178, 206
Yankee Occupation Codes, 180
Yorktown, Virginia, 145
Young, Stark, 88
Yugoslavia, 30

Ziglar, Zig, 204
Zip codes, 180